IMAGES
of America

FILIPINOS IN STOCKTON

In memory of the oldtimers!

Rico Reyes

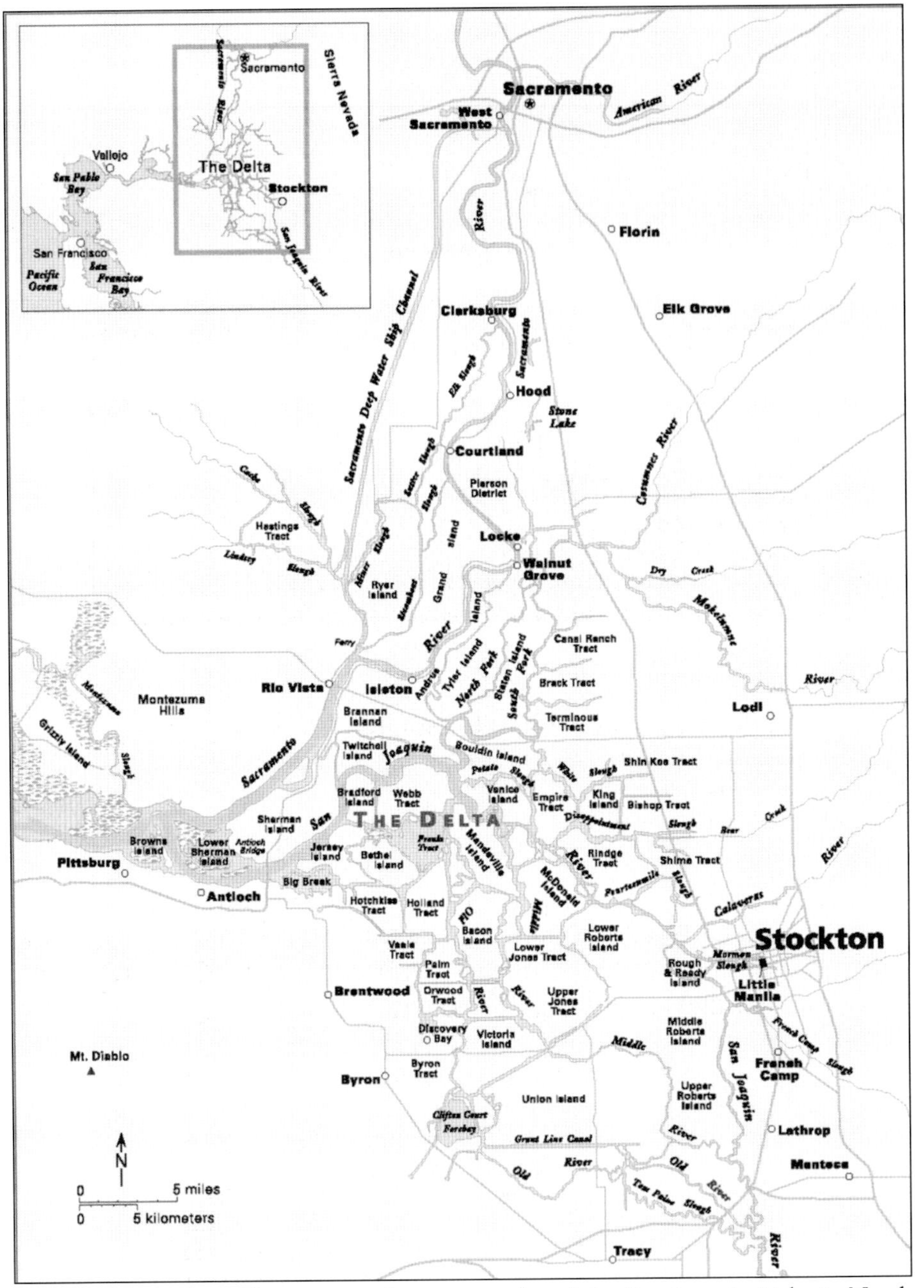

This map shows Stockton's location on the eastern edge of the San Joaquin Delta in Northern California. (Courtesy of Ben Pease.)

ON THE COVER: Filipinas and Filipinos take advantage of a rare day off of work in the fields to gather at a farm near the present site of San Joaquin Delta College in Stockton for an afternoon of music, singing, and dancing in the early 1930s. From left to right are (second row) Victoria Arca, Connie Arca (Fidel), Mary Arca (Inosanto), Asuncion Guevarra (Nicolas), Cecil Arca (the little boy), and Juliana Lazaro. (Photograph by Frank Mancao, courtesy of Filipino American National Historical Society National.)

IMAGES
of America

FILIPINOS IN STOCKTON

Dawn B. Mabalon, Ph.D.; Rico Reyes;
the Stockton Chapter, Filipino American National Historical
Society; and the Little Manila Foundation

ARCADIA
PUBLISHING

ISBN 978-0-7385-5624-6

Published by Arcadia Publishing
Charleston SC, Chicago IL, Portsmouth NH, San Francisco CA

Printed in the United States of America

Library of Congress Catalog Card Number: 2007937764

For all general information contact Arcadia Publishing at:
Telephone 843-853-2070
Fax 843-853-0044
E-mail sales@arcadiapublishing.com
For customer service and orders:
Toll-Free 1-888-313-2665

Visit us on the Internet at www.arcadiapublishing.com

We dedicate this book to the many generations of Filipino Americans in Stockton and San Joaquin County who paved our way; to our families, who put down roots in this community so we could grow and thrive; and to the generations to come.

CONTENTS

Acknowledgments

Our deepest appreciation goes to the many people and organizations whose help made this book possible. This project was truly a product of *bayanihan*, of community effort, generosity, and collaboration. We would like to express our thanks to our coauthors, the Stockton Chapter of the Filipino American National Historical Society and the Little Manila Foundation. Special thanks go to FANHS members and officers Terri Torres, Anita Navalta Bautista, Leatrice Bantillo Perez, Beverly Engkabo, Violet Juanitas Dutra, Angelina Candelario Noveloz, and Art Villaruz. Thank you to our fellow board members of the Little Manila Foundation—especially Adeline B. Suguitan, Dillon Delvo, Elena Mangahas, Rebecca Abellana, Tony Somera, and Florence Quilantang—and our volunteers and interns: Jesse P. Gonzales, Ace Alcantara, Stacey Arquines, Melisa Benal, Desiree Cook, Darrin Olipendo, Matthew Evangelista, Ross Bungcayao, Leanne Dauz, Zachary Aguilar, Jonathan Navarez, Shirley Panugaling, and Alyssa Alcantara.

We want to express our appreciation and gratitude to those who shared their photographs and stories with us for this project: Wilma Bucariza Aguinid; Alma Alcala; Susanne Alcantara; Richard Ancheta; Letty Aspiras; Betty Aynaga; Concepcion M. Bohulano; Kathi Bravo; Laurena Cabanero; Raymond Cablayan; Ed Chavez; Joan May T. Cordova; Fred Cordova; Al Dacanay; Rosaline L. Dickinson; Irene Plaza Edralin; Myrna Elias; Beverly Engkabo; Jimmy and Phyllis Ente; Melanie Espinueva; Maria and James Fabionar/Olamit family; Ted Gabales; Lita R. Galicinao; Katherine Dougherty Gapusan; Tanishia Arbet Gapusan; Manuel (Jay) Castro Gesulga Jr.; Bernie M. Giva; Caroline Bulawit Gray; Melissa Gust/Antaran family; Ivan Hitt Jr.; Arlene Johnson; Andy Imutan; Cheryl Magdael Lauron/Magdael family; Mel Lagasca; Rene Latosa; Lazaro family; Carolina Saqueton Luces; Mabalon family; Shereé A. and Flora Mata; Christopher Mateo; Virginia Navarro; the Nicolas family; Adorle Nieves; Shirley Burnside; Angelina Candelario Noveloz; Helene Bolong Nunes; Evelyn Macavinta Oliveira; Vicky Ramos McElyea; Leatrice Perez; Roy J. Perez; Barbara Caballero Pimental; John Ramirez; George Reyes; Vince and Remy Reyes; Joy Reyna; Dedric Rico; Sharon Monton Robinson; Carlena Padua Rowell; Jose Rubianes; Fernando Ragojo Saldevar; Jericho Saria; Purita Talisayan; Flora May Paguyo Teague; Rudy Tenio; Evangeline Thomas; Sally Tiisen; Maria B. Vea; Clara Villadores; James Villadores; Art Villaruz; Alexis Canillo with Filipino Oral History, Inc.; Grace Tolentino with FILMAPS (Filipino Medical and Allied Professionals); Virginia Navarro with the Association of Filipino American Educators; FANHS Stockton Chapter; the Daguhoy Lodge of the Legionarios del Trabajo, Inc., via Tony Somera; Iloilo Circle; and the Numancia Aid Association.

Thank you to the following individuals for their assistance: reporter Jennifer Torres of the *Record* newspaper and photographers Calixtro Romias and Michael McCollum and their editors at the *Record*; Marissa Aroy, director of *Little Manila: Filipinos in California's Heartland*, for sharing photographs; filmmaker Patricio Ginelsa; and our Arcadia Publishing editor John Poultney. A special thank you to cartographer Ben Pease for the wonderful maps. For allowing us to use their facilities for photograph submissions and scanning, special thanks go to the Community Development Department, City of Stockton; Trinity Presbyterian Church; and Alfonso and Celia Marcelino, for their office at the Filipino Plaza. Special thanks also to the following archivists: Bill Maxwell, Bank of Stockton Photo Archives; Trish Richards, University of the Pacific Holt Atherton Library Special Collections; Catherine Powell, San Francisco State University Labor Archives and Research Center; Tod Ruhstaller and Kimberly Bowden, the Haggin Museum, Stockton, California; Stacey Zwald, Oakland Museum; Cesar Chavez Stockton–San Joaquin Public Library; Clerk of the City of Stockton Katherine Gong-Meissner; and Jeff Liu at Visual Communications in Los Angeles. Drs. Fred and Dorothy Cordova, president emeritus and executive director, respectively, of the Filipino American National Historical Society, deserve special accolades and gratitude for their assistance and for creating the very foundation of the work we do. We are grateful for the support from the Presidential Award at San Francisco State University, the Ford Foundation Diversity Postdoctoral Fellowship, and the Pasker Endowment at the Department of History at SFSU. We would also like to thank our colleagues and staff at our respective academic institutions for their assistance and support.

Finally we want to thank our partners, Jesus P. Gonzales and Andrew Ardizzoia, our parents, Christine Bohulano Bloch and the late Ernesto T. Mabalon and Tony and Rose Reyes, and our families and friends for their love and for their support of this book project and our struggle to preserve Little Manila and this history. We hope that this book is testament, in part, to our everlasting appreciation and to our *utang na loob*, or debt of gratitude, to our families and our forebears.

INTRODUCTION

After the United States colonized the Philippines at the dawn of the 20th century, thousands of Filipinos began immigrating to Hawaii and the United States. When the 1924 Immigration Act excluded Japanese and Chinese laborers, Filipino labor was in high demand in the San Joaquin Delta region because Filipinos, as U.S. nationals, were exempt from the restrictive exclusion laws that barred Japanese and Chinese laborers. By World War II, almost 100,000 Filipinos were living in Hawaii and the United States. Throughout much of the 20th century, Stockton, California, was home to the largest Filipino community outside of the Philippines.

A legend passed down speaks of an old-timer named Villareal, a Filipino who had settled in Stockton around 1898 and encouraged fellow Filipinos to join him there by meeting ships at San Francisco. Then, in the mid-1920s, many *sakadas* (Filipino sugar plantation workers in Hawaii) began to migrate to Stockton and the farms in the surrounding Delta region (see map on page two), drawn by better wages and year-round agricultural work in peaches, grapes, asparagus, tomatoes, sugar beets, celery, and other crops. Soon, encouraged by American teachers who promised unlimited opportunities in America, Filipinos were skipping Hawaii altogether to go straight to San Francisco, where unscrupulous taxi drivers waiting at the docks piled unwitting immigrants into taxicabs for $75 rides to Stockton. By the late 1920s, Filipinos had become the largest ethnic group engaged in San Joaquin County farm labor, and they drove the economic engine of the region. The vast majority of these early Filipino immigrants were very young men from the northern provinces of La Union, Pangasinan, Ilocos Sur, and Ilocos Norte and from provinces in the Visayas, particularly from the islands of Panay, Bohol, Cebu, and Siquijor. Because of strict Catholic gender roles for Filipinas that frowned on unchaperoned travel, most early immigrants were men and the gender ratio was extreme: by some accounts, there were 14 Filipinos to each Filipina in the 1920s.

Life was difficult for early pioneers, who encountered vicious racism and economic hardship. The vast majority of early Pinays and Pinoys (the nickname created by and for Filipinos in America), regardless of their skills or educational attainment, worked in the fields of the Central Valley and San Joaquin Delta. As Asians, they were ineligible for citizenship, so they could not own land or vote. When the Depression devastated the economy, Filipino immigrants were easy scapegoats, especially so in a nation with a long history of anti-Asian repression and exclusion. In 1934, Congress passed the Tydings-McDuffie Act, which granted Philippine independence in a decade but restricted Filipino immigration to 50 per year and reclassified Filipinos as "aliens." In 1935, Congress passed the Filipino Repatriation Act, which offered a one-way ticket home to the Philippines for any immigrant with the condition that he/she never return to the United States.

Stockton was rigidly segregated, and before World War II, Filipinos were not allowed to frequent, much less live, most places north of Main Street. Signs on public places read "Positively No Filipinos Allowed" and "No Dogs and No Filipinos Allowed." The Fox Theater relegated Filipinos to the sides and balcony. In response, Filipinos created their own community: a six-block area in downtown Stockton known as Little Manila that was centered on Lafayette and El Dorado Streets near Chinatown and Nihonmachi. Because the neighborhood drew thousands of Filipinos from all over the nation, Stockton's Little Manila became the heart of Filipino America and a crossroads for a rapidly growing national ethnic community. For thousands of Filipinos who worked and lived in San Joaquin County and in the Delta, Stockton was the "big city," and Little Manila was an important destination.

World War II brought dramatic changes for the community. Little Manila expanded as Filipinos took over storefronts left empty by the incarceration of Japanese Americans. Enlistment in the newly created 1st and 2nd Filipino Infantry Regiments allowed Filipinos to become U.S. citizens, to take advantage of the GI Bill, and to fight overseas to defend the Philippines. The 1945 War Brides Act enabled these veterans to bring back war brides from the Philippines, and the 1946 Luce-Cellar Act gave all Filipinos the right to naturalize. With citizenship, Filipinos were finally able to buy homes and farmland and petition for spouses and children from the Philippines. The community experienced its own postwar baby boom, and weekends were always centered on community events seeing friends and family in Little Manila.

But in the late 1950s, the City of Stockton bulldozed several blocks of Little Manila, Chinatown, and Nihonmachi for the West End Redevelopment Project, and in 1970, the state built the Crosstown Freeway through two of the remaining four blocks of Little Manila. As a result of the demolitions, hundreds of poor, elderly Filipinos were evicted and the vibrant community was almost destroyed. By the 1990s, only two blocks, a handful of Filipino American organizations, and several dozen old-timers remained. Many young people in the community never learned about the historic significance of the neighborhood because it had been wiped off of the map before their birth. Despite the demolitions, the community continued to grow and thrive. Some buildings survived. Organizations built their own housing in and near Little Manila for aging members. The Associated Filipino Organizations (AFO) built the Filipino Center (now Filipino Plaza), which opened on August 12, 1972, at 6 West Main Street in downtown. The AFO's annual Barrio Fiesta, always held the second week of August, commemorates and celebrates the historic opening of the complex.

The entire city of Stockton became a Little Manila as Filipinos left the city's core and settled in new neighborhoods in the north and west in the 1960s and 1970s. By the 1970s, thousands of Filipinos began immigrating to the West Coast as a result of the 1965 Immigration Act, which allowed for a 20,000 annual quota or Filipino immigrants and continued to allow family reunification above immigration quotas. Because of immigration visa preferences that favored professionals, many new immigrants to Stockton were college educated. Some of the new immigrants were the family members of pioneers who had settled in Stockton before World War II. Others were Filipino American military families who had settled in Stockton because of the Rough and Ready military base, the Sharpe Army Depot in Tracy, or the nearby navy base in Vallejo.

In the past four decades, newcomers and longtime Filipino Stocktonians have created a rich and diverse community. According to the 1990 Census, Filipino Americans constituted the largest Asian American community in San Joaquin County, and there has been a renewed interest in community history in the last two decades. The Filipino American National Historical Society chose Stockton for the site of its planned Filipino American National Museum. The Stockton Chapter of the Filipino American Historical Society was founded in 1992; they led the campaign to designate the Little Manila Historic Site in the blocks surrounding El Dorado and Lafayette Streets downtown in 2000. Since 2000, the Little Manila Foundation has endeavored to revitalize the area with historic banners and signs and to prevent more demolition and displacement.

When we asked members of the community to share photographs for this book project, we were rewarded with an astounding array of images from every decade and from every aspect of Filipino American life. The photographs together weave a tapestry of diverse experiences: they speak of shared struggles, triumphs, celebrations, and joy. Each photograph told its own incredible story. Sadly, because of space considerations, we could not include every photograph submitted for this book. We hope that the images presented here inspire future projects that explore the history of Filipinos in Stockton. Consider this book a place to begin the recovery of the history of the historic heart of Filipino America.

One

The First Generations

Pinay and Pinoy Pioneers

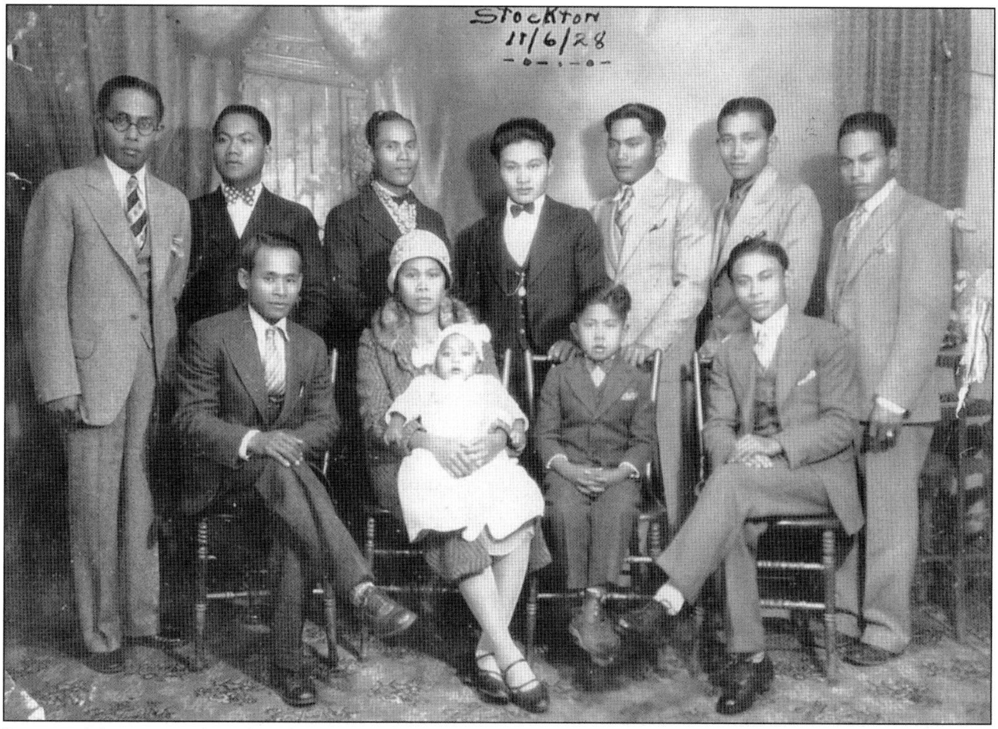

Pictured here is a family who arrived in Stockton in the 1920s. Thousands of pioneers came from the turn of the 20th century to World War II, as American colonialism transformed life for Filipinos. Among the first who came to the area were students and former sugarcane workers from Hawaii. American teachers in the Philippines spoke of limitless opportunities in the United States and extolled the virtues of an American education, which inspired a generation of Filipino immigrants to study in the United States. The American colonial *pensionada/o* program sent Filipinos to American universities in the first decades of the 20th century. Several attended UC Berkeley, and from 1915 to 1923, more than 15 Filipinos attended College of the Pacific (now University of the Pacific). Filipinos began leaving Hawaii for work in the San Joaquin Delta beginning in the 1910s. In one old-timer's words, immigrants hoped "to pick gold off the streets." But it would not be so. Because of racism, most never worked outside of the fields; very few were able to complete college. Nevertheless, these men, women, and families persevered to put down roots in the San Joaquin Delta. Pinay and Pinoy pioneers created a strong and stable community for the generations that followed. (Courtesy of Sharon Monton Robinson.)

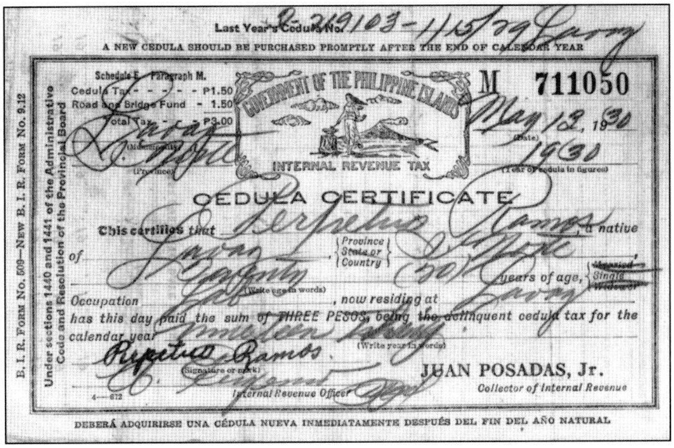

Last Year's Cedula No. 2-219103-115/29 Laoag
A NEW CEDULA SHOULD BE PURCHASED PROMPTLY AFTER THE END OF CALENDAR YEAR

Schedule E Paragraph M.
Cedula Tax - - - - P1.50
Road and Bridge Fund - 1.50
Total Tax - - - P3.00

GOVERNMENT OF THE PHILIPPINE ISLANDS
INTERNAL REVENUE TAX

M 711050

May 12, 1930
(Date)
1930
(Year of cedula in figures)

CEDULA CERTIFICATE

This certifies that Perfecto Ramos a native of Laoag, I. Norte (Province, State or Country), Twenty (30) years of age, Single
Occupation ..., now residing at Laoag
has this day paid the sum of THREE PESOS, being the delinquent cedula tax for the calendar year Nineteen Thirty

Perfecto Ramos
(Signature or mark)

Internal Revenue Officer

JUAN POSADAS, Jr.
Collector of Internal Revenue

B. I. R. FORM No. 509—New B. I. R. FORM No. 9.12
Under sections 1440 and 1441 of the Administrative Code and Resolution of the Provincial Board

DEBERÁ ADQUIRIRSE UNA CÉDULA NUEVA INMEDIATAMENTE DESPUÉS DEL FIN DEL AÑO NATURAL

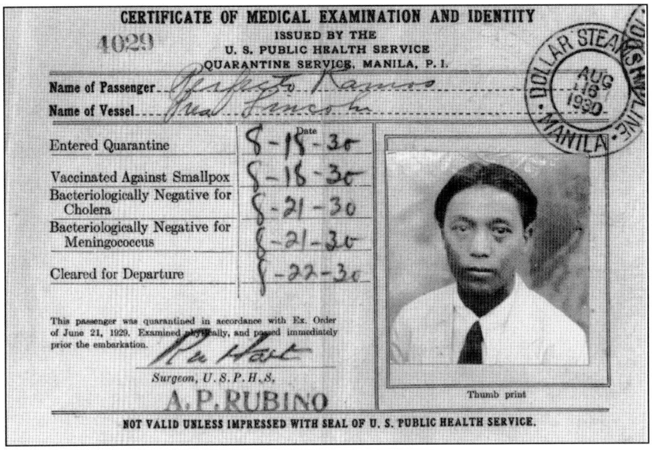

CERTIFICATE OF MEDICAL EXAMINATION AND IDENTITY
ISSUED BY THE
U. S. PUBLIC HEALTH SERVICE
QUARANTINE SERVICE, MANILA, P. I.

4029

DOLLAR STEAMSHIP LINE
AUG 16 1930
MANILA

Name of Passenger Perfecto Ramos
Name of Vessel Pres. Lincoln

	Date
Entered Quarantine	8-15-30
Vaccinated Against Smallpox	8-16-30
Bacteriologically Negative for Cholera	8-21-30
Bacteriologically Negative for Meningococcus	8-21-30
Cleared for Departure	8-22-30

This passenger was quarantined in accordance with Ex. Order of June 21, 1929. Examined physically, and passed immediately prior the embarkation.

Surgeon, U. S. P. H. S.
A. P. RUBINO

Thumb print

NOT VALID UNLESS IMPRESSED WITH SEAL OF U. S. PUBLIC HEALTH SERVICE.

Because Filipino immigrants were classified as U.S. nationals, they could enter the United States freely before 1934, when the Tydings-McDuffie Act classified Filipinos as "aliens" and restricted entry to only 50 Filipinos annually. Perfecto Ramos saved his immigration card and *cedula* (certification of taxes paid). Ramos raised a family and farmed in Lathrop, near Stockton. (Courtesy of Vicky Ramos McElyea.)

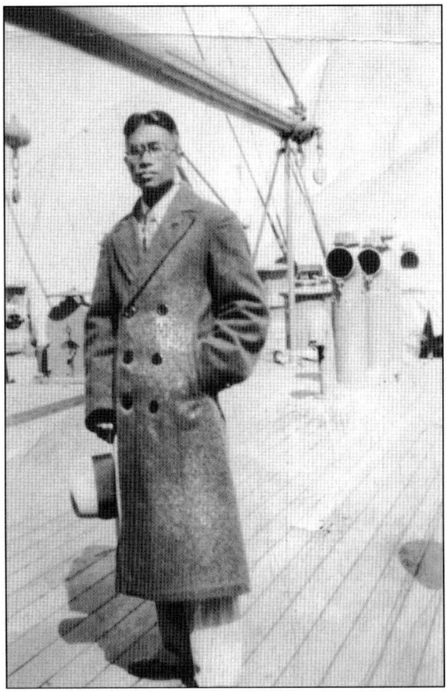

Claro Candelario is pictured here en route to the United States in 1930. A teacher from La Union, Ilocos Sur, Candelario worked as a houseboy in Los Angeles. He befriended Carlos Bulosan, and they moved to Stockton in 1939. Candelario, who owned the Luzon Café on Lafayette Street and inspired the character "Claro" in Bulosan's *America Is in the Heart*, was a venerable labor activist and charismatic community leader in Stockton. (Courtesy of Angelina Candelario Novolezo.)

The advent of affordable, third-class passenger tickets on the Dollar Steamship Presidential Liners in 1925 enabled thousands of Filipinos to travel from Manila to San Francisco and Seattle beginning in the mid-1920s. Thousands of immigrants took the Presidential steamship liners to America. Here Mr. and Mrs. D. E. Diamante and friends pose on the *President McKinley* as it prepares to land in the United States. (Courtesy of FANHS Stockton.)

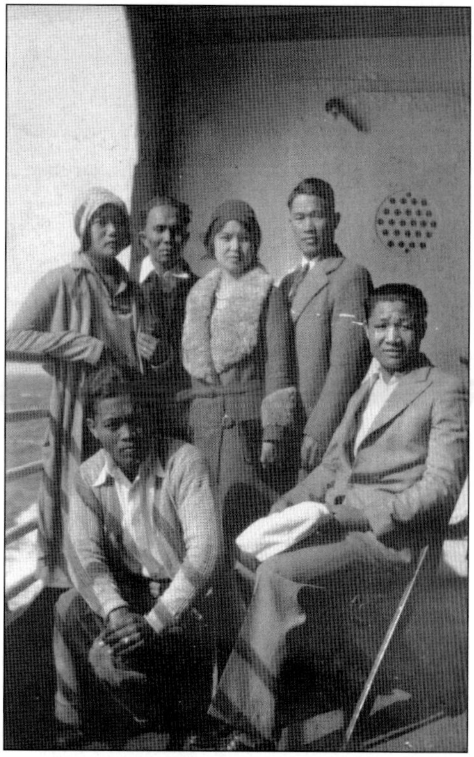

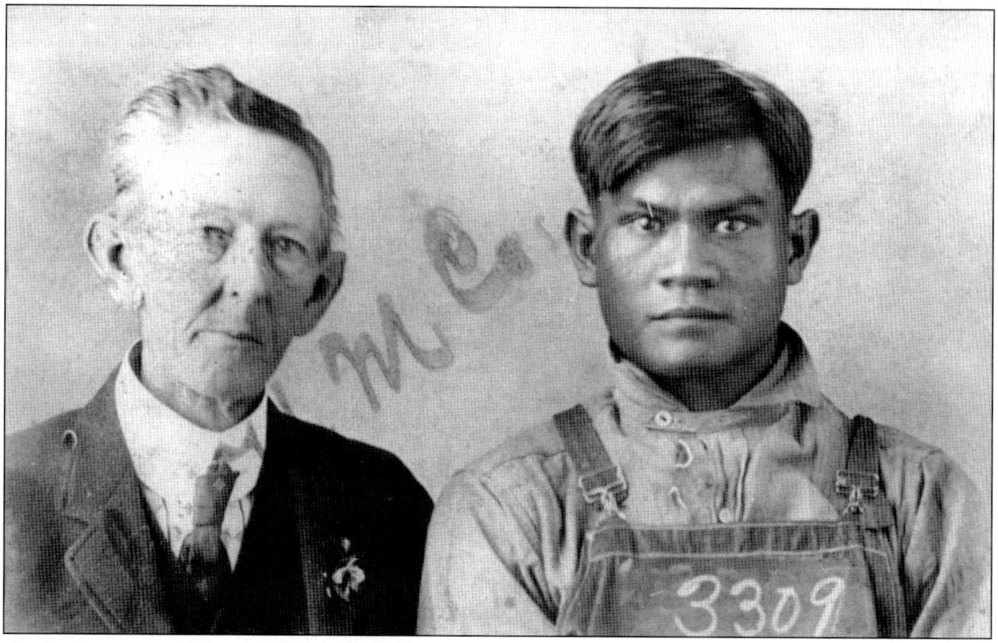

Cirilo Yongque Juanitas, right, was hired by Holt Manufacturing in Stockton in 1917. Juanitas left Barbaza, Antique, Panay, for Hawaii in 1913, then went to Stockton, where he opened a pool hall/candy store on El Dorado Street in 1922. He worked on farms; owned the Quezon Hotel, two grocery stores, and a farm near Cherokee Road; and was a partner in the Manila Inn Tavern. He raised a large family in Stockton. (Courtesy of FANHS Stockton.)

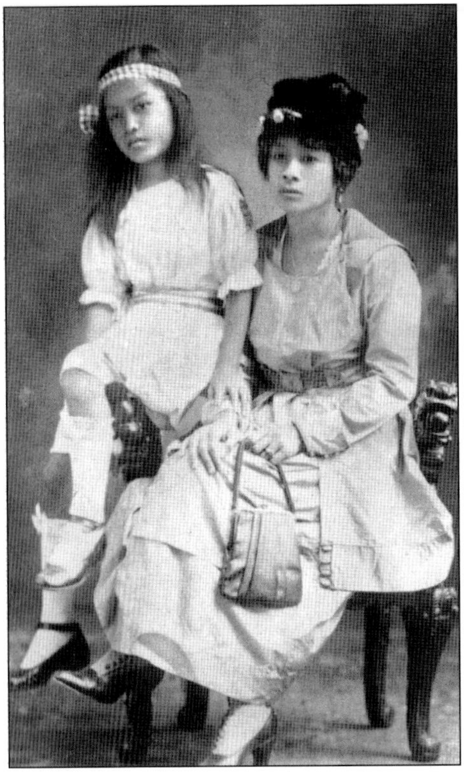

In 1918, Cebu native Remedios Tenedor (the young girl) with her aunt, Fortunata Montayre Naranda, commemorated their departure from Hawaii for Stockton with a formal portrait. Remedios's story was typical of many pioneers: her family had worked in sugarcane in the 1910s, moved to Honolulu, then on to Stockton for better opportunities. The family started a business in Stockton and became migrant farm workers in the 1920s. Remedios married and settled in Los Angeles after World War II. (Courtesy of FANHS National.)

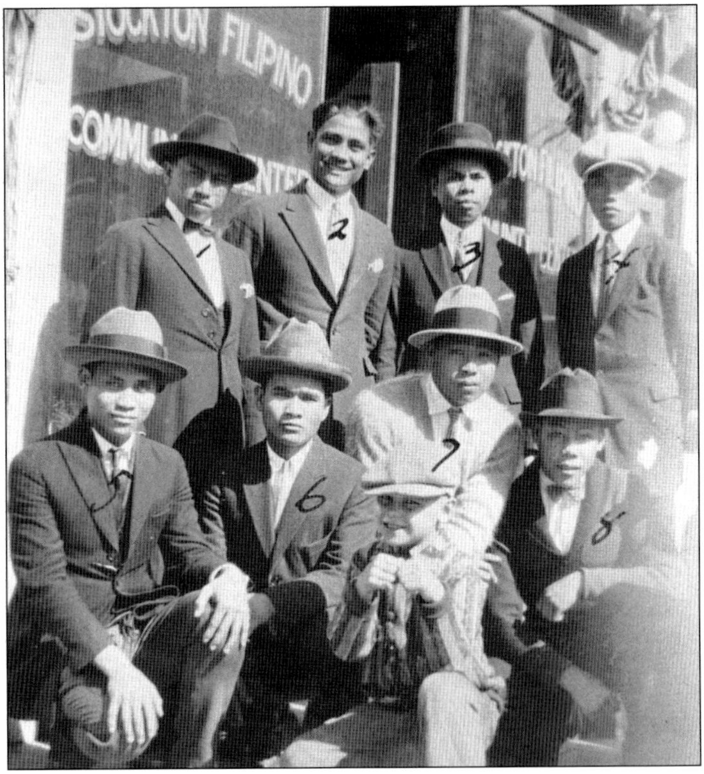

Alejandro Ancheta, number 5, is shown with friends in front of the Filipino Community Center at 111 East Lafayette Street in 1924. Filipino businesses and organizations were just beginning to take root in the area. Ancheta later became a pastor of the Bethany Temple, a Filipino evangelical congregation still in existence in Stockton today. (Courtesy of Photographic Collections, Visual Communications.)

In the 1920s, two sharply dressed unidentified men and a little girl celebrate their arrival in the heart of Filipino America with a photograph inscribed: "Our First Day in Stockton." (Courtesy of Photographic Collections, Visual Communications.)

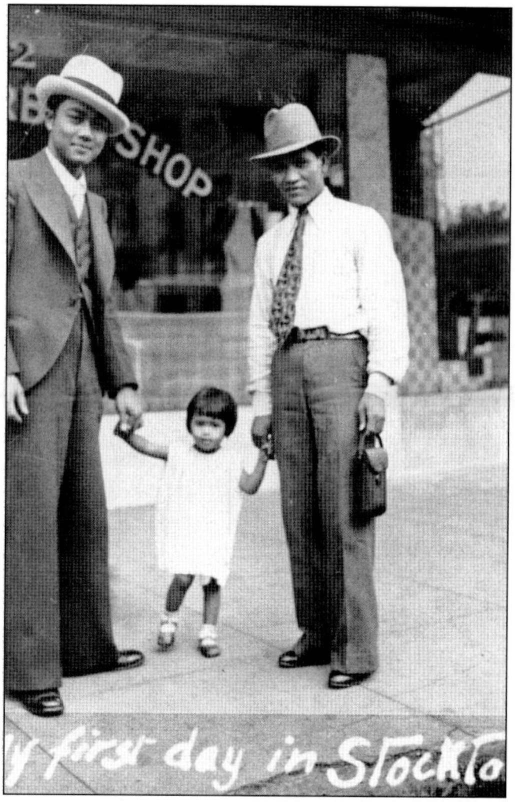

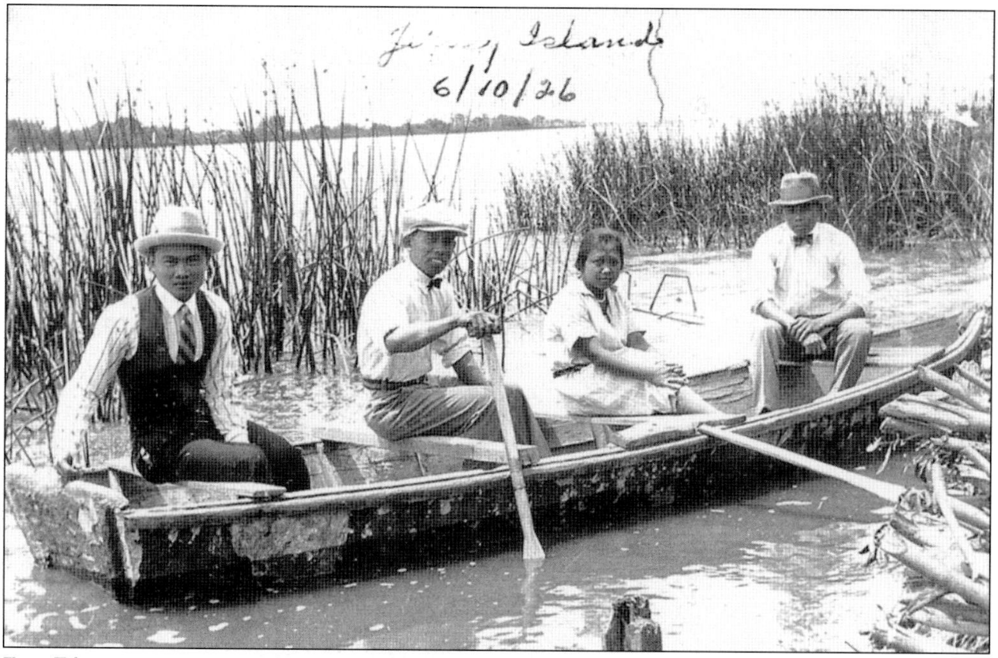

Four Filipinos pose in a rowboat on Jersey Island in 1926. Ferries and small boats provided transport to and between the various Delta islands, where Filipinos labored on farms and lived in camps. (Courtesy of the Sharon Monton Robinson.)

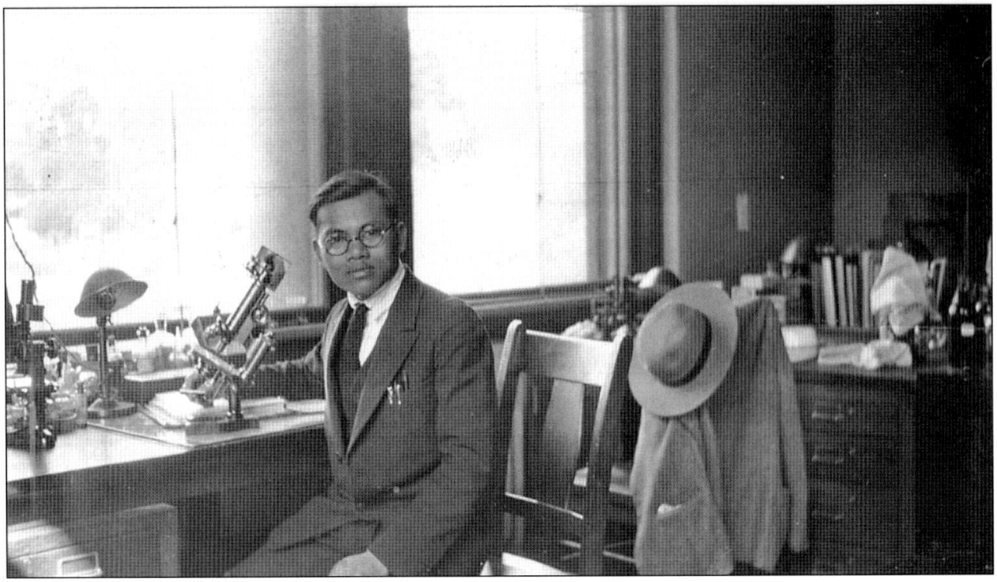

Primo Villaruz, a native of Capiz, Panay, was a pensionado who graduated from UC Berkeley in 1927 and settled in Stockton, where he met his wife, Rita, and they raised several children. He was the first Filipino chemist hired by the California Water Service to oversee the purification of the local water supply. Villaruz was elected the first president of the Filipino Community of Stockton and Vicinity in 1930. (Courtesy of Art Villaruz.)

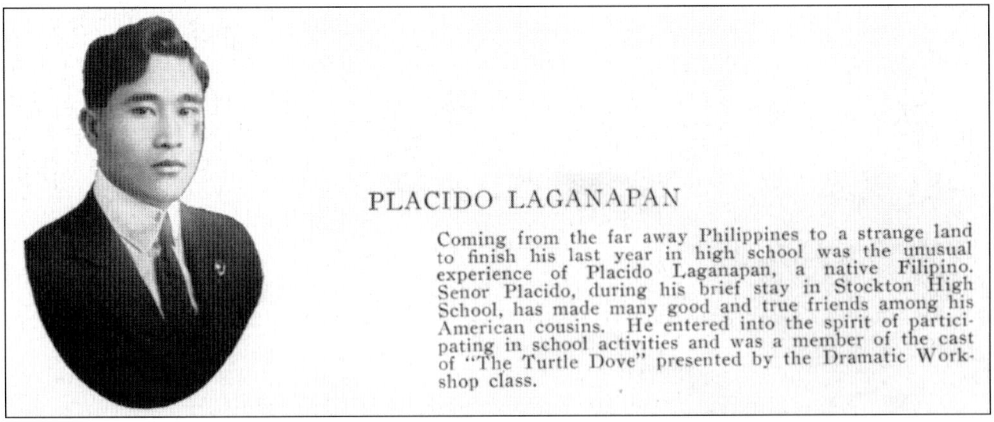

PLACIDO LAGANAPAN

Coming from the far away Philippines to a strange land to finish his last year in high school was the unusual experience of Placido Laganapan, a native Filipino. Senor Placido, during his brief stay in Stockton High School, has made many good and true friends among his American cousins. He entered into the spirit of participating in school activities and was a member of the cast of "The Turtle Dove" presented by the Dramatic Workshop class.

Many Filipinos arrived in Stockton and attended school while working in the fields or in domestic or service work. Placido Laganapan attended Stockton High School in 1922. This picture was in the Stockton High School yearbook, the *Guard and Tackle*. (Courtesy of the Stockton Public Library.)

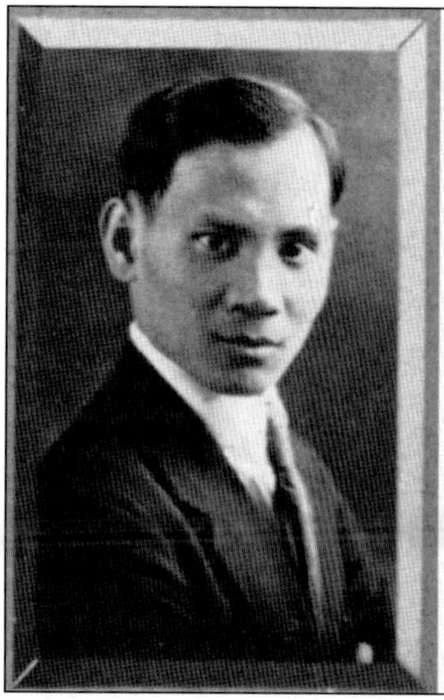

IGNACIO CRISTOBAL
Academic
This was a stranger from across the sea, the far away Philippines, but he was well liked by all who knew him. During the time he spent in S. H. S., his especial hobbies were journalism and poetry. In fact, Ignacio fully expects to run a newspaper or magazine in his home land.

Ignacio Cristobal was attending Stockton High School in 1923. Cristobal, like thousands of his compatriots, was probably preparing to attend college in the United States. (Courtesy of the Stockton Public Library.)

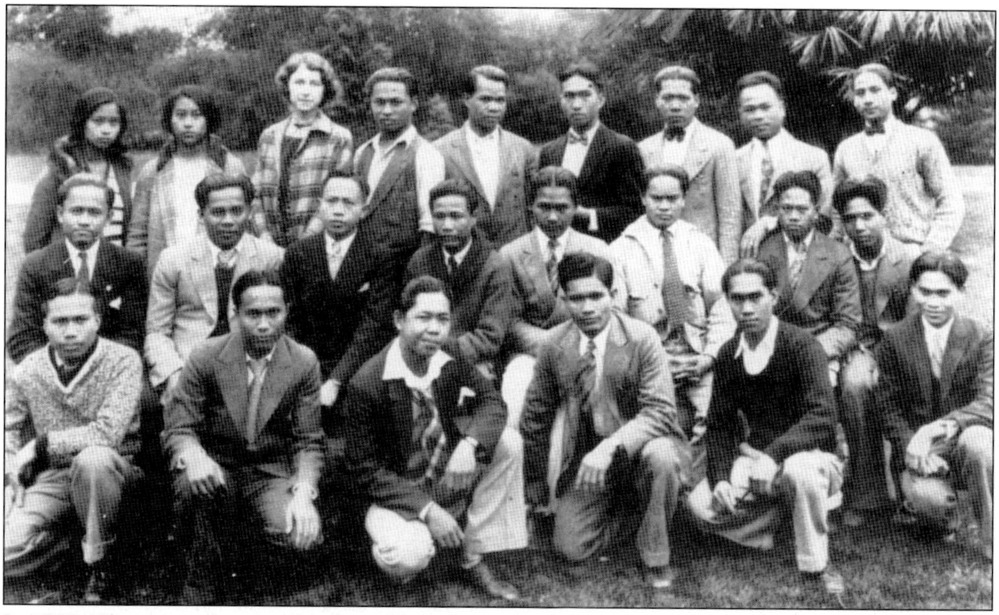

In 1929, Filipino students at Stockton High formed a club and are pictured in the school yearbook, the *Guard and Tackle*. Their officers for the fall semester included Daniel Dancel, president; Hoyolito Sajonia, vice president; Atanasio L. Alcala, secretary-treasurer; and Simplicio Bilinario, sergeant-at-arms. Spring semester officers were Juan Montermeso, president; Simplicio Bilinario, vice-president; Mary Arca (third row, second from left, next to her sister, Flora Arca), secretary-treasurer; and Eulalio Aguinaldo, sergeant-at-arms. Eulalio Cablayan is second from the right in the first row. (Courtesy of Raymond Cablayan and the Stockton Public Library.)

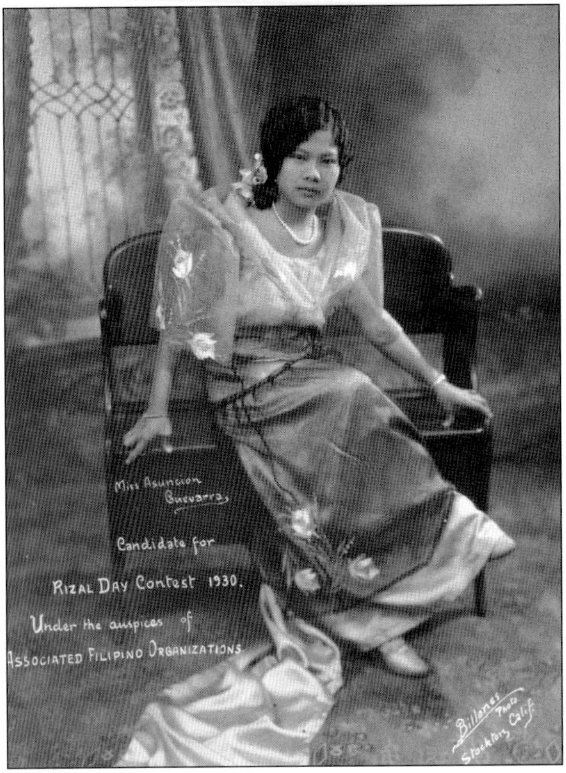

Asuncion Guevarra left Iloilo, Panay, and arrived in the United States in 1929 with her mother and stepfather, Placido and Juliana Lazaro. She married a local barber, Sixto Nicolas; they settled in Stockton, and raised a family. Here she is pictured in 1930 running for Rizal Day queen. Photographs like these were distributed during queen contests to drum up ticket sales. (Photograph by John Y. Billones, courtesy of FANHS Stockton.)

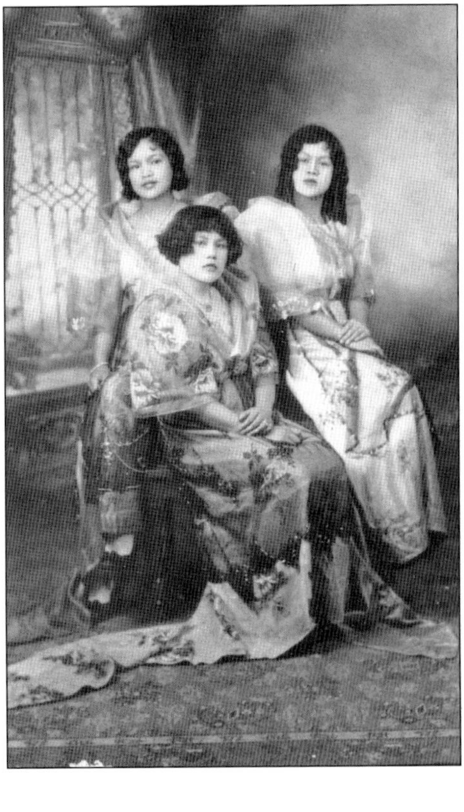

Margarita Balucas and her daughters Feling and Catherine pose for local Filipino photographer John Y. Billones around the 1920s or 1930s. Balucas had come to Stockton from Hawaii, and she owned a pool hall and restaurant in Little Manila. Most Pinoys took formal portraits in American suits to embody American modernity, but Pinays often wore Filipina dress in formal portraits, perhaps to symbolize a homeland left behind. (Photograph by John Y. Billones, courtesy of FANHS National.)

Pinoys bought McIntosh suits and posed for glamorous formal studio portraits to be sent home; this inspired more immigration. Crouching at left is Fructuoso Monton, who left Tubigon, Bohol, and arrived in the United States on September 18, 1924. He was a founding member of the Worshipful Daguhoy Lodge, Legionarios del Trabajo. He and his wife, Susanna Monton, raised their family in Stockton. (Courtesy of Sharon Monton Robinson.)

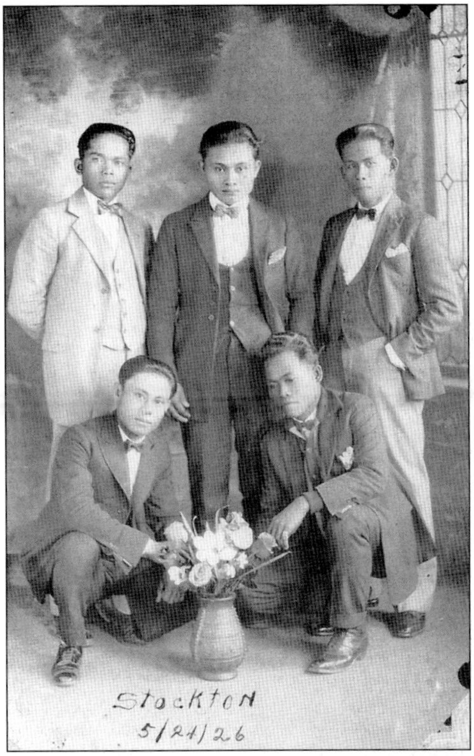

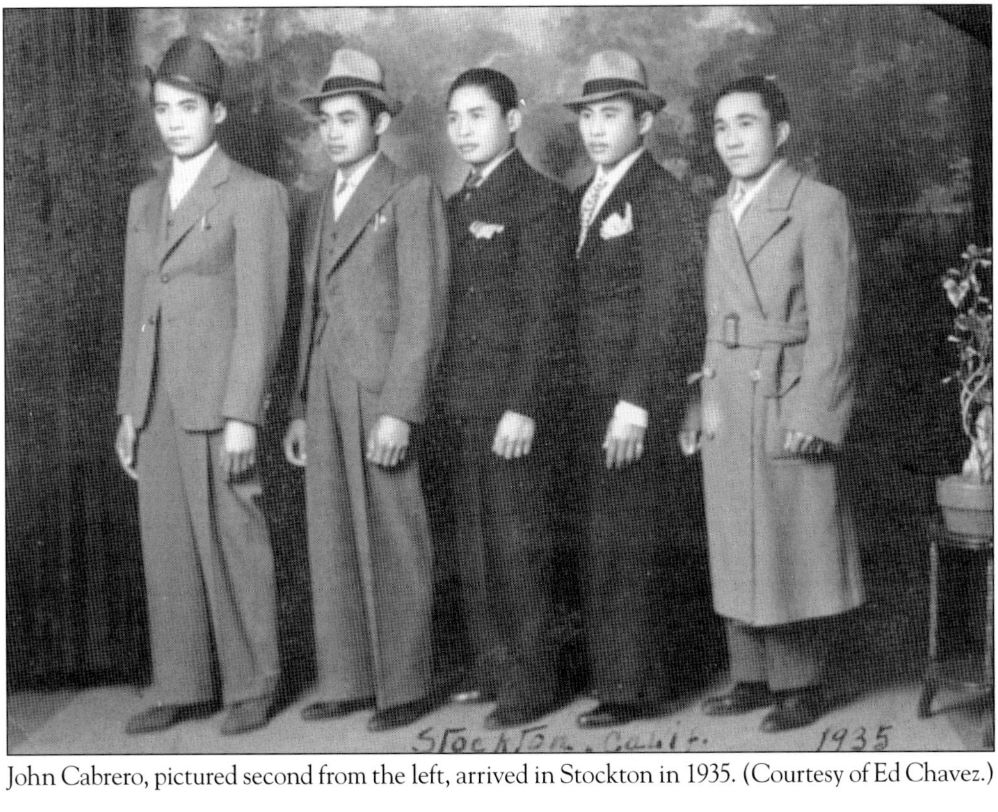

John Cabrero, pictured second from the left, arrived in Stockton in 1935. (Courtesy of Ed Chavez.)

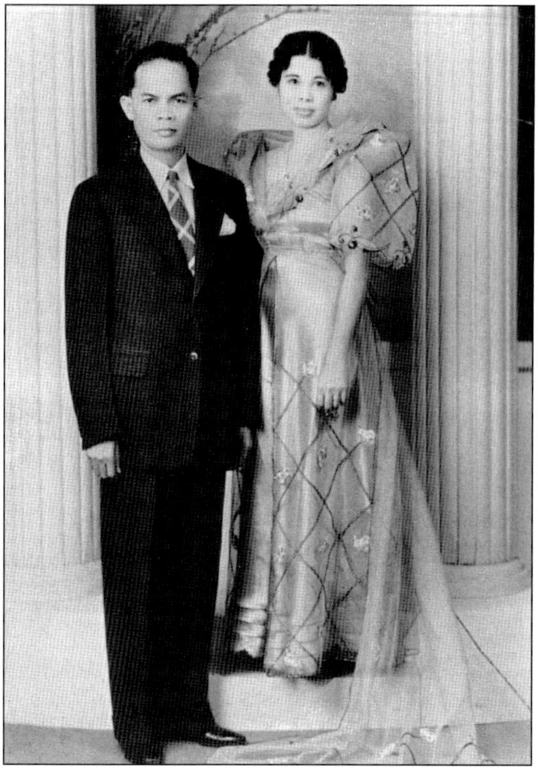

Demetrio and Anna Ente are shown in Stockton in the 1930s. Ente left Loboc, Bohol, and arrived in Seattle in 1917, where he met and married Manila-born Anna Merrill. In 1938, he moved his Seattle-based Rizal Social Club, a dance hall and nightclub, to Little Manila at 138 East Lafayette Street. In 1947, he built the Filipino Recreation Center at East Lafayette and Hunter Streets (which became the American Federation of Labor Hall and now Emerald Restaurant). He also farmed onions and leased two Little Manila hotels: the White and the MacArthur. Ente once owned the most palatial home in Stockton, the Wong Mansion on Clay Street. (Courtesy of Jimmy Ente.)

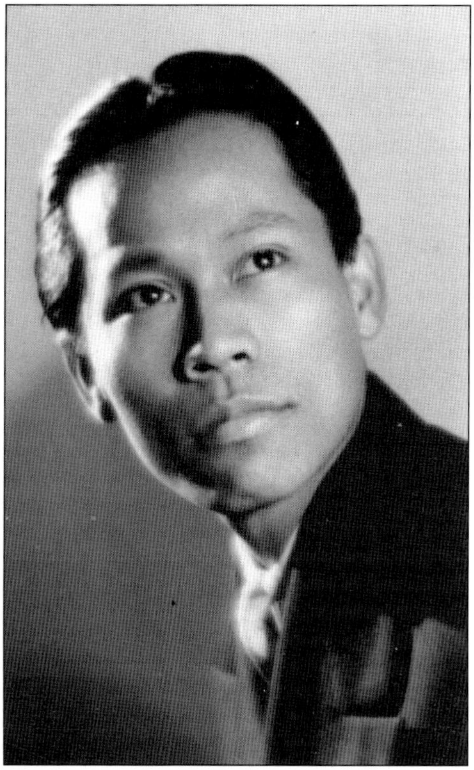

In 1939, writer/activist Carlos Bulosan of Magusmana, Pangasinan, moved to Stockton with Claro Candelario to campaign for Filipino citizenship with the Committee for the Protection of Filipino Rights. Bulosan lived intermittently in Little Manila at 110 South El Dorado Street until his death in 1956. Stockton plays a key role in Bulosan's 1943 novel *America Is in the Heart.* (Photograph by Claro Candelario, courtesy of Angelina Candelario Novolezo.)

Some Filipinas who immigrated to Stockton in the 1920s had college degrees, but few were able to work as professionals. Lourdes B. Campos, a nurse, immigrated to Stockton in 1929. (Courtesy of Leatrice Bantillo Perez.)

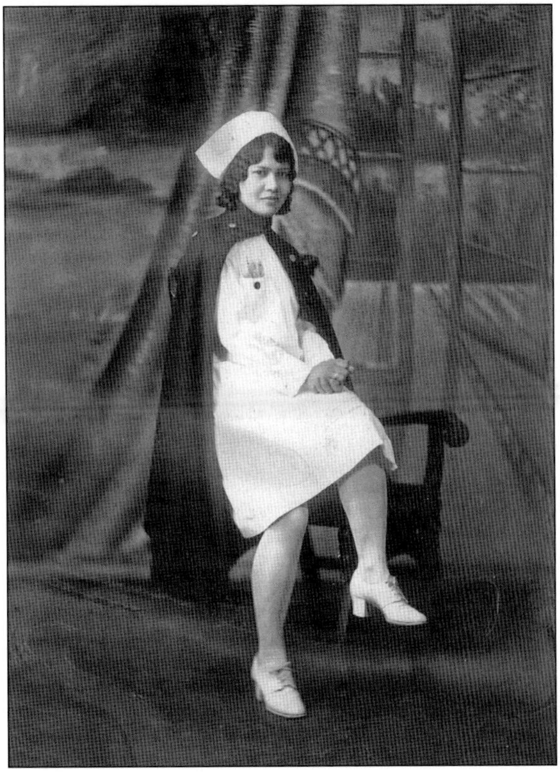

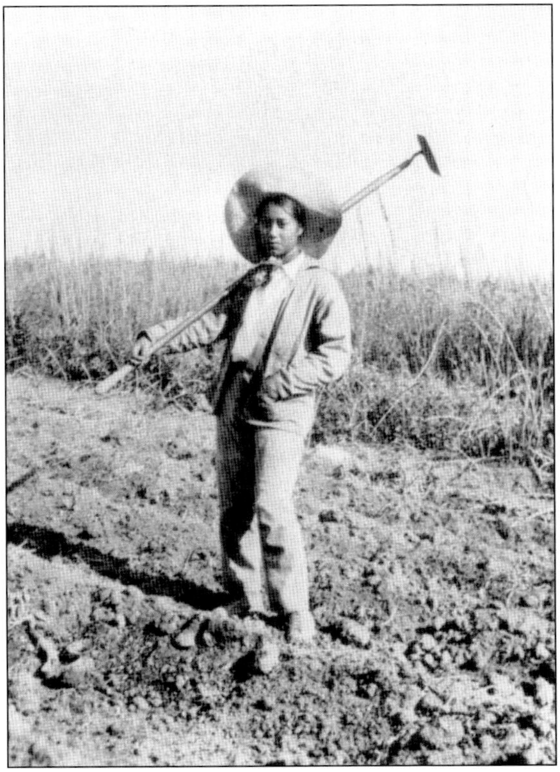

Hawaii-born Mary Arca migrated to Stockton with her family in 1923 and worked in the fields to help support her family. She and her husband, Sebastian Inosanto, became respected labor contractors, union activists with the Filipino Agricultural Laborers Association, and lauded community leaders. In the 1940s, Mary's sister Flora (Arca) Mata became the first Pinay teacher in Stockton. After World War II, Mary finished college and became the second. (Courtesy of Filipino Oral History Project, Inc.)

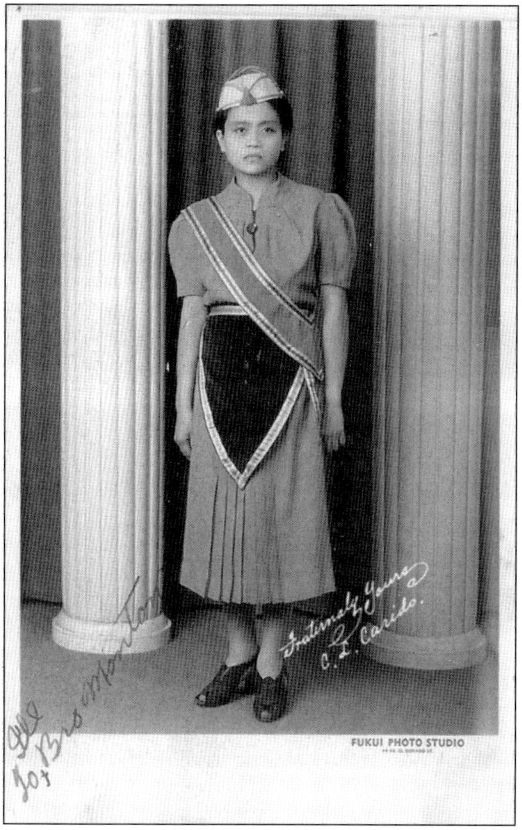

Camila Labor Carido was born in Hinundayan, Leyte, and immigrated to the United States in 1929 as a teenager to join her father, Epifiano. She was a founding member of the Teodora Alonzo Lodge, the first women's lodge of the Legionarios del Trabajo in America. Here she is pictured in her elaborate lodge regalia in the 1930s. (Photograph by Fukui Studio, courtesy of Sharon Monton Robinson.)

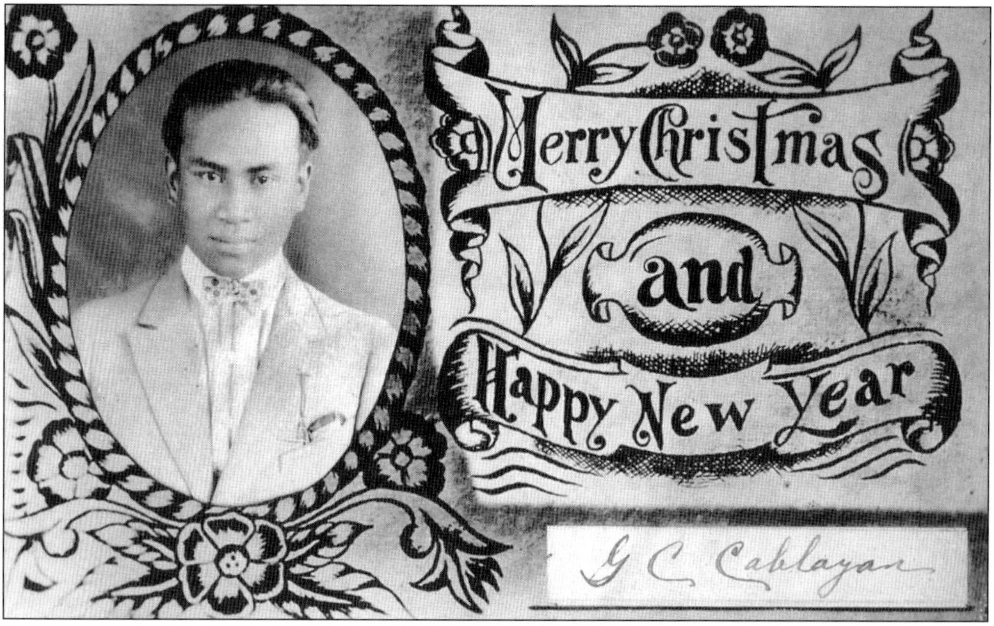

Immigrants quickly adopted the custom of sending Christmas greetings to one another and home to the Philippines. George Cablayan sent this holiday card to friends and family in the 1920s. (Courtesy of Raymond Cablayan.)

Life in America allowed immigrant Pinoys to play with different personas and identities. This Pinoy dressed as a cowboy for a formal portrait taken in Little Manila in the 1930s. (Courtesy of the Haggin Museum, Stockton, California.)

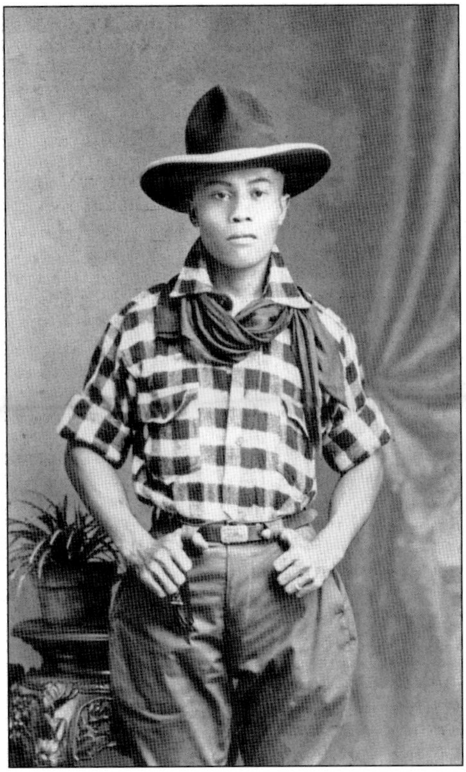

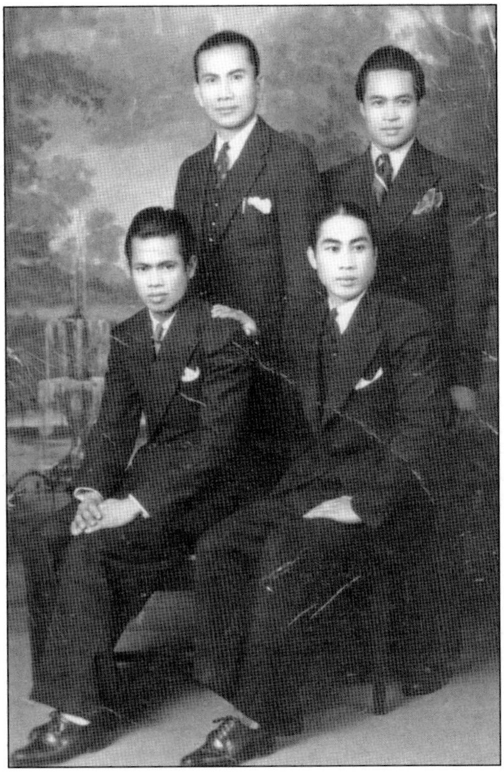

Esteban "Steve" Acacio Gapusan (second row, on right) left Ilocos Norte in 1926 for Stockton. He worked in the fields in San Joaquin County, and he and his wife, Katherine, raised five children. He is pictured with his relatives Tony (to his left) and below, from left to right, his nephew Frank Mateo and Florencio (last name unknown). (Courtesy of Kathrine and Tanishia Gapusan.)

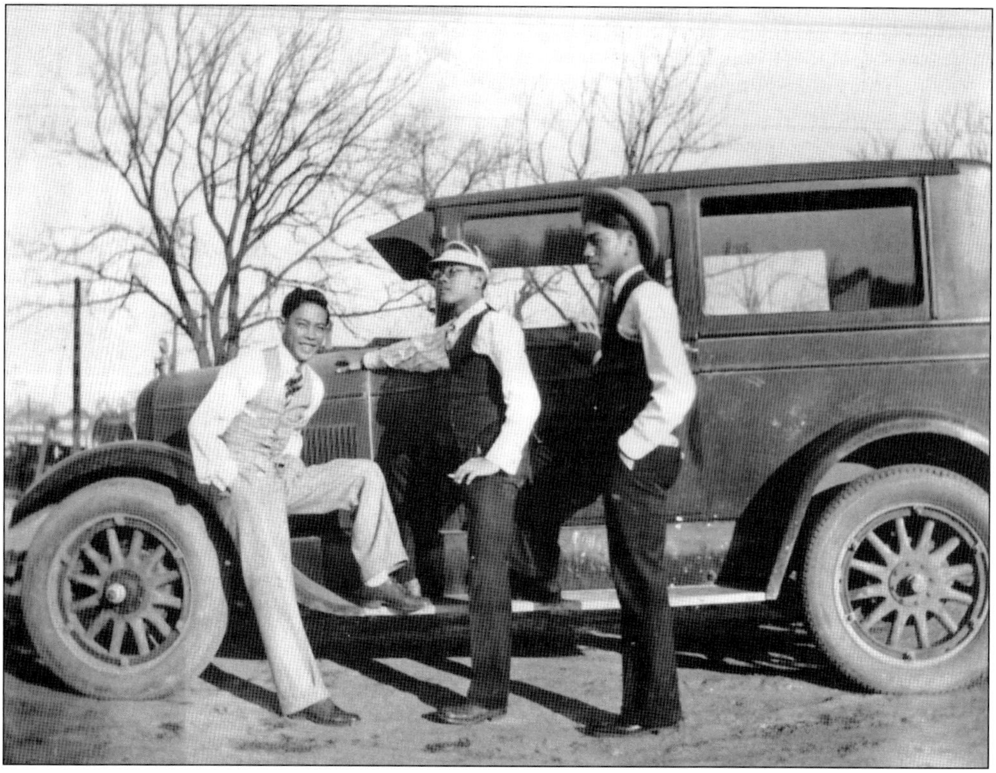

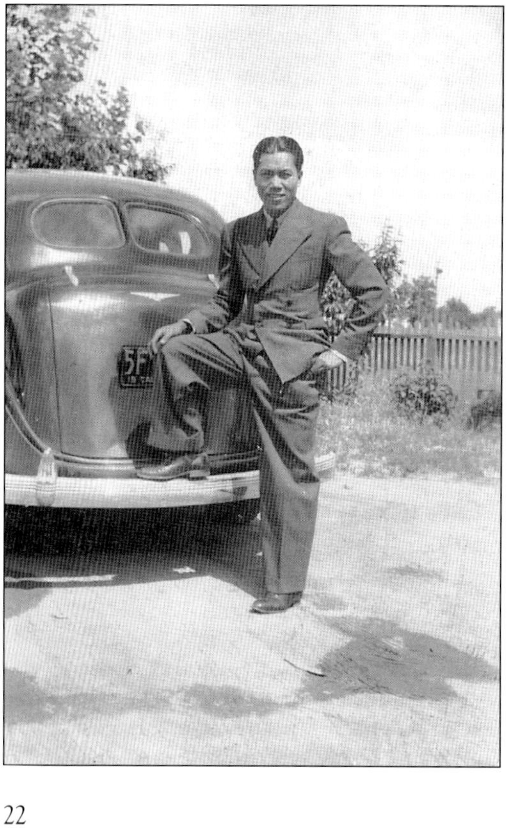

After the purchase of a sharp suit, a car was the commodity Filipino immigrants most wanted. Many pooled their money and shared a car. This might have been the case for these three friends in Stockton. (Courtesy of FANHS Stockton.)

Isaac Romena is shown here in April 1937 in a sharp suit with his car in a classic 1930s Pinoy photograph. (Courtesy of Arlene Johnson.)

Several Filipino pioneer families settled in Stockton. Pictured here is the Cano family in 1936 in the *campo* on Terminous Island near Highway 4. From left to right are George, Faustina Juntilla, Laura, Felicidad "Phyllis" (Ente), Constancia "Connie" (Estante), and Toribio "Terry" (Rosal). (Courtesy of Phyllis Ente.)

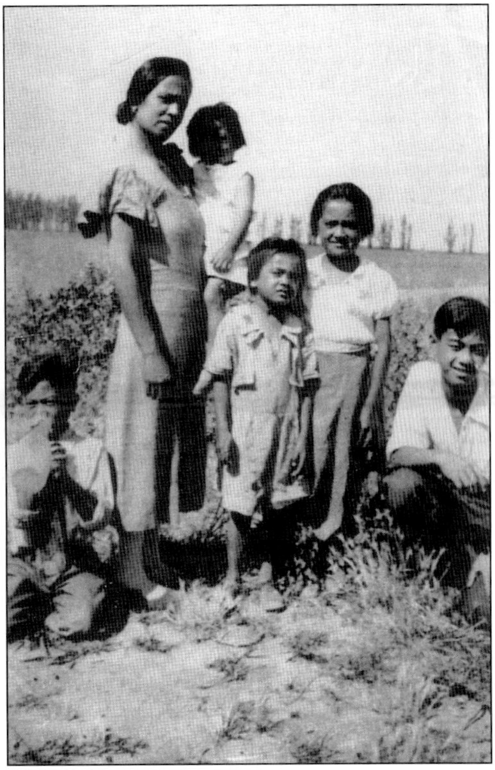

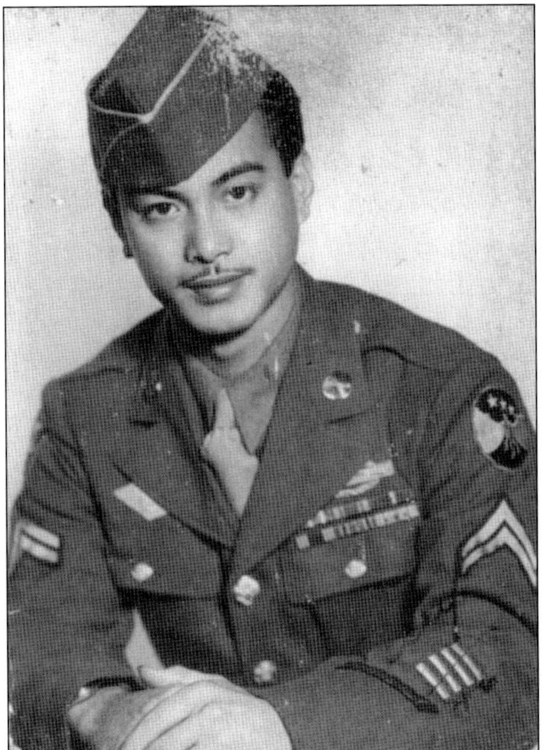

Second-generation Toribio "Terry" Rosal was one of many Filipinos who joined the 1st and 2nd Filipino Infantry Regiments and served in the Philippines during World War II. These veterans received naturalization and all Veterans Administration and GI Bill benefits. Rosal returned and became a leader of the Manuel A. Roxas Post of the American Legion and a member of the Legionarios del Trabajo. He and his wife, Hawaii-born Emily Rosal, raised their family in Stockton. (Courtesy of Emily Rosal.)

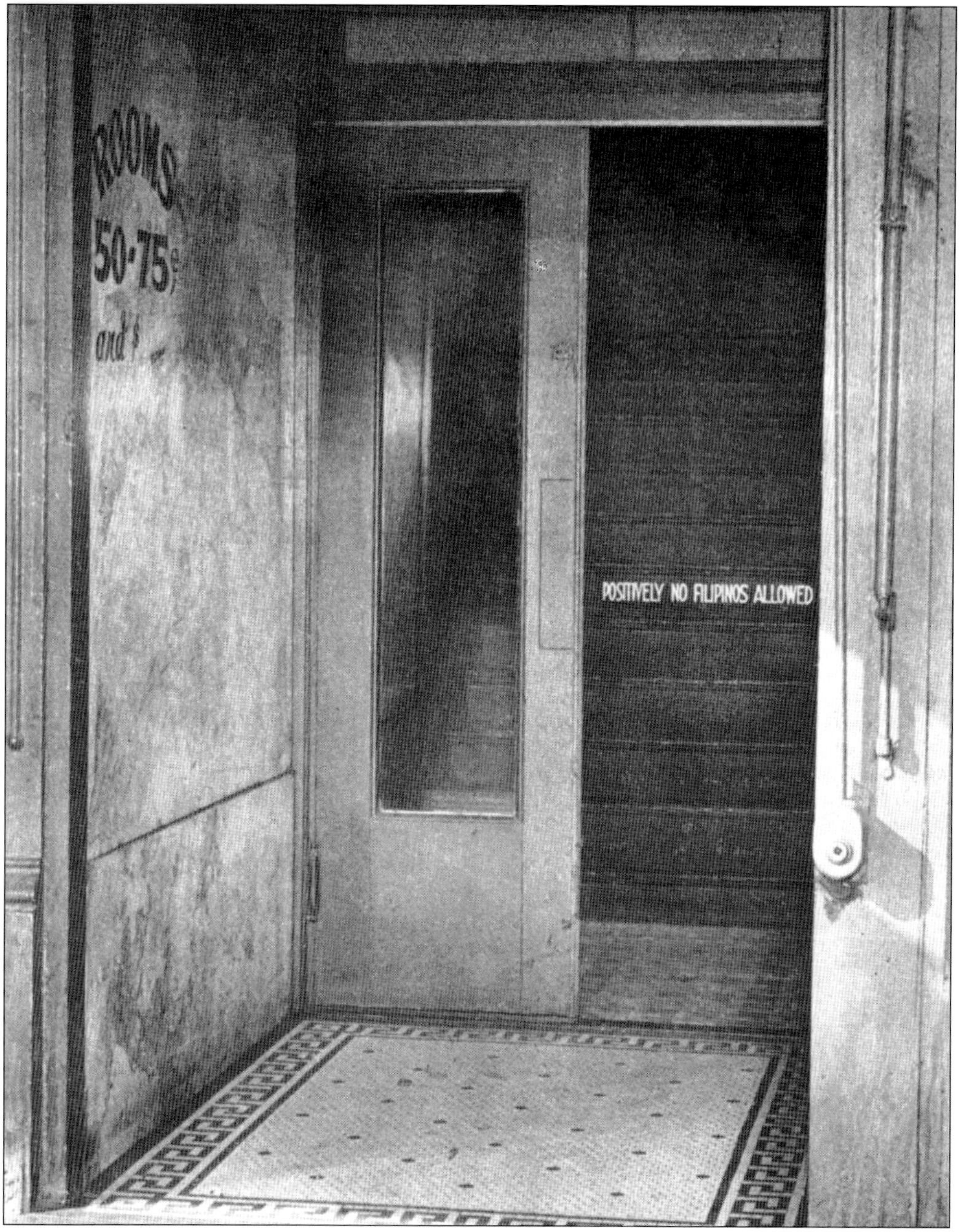

This Stockton hotel, photographed in 1945, was only one of many area establishments, including restaurants, public pools, department stores, and other public places that barred Filipinos. Many longtime residents remember signs that read "No Filipinos and Dogs Allowed." Stockton was rigidly segregated, and only whites could live north of Main Street until after the 1960s. (Courtesy of FANHS National.)

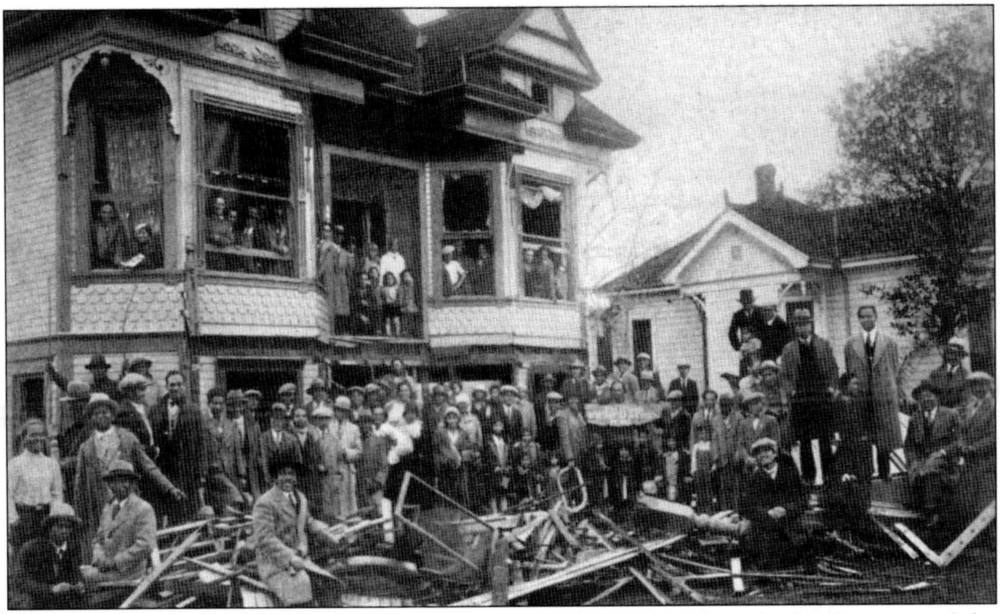

Shortly after midnight on January 29, 1930, a group threw a bomb at the headquarters of the Filipino Federation of America (FFA) building at 2049 South San Joaquin Street, destroying the front of the building. The bombing occurred as white mobs were attacking Filipinos throughout the state. Only one person was injured during the bombing, for which no one was ever prosecuted. The FFA quickly rebuilt its porch. The federation was founded in December 1925 in Los Angeles, and membership consisted of thousands of former *sakadas*. The FFA was a mutual aid and quasi-religious society; their political and spiritual leader was the controversial Hilario Moncado. Though the original building is no longer there, the FFA maintains its sprawling headquarters on the same site today. (Courtesy of FANHS Stockton.)

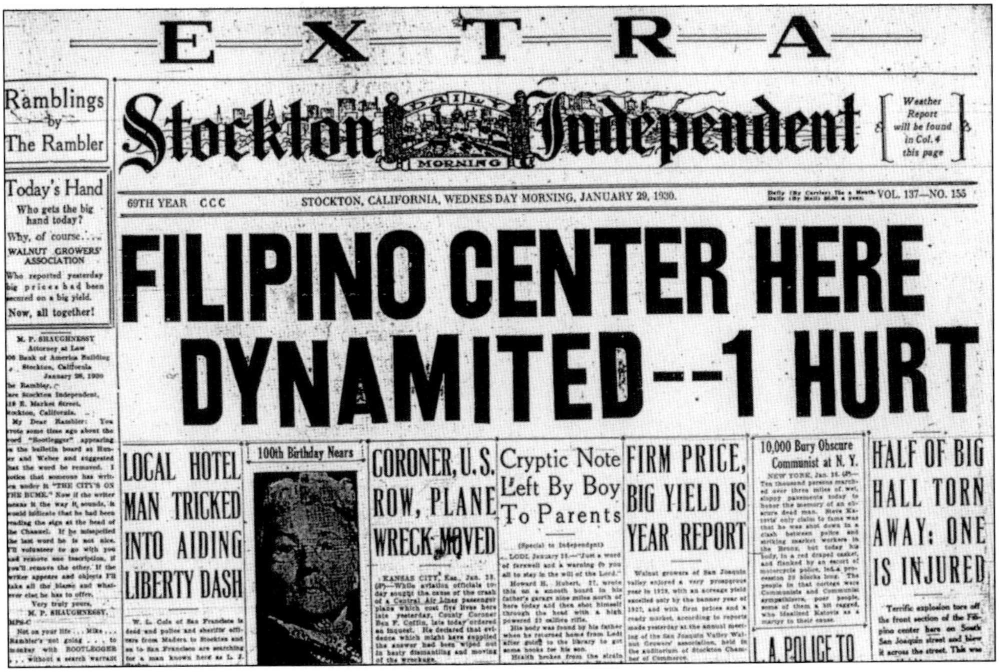

E X T R A

Ramblings by The Rambler

Stockton Daily Independent Morning

Weather Report will be found in Col. 4 this page

69TH YEAR CCC — STOCKTON, CALIFORNIA, WEDNESDAY MORNING, JANUARY 29, 1930. — VOL. 137—NO. 155

FILIPINO CENTER HERE DYNAMITED--1 HURT

Today's Hand

Who gets the big hand today?

Why, of course. . . . WALNUT GROWERS' ASSOCIATION

Who reported yesterday big prices had been secured on a big yield.

Now, all together!

M. P. SHAUGHNESSY
Attorney at Law
[illegible] Bank of America Building
Stockton, California
January 28, 1930

The Rambler,
Care Stockton Independent,
[illegible] E. Market Street,
Stockton, California.

My Dear Rambler: You wrote some time ago about the word "Bootlegger" appearing on the bulletin board at Hunter and Weber and suggested that the word be removed. I notice that someone has written under it "THE CITY'S ON THE BUMS." Now if the writer means it the way it sounds, it would indicate that he had been reading the sign at the head of the Channel. If he misspelled the last word he is not nice. I'll volunteer to go with you and remove one inscription, if you'll remove the other. If the writer appears and objects I'll take all the blame and whatever else he has to offer.

Very truly yours,
M. P. SHAUGHNESSY.
MPS-C

Not on your life . . . Mike . . . Rambler's not going . . . to monkey with BOOTLEGGER . . . without a search warrant

LOCAL HOTEL MAN TRICKED INTO AIDING LIBERTY DASH

W. L. Cole of San Francisco is dead and police and sheriffs' officers from Madera to Stockton and on to San Francisco are searching for a man known here as L. J.

100th Birthday Nears

CORONER, U.S. ROW, PLANE WRECK MOVED

KANSAS CITY, Kas., Jan. 28. (AP)—While aviation officials today sought the cause of the crash of a Central Air Lines passenger plane which cost five lives here late yesterday, County Coroner Ben F. Coffin, late today ordered an inquest. He declared that evidence which might have supplied the answer had been wiped out in hasty dismantling and moving of the wreckage.

Cryptic Note Left By Boy To Parents

(Special to Independent)

LODI, January 28.—"Just a word of farewell and a warning to you all to stay in the will of the Lord."

Howard H. Hubert, 27, wrote this on a smooth board in his father's garage nine miles north of here today and then shot himself through the head with a high powered 22 calibre rifle.

His body was found by his father when he returned home from Lodi after going to the library to get some books for his son.

Health broken from the strain

FIRM PRICE, BIG YIELD IS YEAR REPORT

Walnut growers of San Joaquin valley enjoyed a very prosperous year in 1929, with an acreage yield excelled only by the banner year of 1927, and with firm prices and a ready market, according to reports made yesterday at the annual meeting of the San Joaquin Valley Walnut Growers' association, held in the auditorium of Stockton Chamber of Commerce.

10,000 Bury Obscure Communist at N. Y.

NEW YORK, Jan. 28. (AP)—Ten thousand persons marched over three miles of wet, sloppy pavements today to honor the memory of an obscure dead man. Steve Katovis' only claim to fame was that he was shot down in a clash between police and striking market workers in the Bronx, but today his body, in a red draped casket, and flanked by an escort of motorcycle police, led a procession 20 blocks long. The people in that cortege were Communists and Communist sympathizers, poor people, some of them a bit ragged, who idealized Katovis as a martyr to their cause.

L. A. POLICE TO

HALF OF BIG HALL TORN AWAY: ONE IS INJURED

Terrific explosion tore off the front section of the Filipino center here on South San Joaquin street and blew it across the street. This was

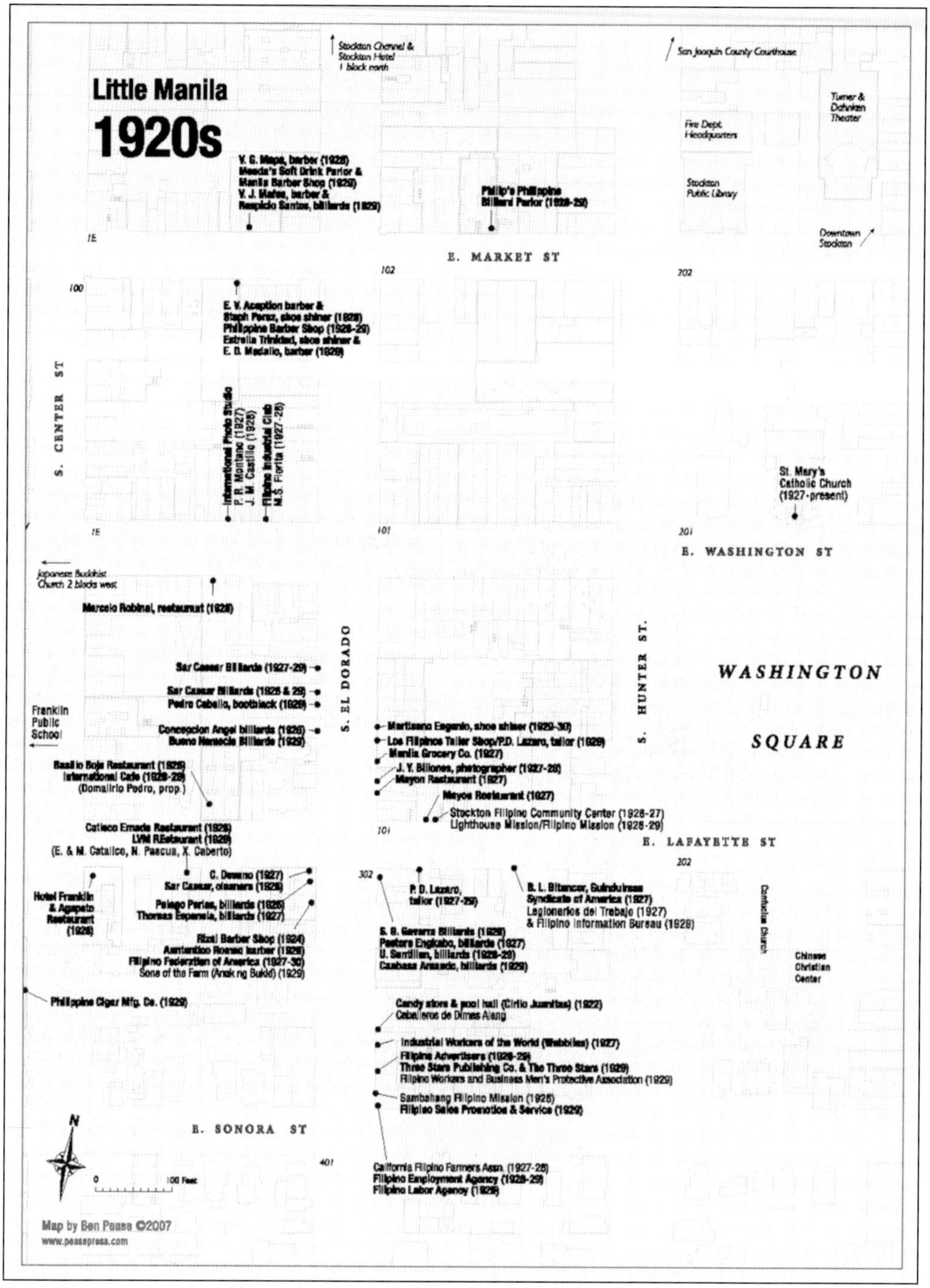

City directories and oral histories show a growing Filipino presence downtown near Chinatown and Nihonmachi (Japantown), near the intersection of Lafayette and El Dorado Streets. Filipinos were barred from any neighborhoods north of Main Street, a block north of Market Street. (Courtesy of Ben Pease.)

Two

WORKING TO SURVIVE
LABOR AND LABOR UNIONS

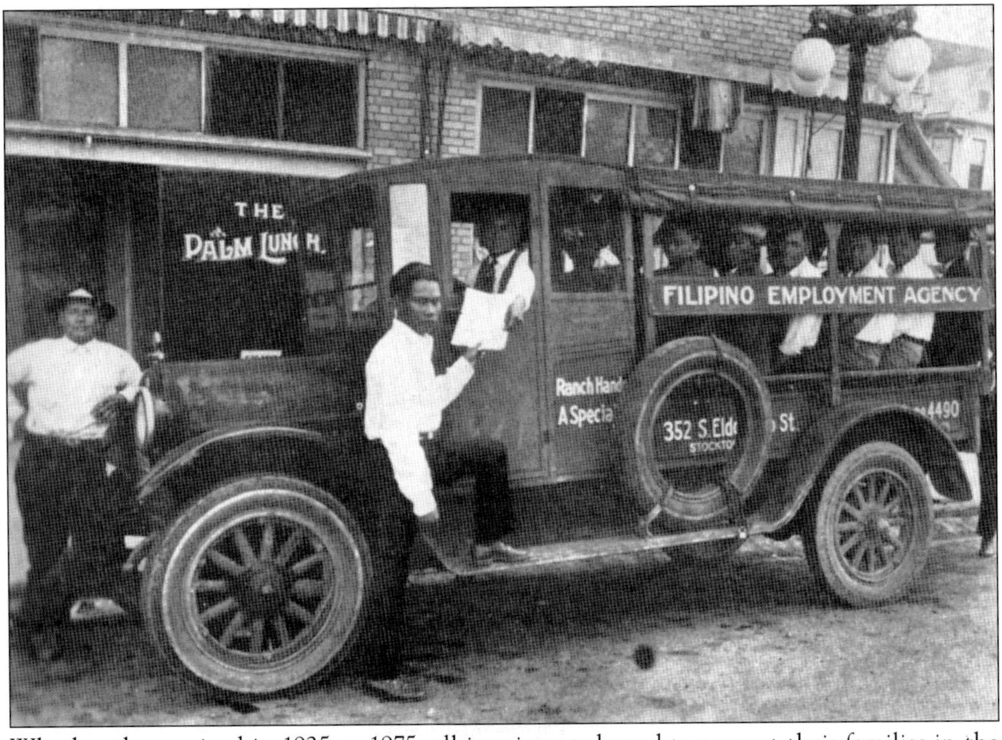

Whether they arrived in 1925 or 1975, all immigrants hoped to support their families in the United States as well as send money home to the Philippines, but even the most highly educated immigrants were barred from white-collar jobs until recently. Through the 20th century, Filipinos in Stockton have played an integral role in the San Joaquin Delta agricultural economy. By the 1920s, Filipino farm labor contractors were recruiting workers in Little Manila and transporting them to farms in the San Joaquin Delta. Filipinos soon attained a reputation for highly skilled and efficient labor everywhere they worked: in grapes, sugar beets, potatoes, celery, peaches, pruning, tomatoes, and especially asparagus. They developed close ties in their *campo* work crews, which usually consisted of Filipinos from the same town or region. Filipinos took great pride and dignity in their work, which was why they formed powerful, militant labor unions. After World War II, Stockton became home to many more immigrant and American-born Filipino professionals. (Photograph by John Y. Billones, courtesy of FANHS Stockton.)

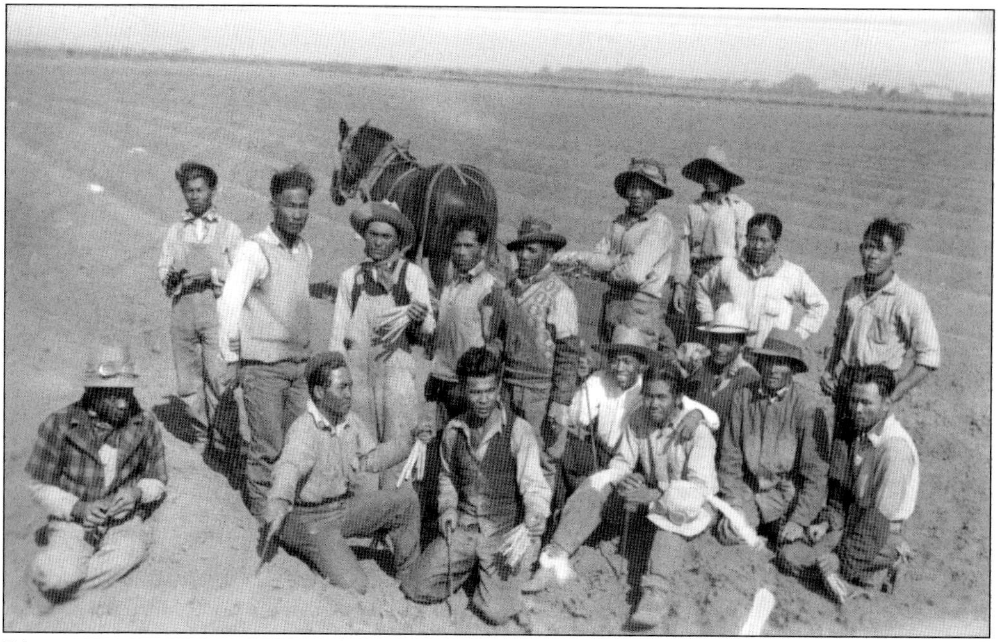

Filipino asparagus cutters pause during their workday. Asparagus season was lucrative for skilled Filipinos who could cut at amazing speeds, but work was grueling, since peat dust was harsh and itchy and the heat was relentless. (Photograph by Frank Mancao, courtesy of FANHS National.)

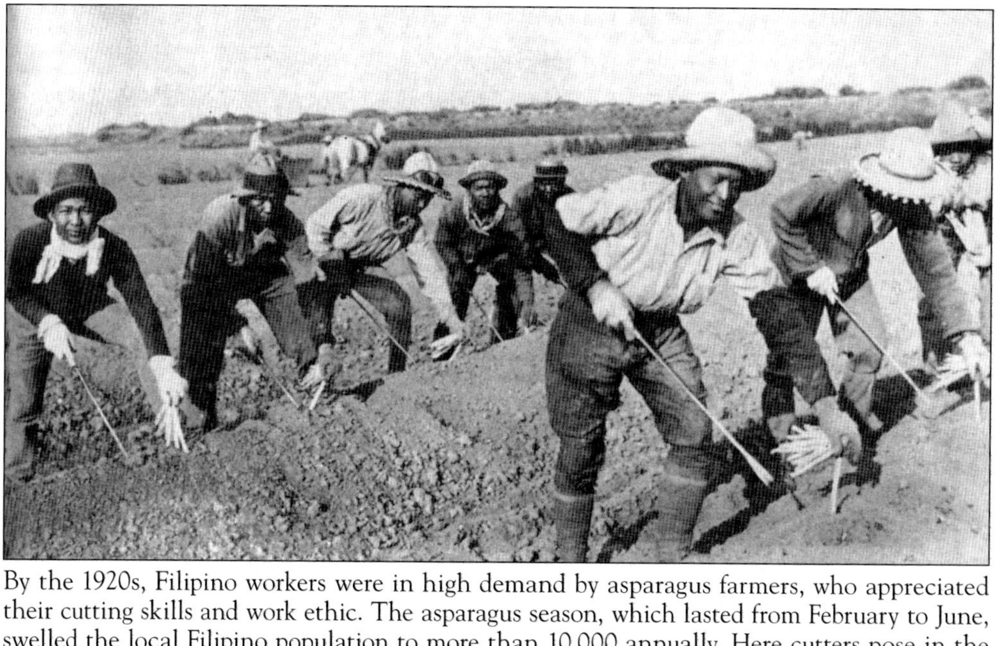

By the 1920s, Filipino workers were in high demand by asparagus farmers, who appreciated their cutting skills and work ethic. The asparagus season, which lasted from February to June, swelled the local Filipino population to more than 10,000 annually. Here cutters pose in the 1920s. Asparagus is still cut spear by spear by hand. (Photograph by John Y. Billones, courtesy of FANHS Stockton.)

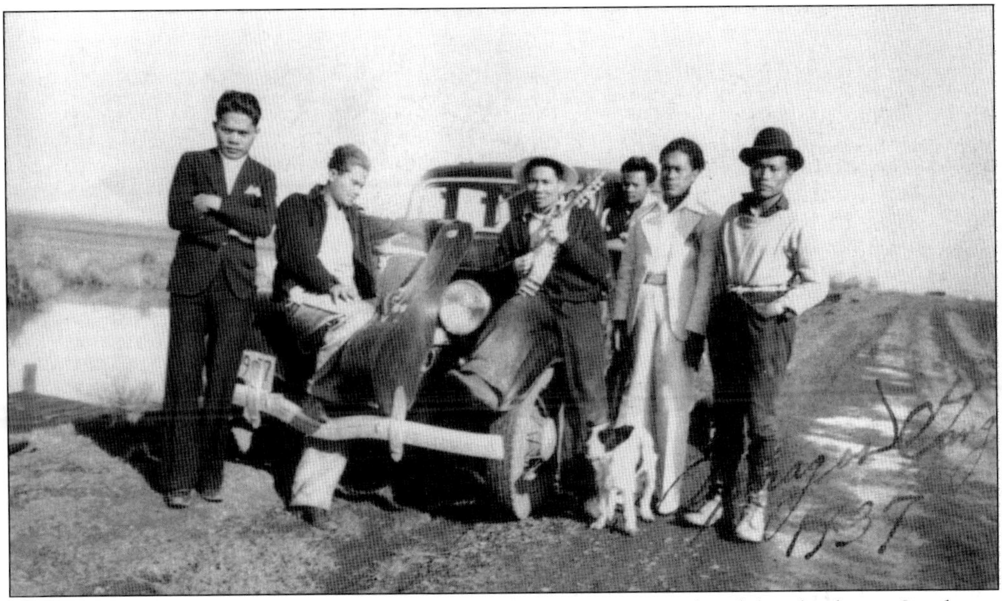

Cipriano "Rudy" Delvo (in the black hat on right) became a tireless labor leader in Stockton, organizing workers for the 1948–1949 asparagus strikes for Local 7, for the 1965 Delano Grape Strike, and during the grape boycotts in the 1970s. Here Delvo is with friends from his labor camp in a photograph he titled "Asparagus Gang," *c.* 1930s. (Courtesy of Dillon Delvo.)

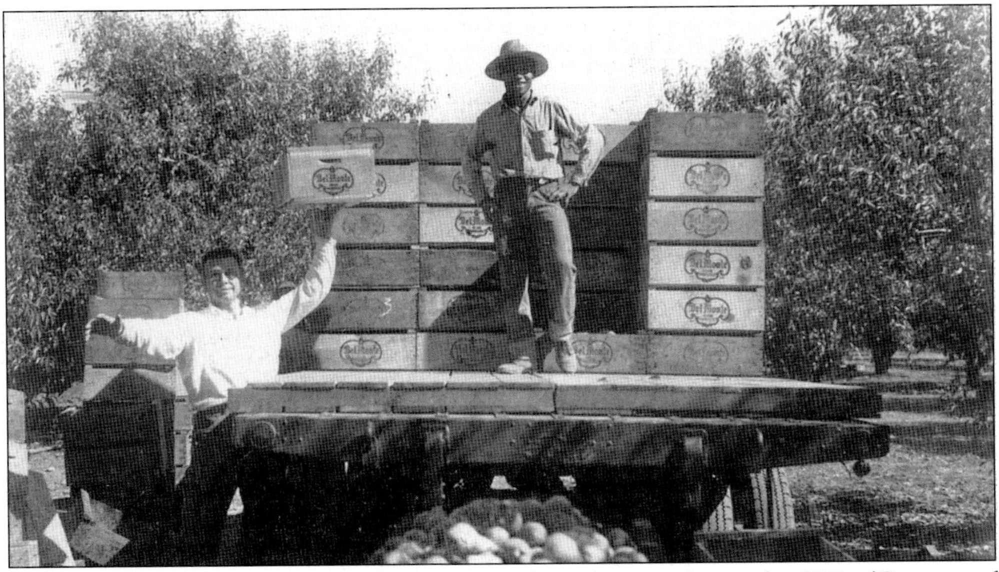

A Pinoy working in peaches for Del Monte poses for a photographer in the 1930s. (Courtesy of Tony Somera.)

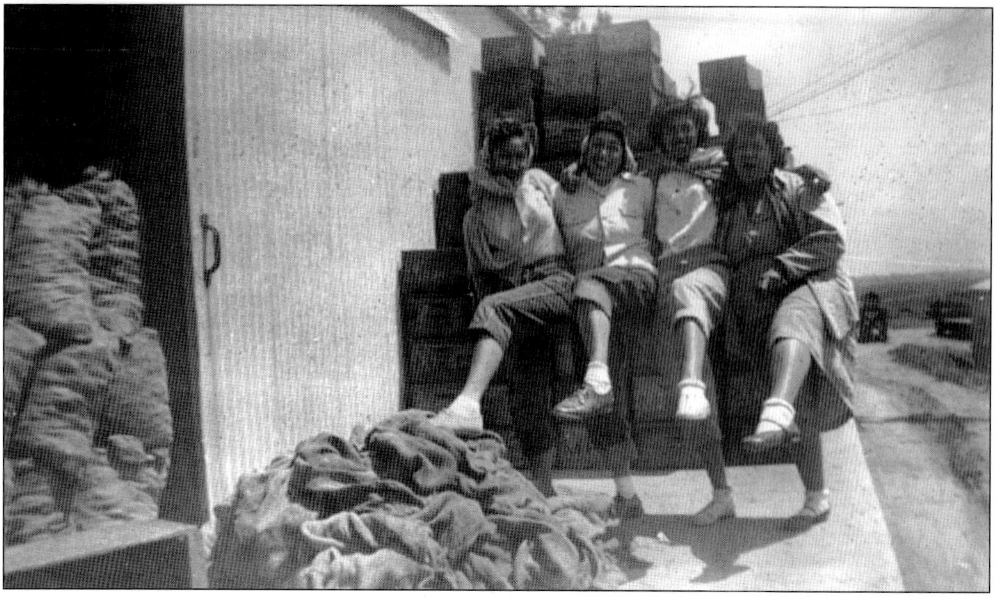

Ida Silva Cabrero and friends at a potato packing shed take a break around the 1940s. (Courtesy of Ed Chavez.)

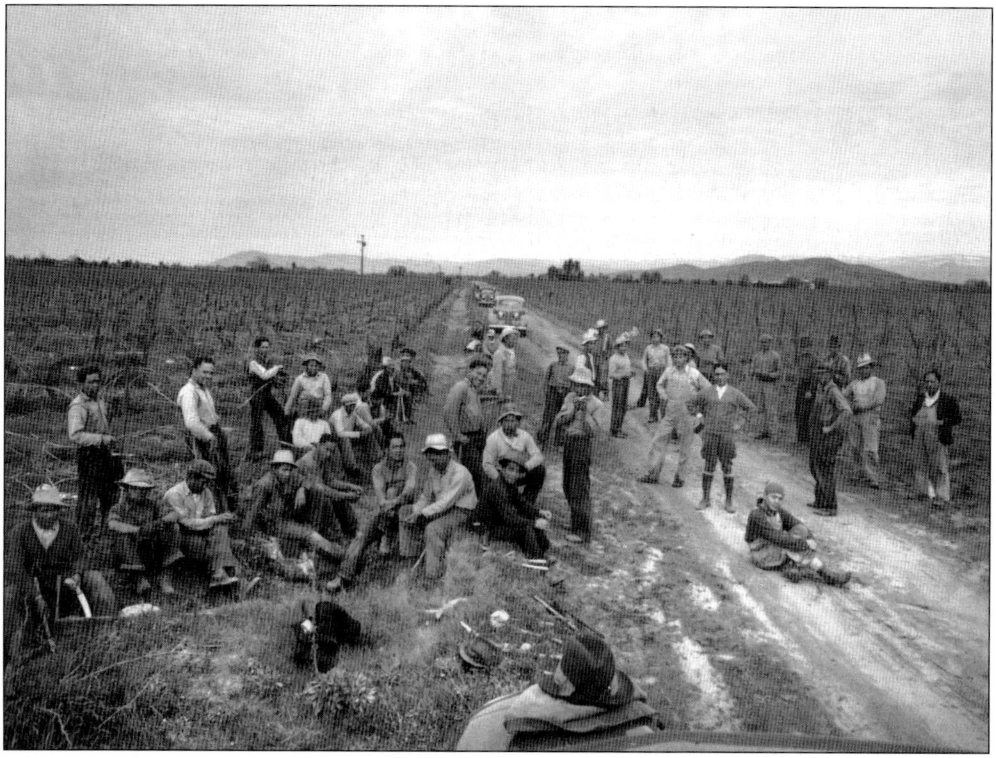

Filipinos working in grape pruning are shown at the end of their workday. Pruning season started in late fall. (Photograph by Frank Mancao, courtesy of FANHS National.)

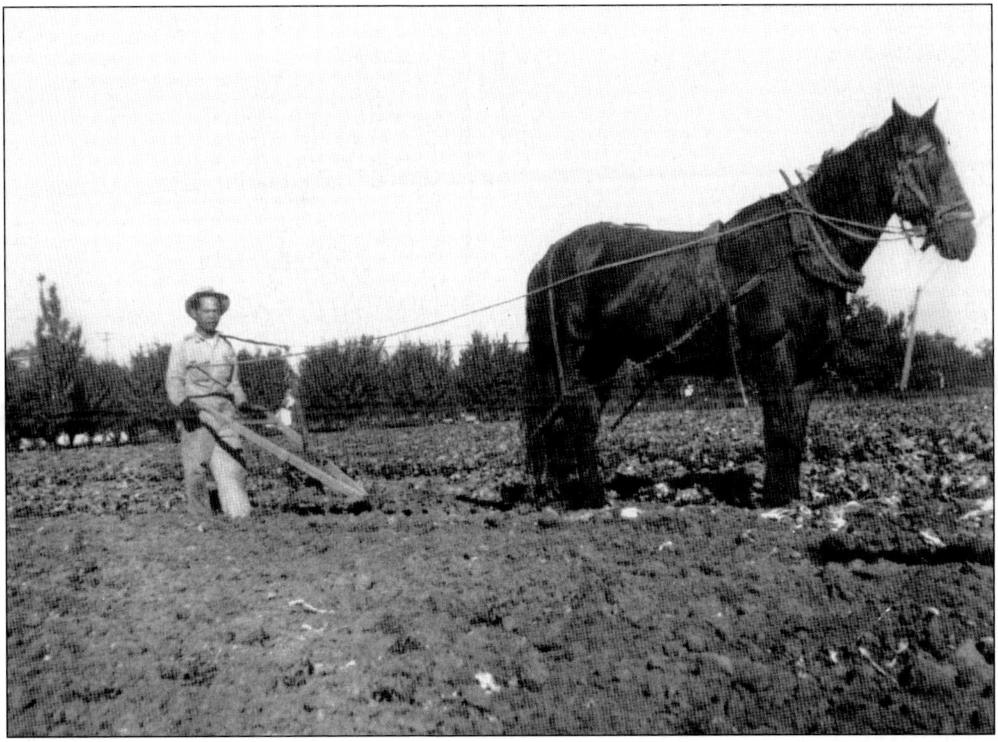

Celestino "Chester" Serna Somera plows a field in the 1930s. Somera, a native of Cabugan, Ilocos Sur, came to Stockton in 1930 and became a member of the Legionarios del Trabajo. (Courtesy of Tony Somera.)

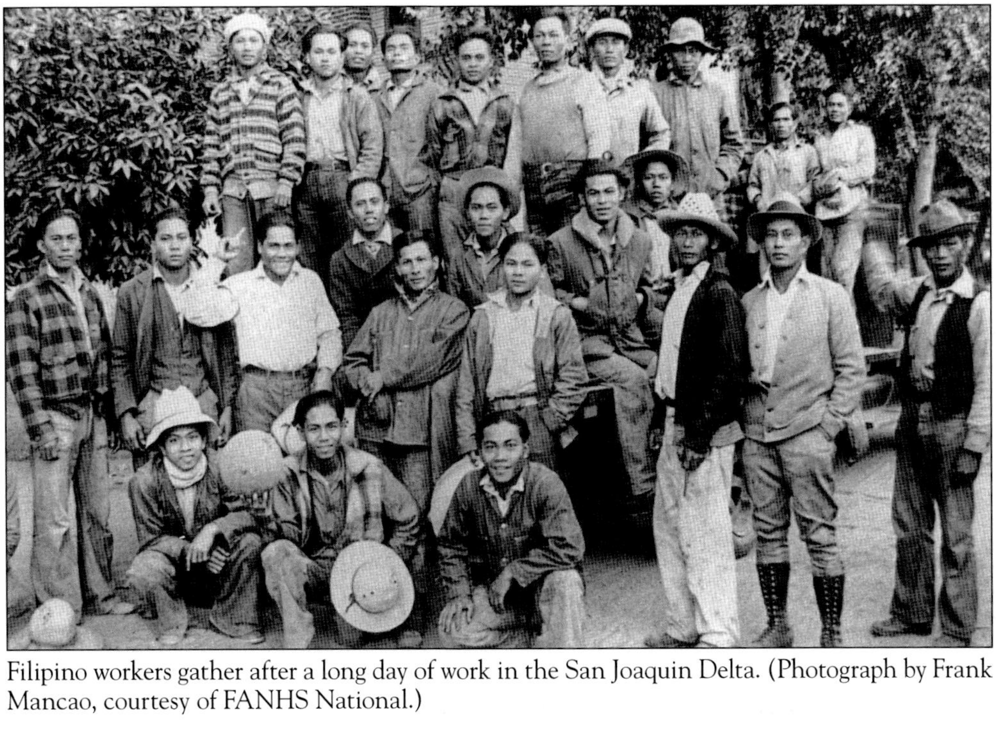

Filipino workers gather after a long day of work in the San Joaquin Delta. (Photograph by Frank Mancao, courtesy of FANHS National.)

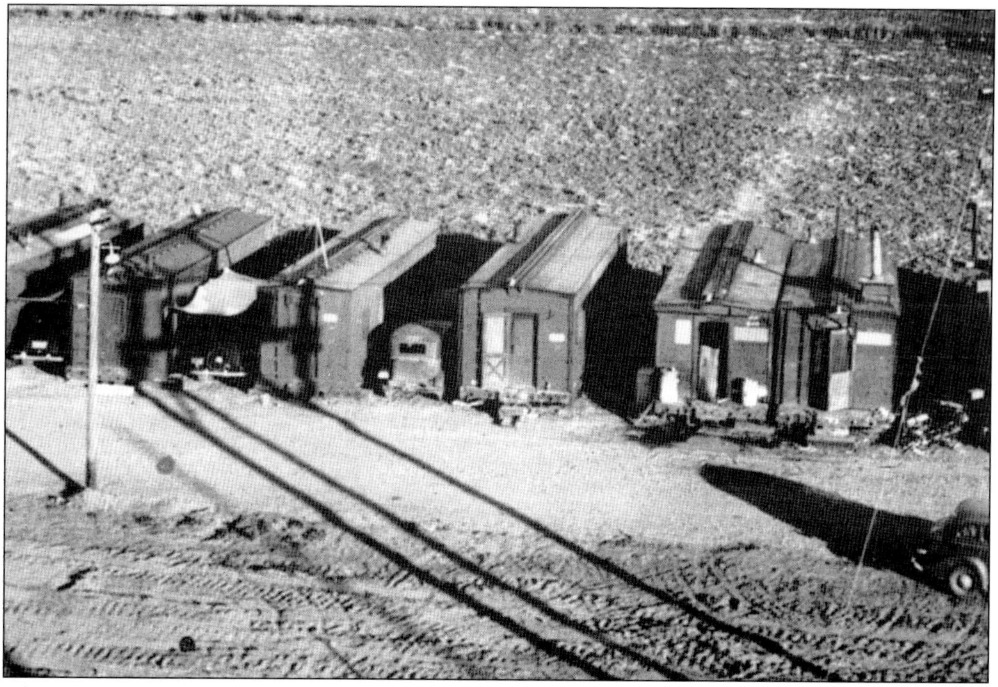

Filipino workers were forced to live in dilapidated housing on Delta farms. Typical housing included shacks, broken down barns, and, shown here in this photograph, converted boxcars. These were on Terminous Island in the 1930s or 1940s. (Courtesy of the Bank of Stockton Photo Collection.)

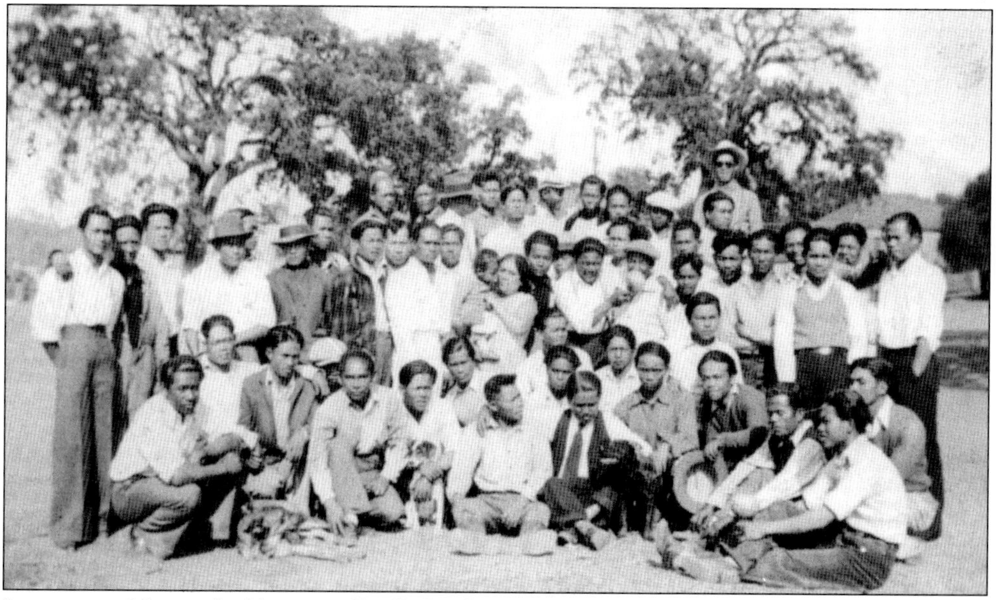

Leoncio and Lucia (holding son Fred) Cordova, of Numancia, Aklan, headed a labor camp southwest of Stockton at Middle River in the Delta in the 1930s. Most of the workers were probably related to the Cordovas or came from the same region. Ilocanos and Visayans tended to gather in camps organized depending on region, dialect, and hometown. Fred and his wife, Dorothy, Cordova are the founders of the Filipino American National Historical Society. (Courtesy of FANHS National.)

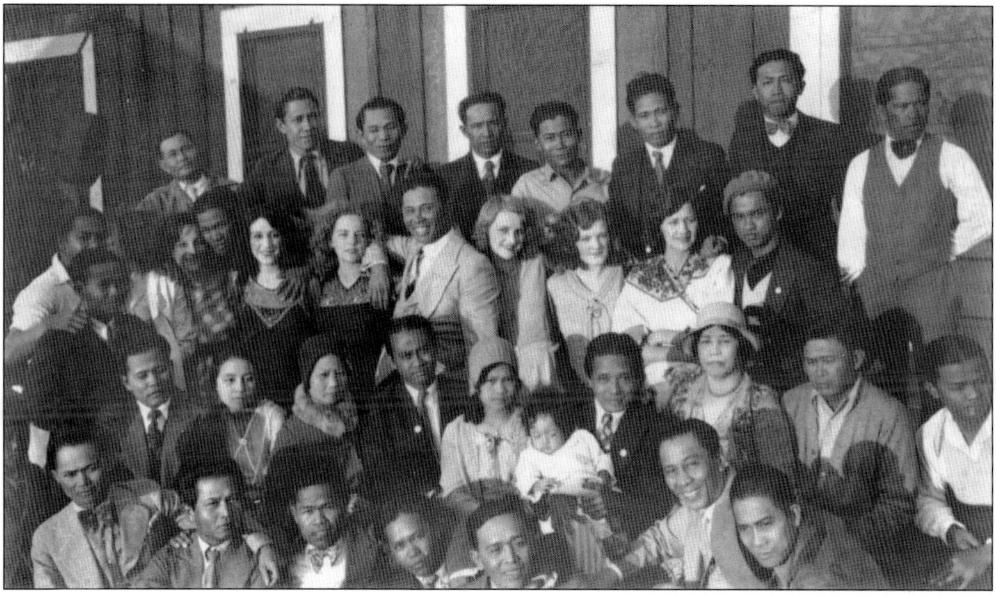

On some days after work, labor contractors brought in ladies to entertain workers in the *campo*. Here Pinays visiting their friends and relatives in the *campo* near Stockton are caught in an awkward moment with their relatives and these working women in a classic Frank Mancao *campo* portrait from the early 1930s. (Courtesy FANHS National.)

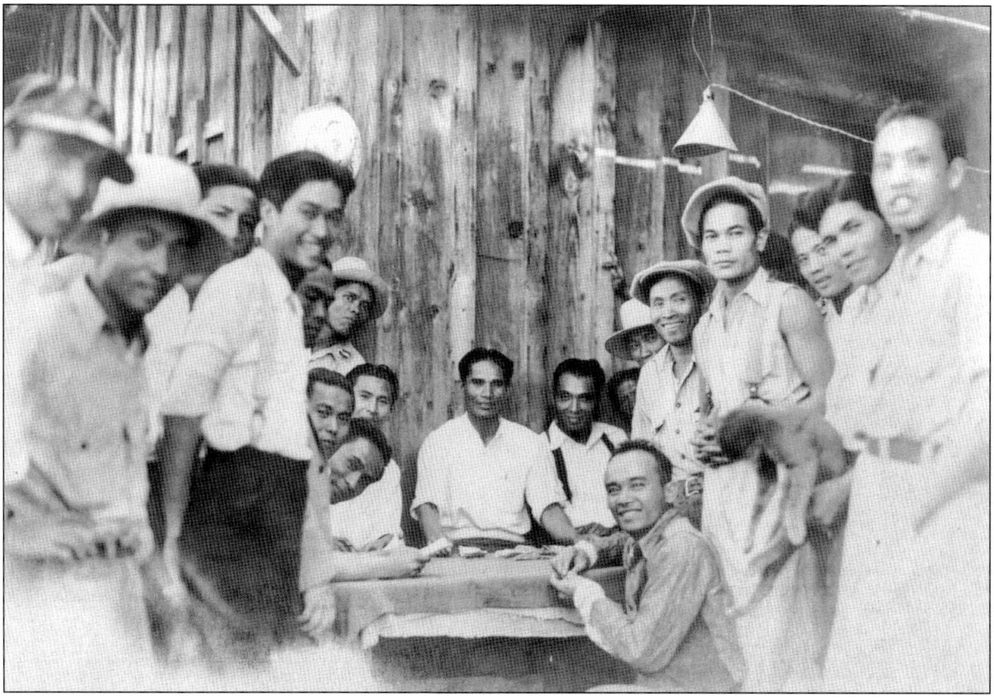

Popular pastimes after work in the campo and cannery included gambling. Here a group of workers pose for a photographer in the middle of a card game in a *campo* in the delta. (Courtesy of FANHS National.)

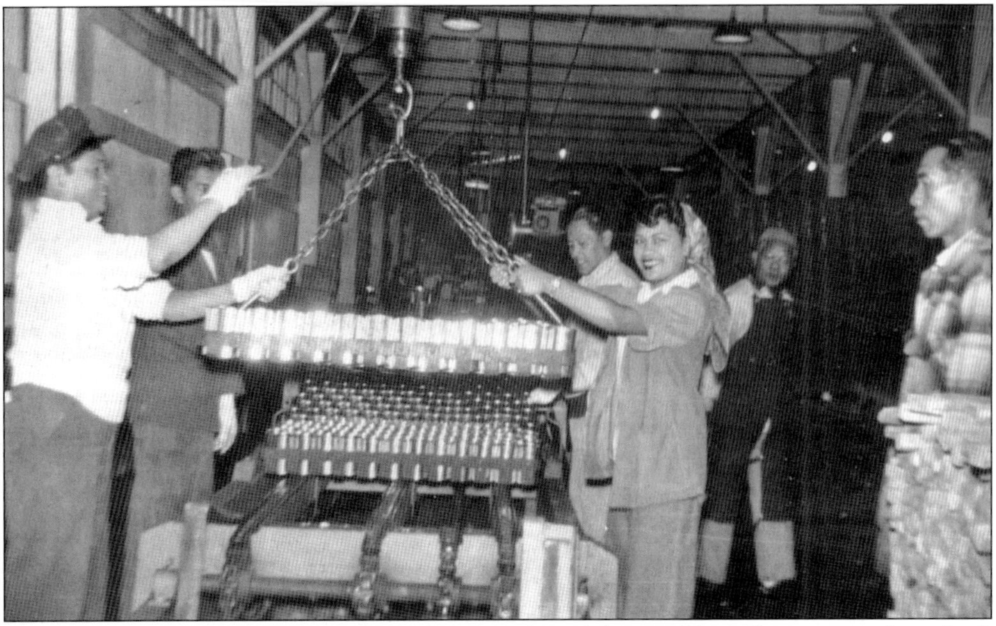

Work was hard and conditions were hazardous, but if one didn't gamble it all away, a good paycheck was one's reward after a long summer in Alaska. Here is a rare photograph of a Stockton Pinay *Alaskera* with Pablo Mabalon (in the black apron) in a cannery in the 1940s. Most workers were men, but some Pinays worked in the canneries, especially during World War II labor shortages. (Courtesy of the Mabalon family collection.)

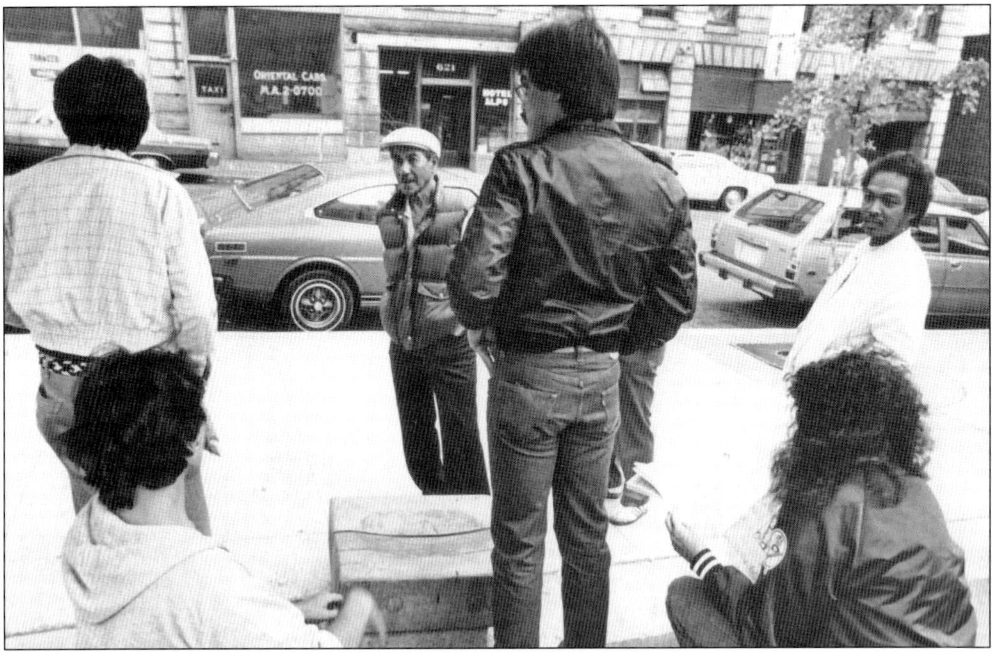

Every summer, thousands of Filipinos left Stockton to work in Alaskan salmon canneries. Two of these *Alaskeros* were Stockton residents Melanio Ancheta, facing the camera on the right, and Marcelo Ancheta, left, waiting in Seattle's International District in July 1981 for their departure to the canneries. (Courtesy of Richard Ancheta.)

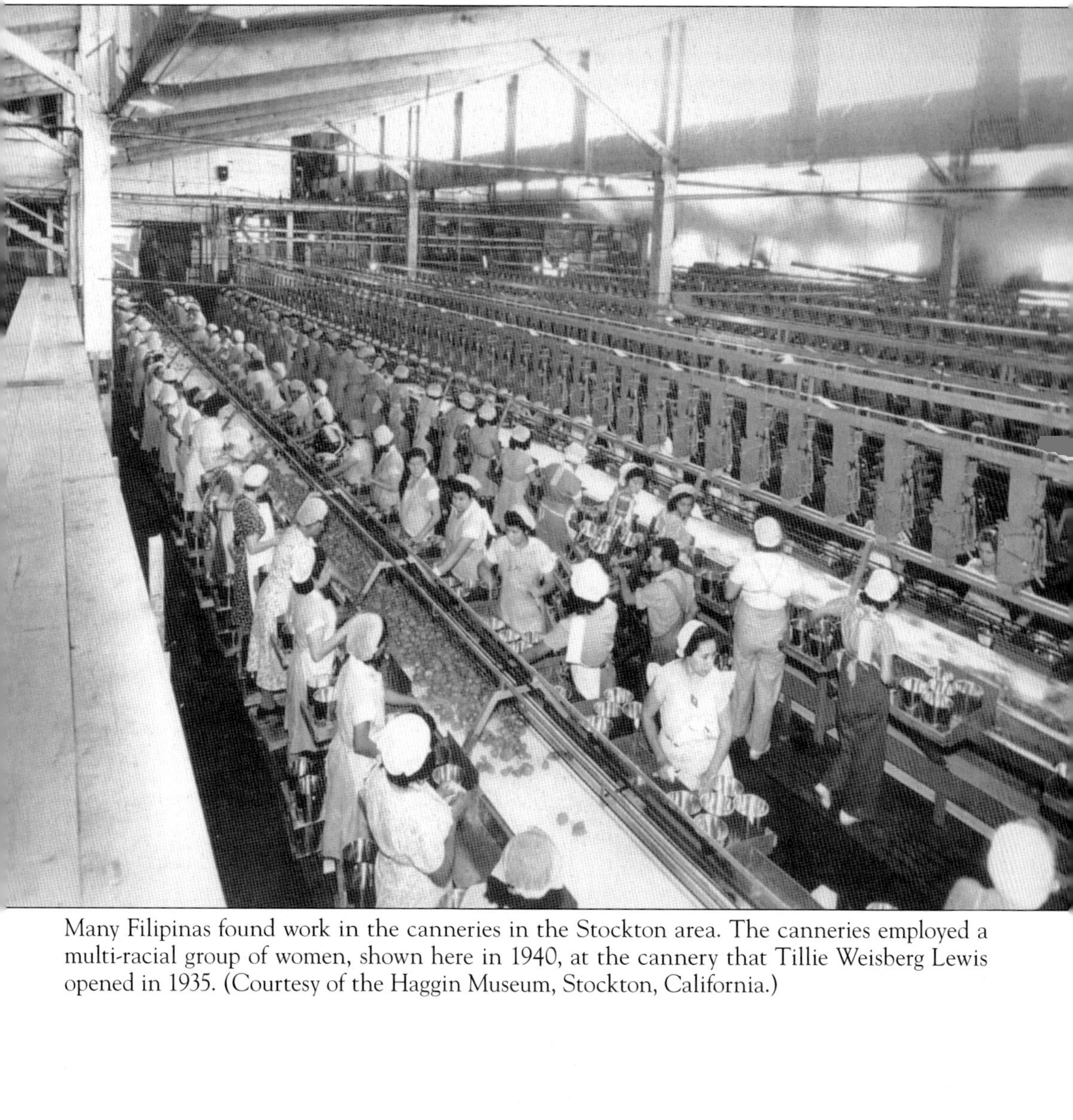

Many Filipinas found work in the canneries in the Stockton area. The canneries employed a multi-racial group of women, shown here in 1940, at the cannery that Tillie Weisberg Lewis opened in 1935. (Courtesy of the Haggin Museum, Stockton, California.)

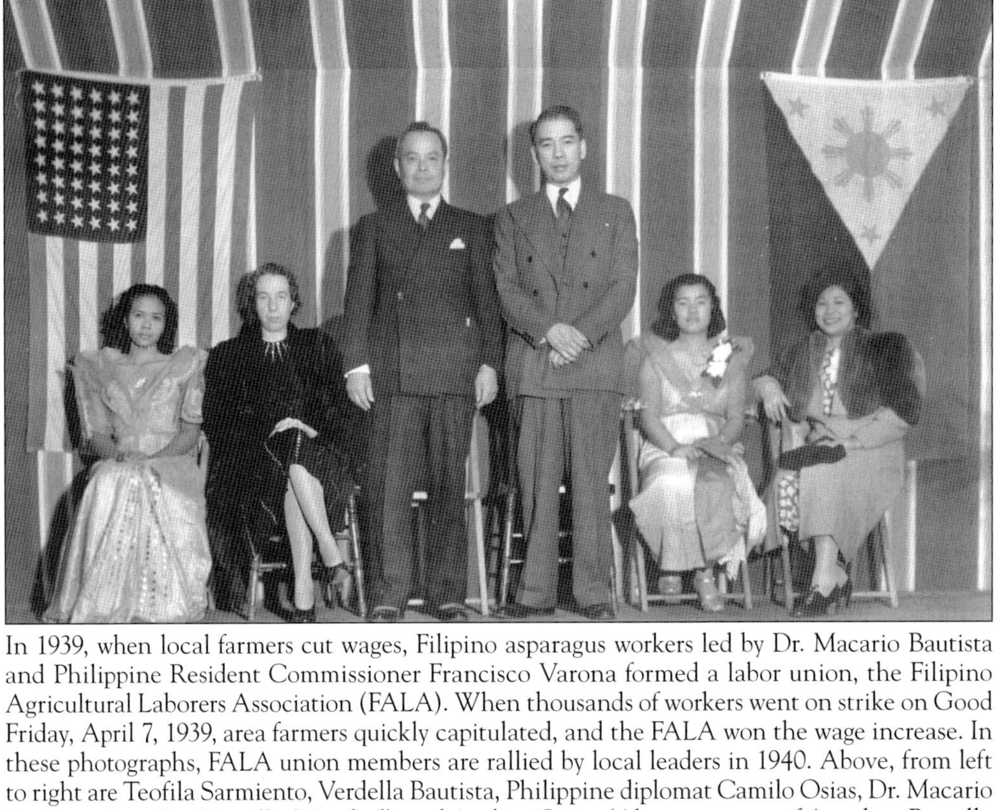

In 1939, when local farmers cut wages, Filipino asparagus workers led by Dr. Macario Bautista and Philippine Resident Commissioner Francisco Varona formed a labor union, the Filipino Agricultural Laborers Association (FALA). When thousands of workers went on strike on Good Friday, April 7, 1939, area farmers quickly capitulated, and the FALA won the wage increase. In these photographs, FALA union members are rallied by local leaders in 1940. Above, from left to right are Teofila Sarmiento, Verdella Bautista, Philippine diplomat Camilo Osias, Dr. Macario Bautista, Angelina Bantillo (Magdael), and Avelina Osias. (Above courtesy of Angelina Bantillo Magdael family collection; below courtesy of Special Collections, University of the Pacific.)

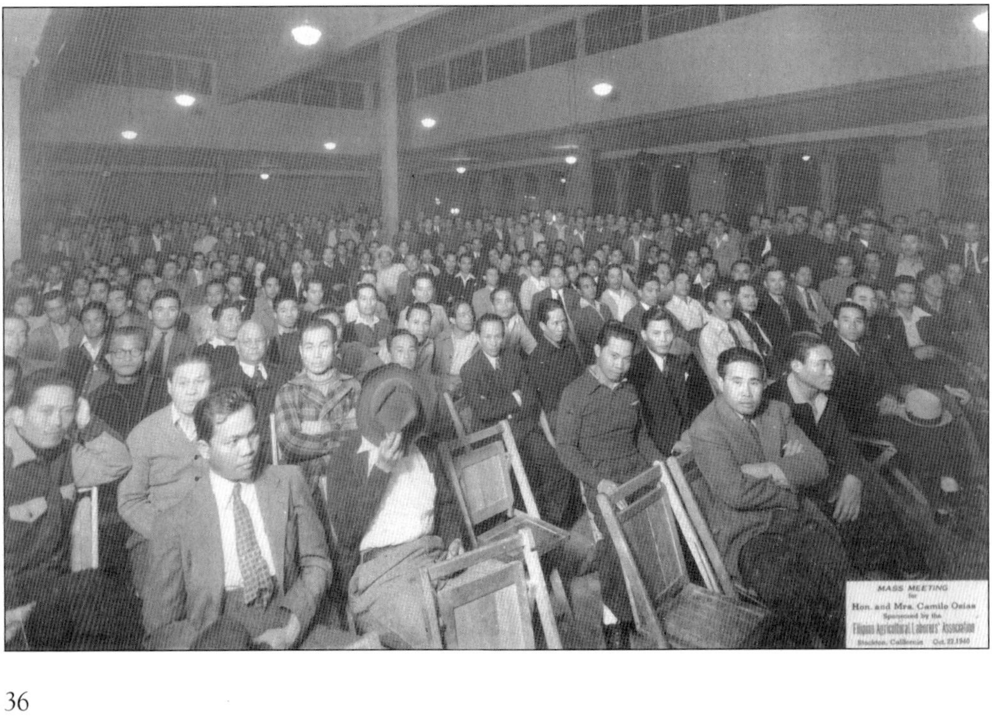

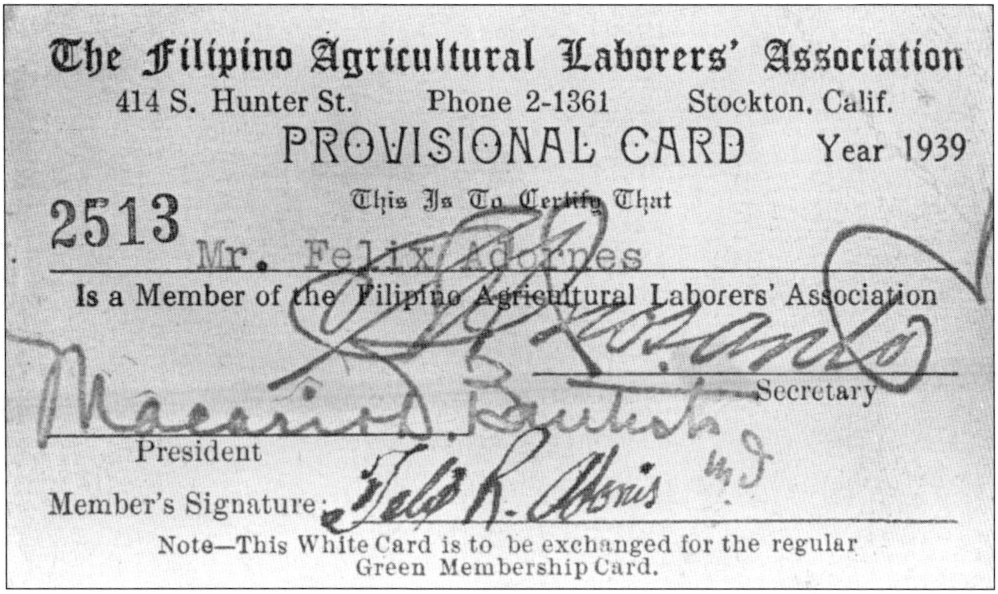
The Filipino Agricultural Laborers' Association
414 S. Hunter St. Phone 2-1361 Stockton, Calif.
PROVISIONAL CARD Year 1939
2513
This Is To Certify That
Mr. Felix Adornes
Is a Member of the Filipino Agricultural Laborers' Association
Secretary
President
Member's Signature
Note—This White Card is to be exchanged for the regular Green Membership Card.

The FALA membership card of Felix Adornes is signed by Sec. Sebastian Inosanto and Pres. Dr. Macario Bautista. The FALA was highly organized, militant, and powerful. However, anti-union activity from white and Japanese American farmers and the advent of World War II caused the union's demise. (Courtesy of Photographic Collections, Visual Communications.)

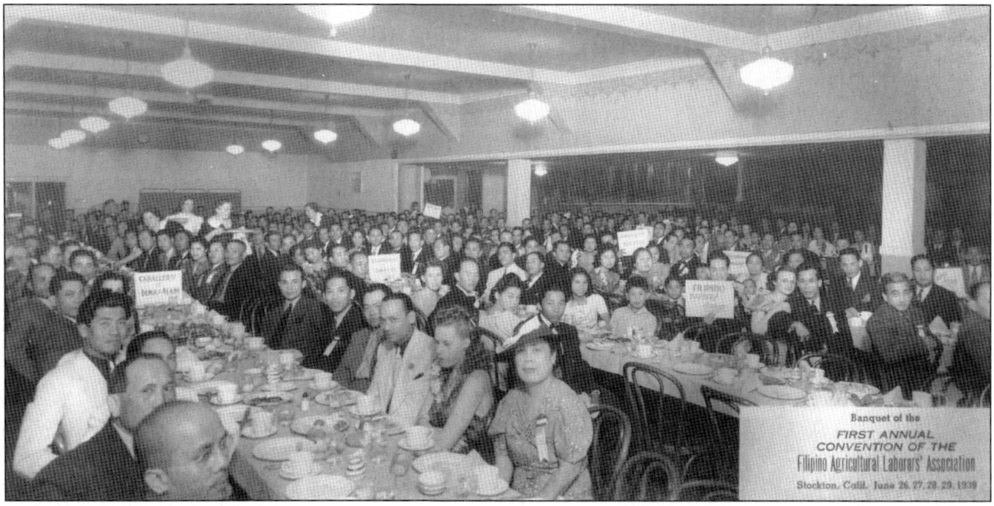

The FALA went on to organize strikes in celery and in other crops. Here the union holds its first convention in 1939 with the Stockton community. The union had just won a significant victory in that spring's asparagus harvest by forcing farmers to maintain wage levels. (Courtesy of the Iloilo Circle.)

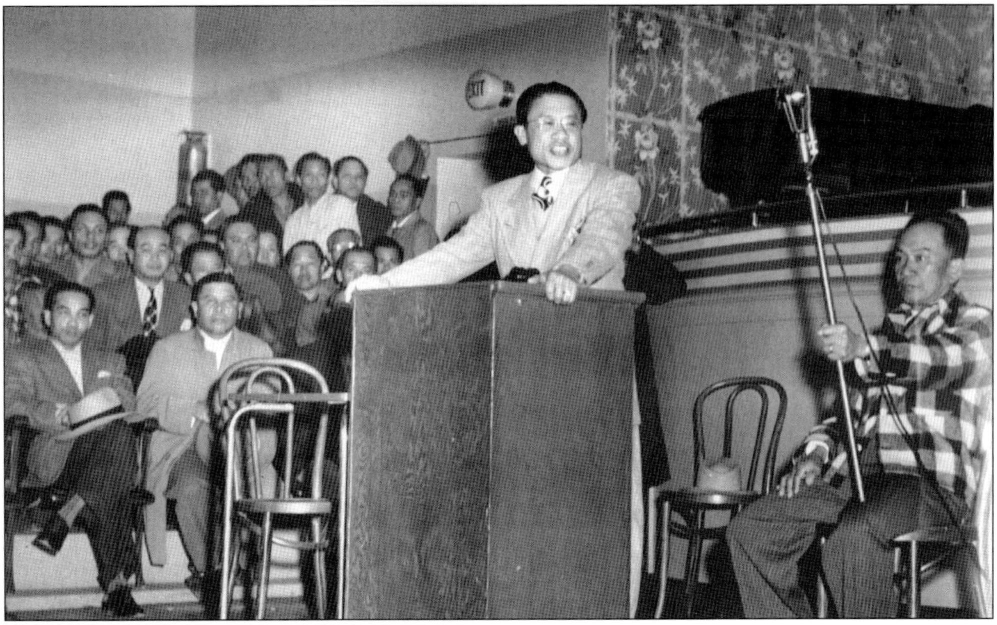

Claro Candelario, at the podium, exhorts his fellow workers to go on strike with Local 7 against the asparagus farmers in 1948 at the American Federation of Labor Hall, formerly the Filipino Recreation Center, at 144 East Lafayette Street. The strike failed because of community divisions and the red-baiting of union leaders by farmers, police, and conservative Filipinos. (Courtesy of Angelina Candelario Noveloz.)

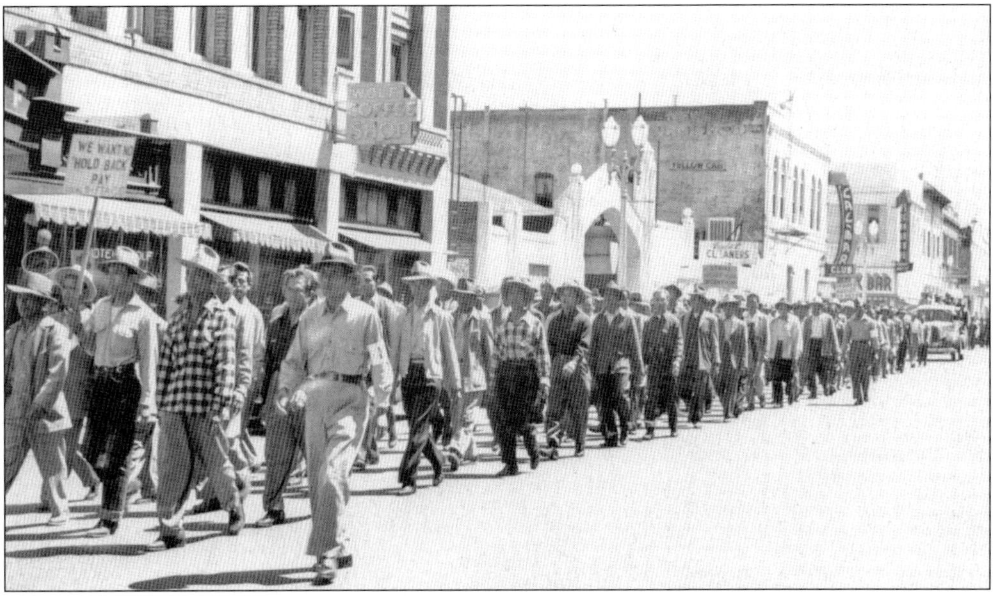

Here more than 1,500 asparagus workers march in downtown Stockton in May 1948. Thousands of workers—including labor leaders Rudy Delvo, Larry Itliong, Chris Mensalvas, and Ernesto Mangaoang and a young Philip Vera Cruz—participated in this 1948–1949 strike, which was headquartered at the Mariposa Hotel at 130 East Lafayette Street. Veterans of the strike would go on to form the Agricultural Workers Organizing Committee (AWOC), which began the Delano Grape Strike in September 1965. (Courtesy of FANHS Stockton.)

Stocktonian Larry Itliong, right, shown here with Pete Velasco, left, at a United Farm Workers (UFW) event in the late 1960s, was sent from Stockton to organize Delano grape workers with the Agricultural Workers Organizing Committee in 1965. He led the historic 1965 grape strike and persuaded Cesar Chavez to join with the Filipino strikers. From this came the United Farm Workers Organizing Committee, organized in 1966. (Courtesy of the San Francisco State University Labor Archives and Research Center.)

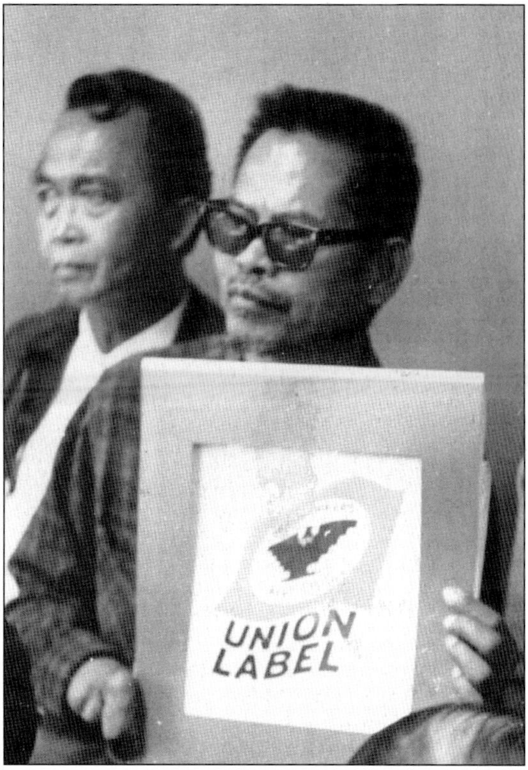

Stocktonian Andy Imutan, left, was a prominent leader during the Delano Grape Strike and continued his involvement in the UFW after Larry Itliong retired from the union in 1971. Here he takes Cesar Chavez, right, to Stockton during the grape boycott in the 1970s and shows him the *Ang Pilipino* community newspaper. (Courtesy of Andy Imutan.)

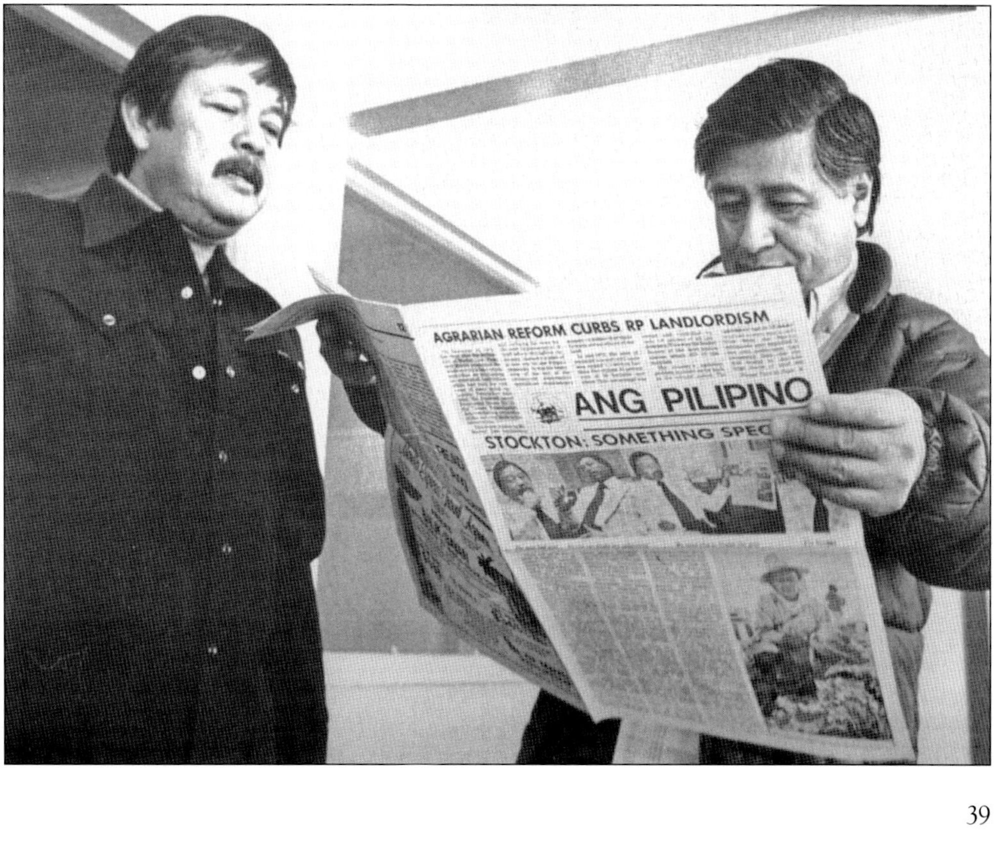

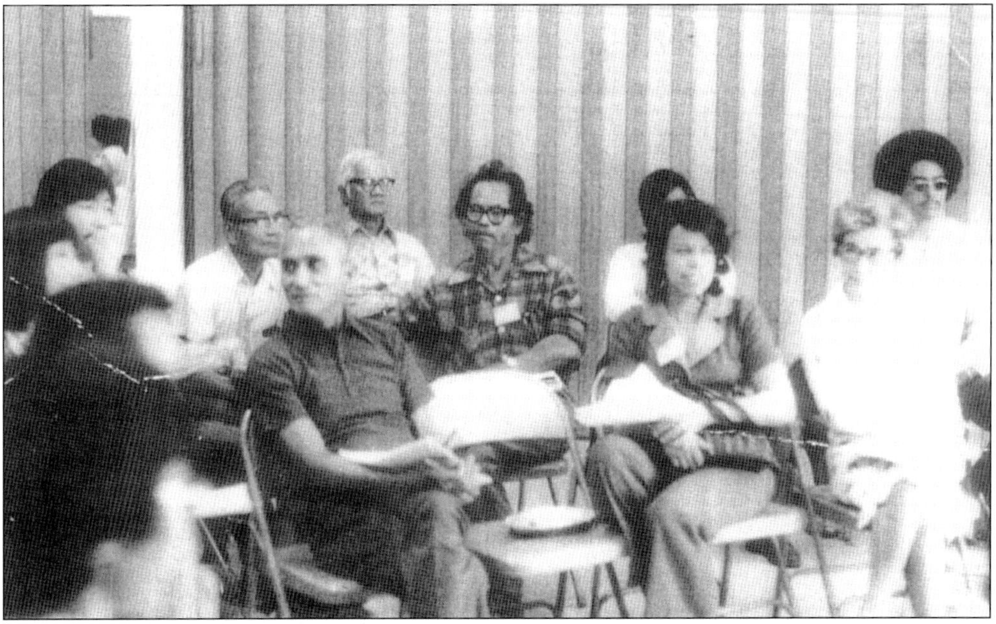

Larry Itliong continued his labor activism after leaving the United Farm Workers in 1971. Here Itliong (center, in plaid shirt) helps locals plan a strike on the Safeway grocery chain in 1974. Also in the photograph are local leaders C. Tamayo (in white shirt to the left of Itliong), Apolinar Sangalang, and on the far right, second-generation Pinoy Mel Lagasca. (Courtesy of Mel Lagasca.)

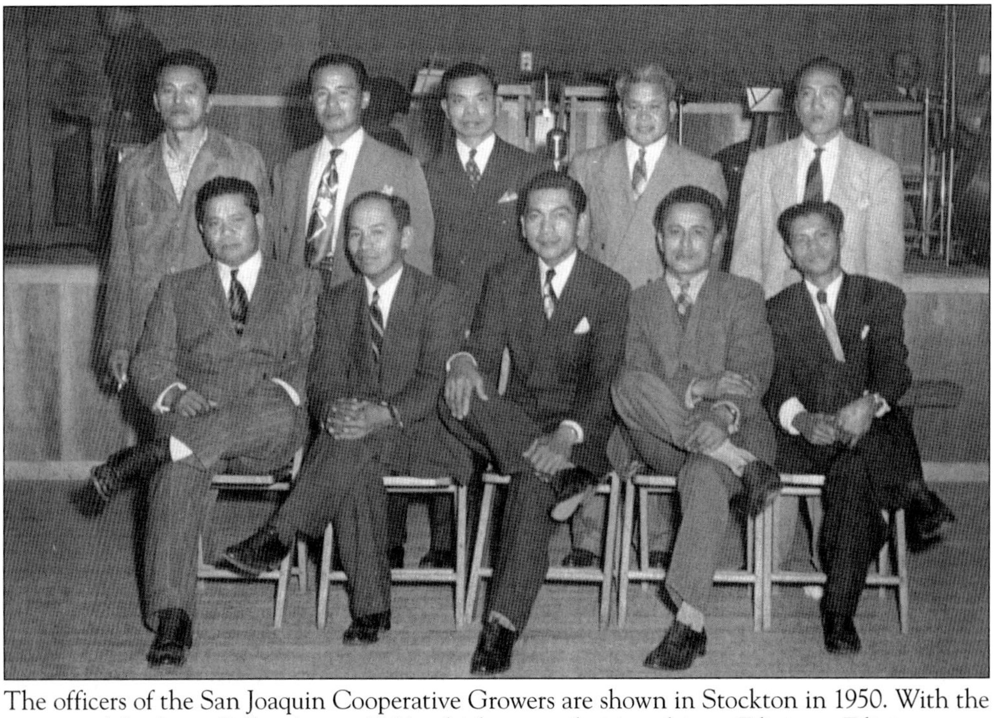

The officers of the San Joaquin Cooperative Growers are shown in Stockton in 1950. With the passage of the Luce-Celler Act in 1946, which granted citizenship to Filipinos, Filipinos were able to purchase farms. (Courtesy of FANHS Stockton.)

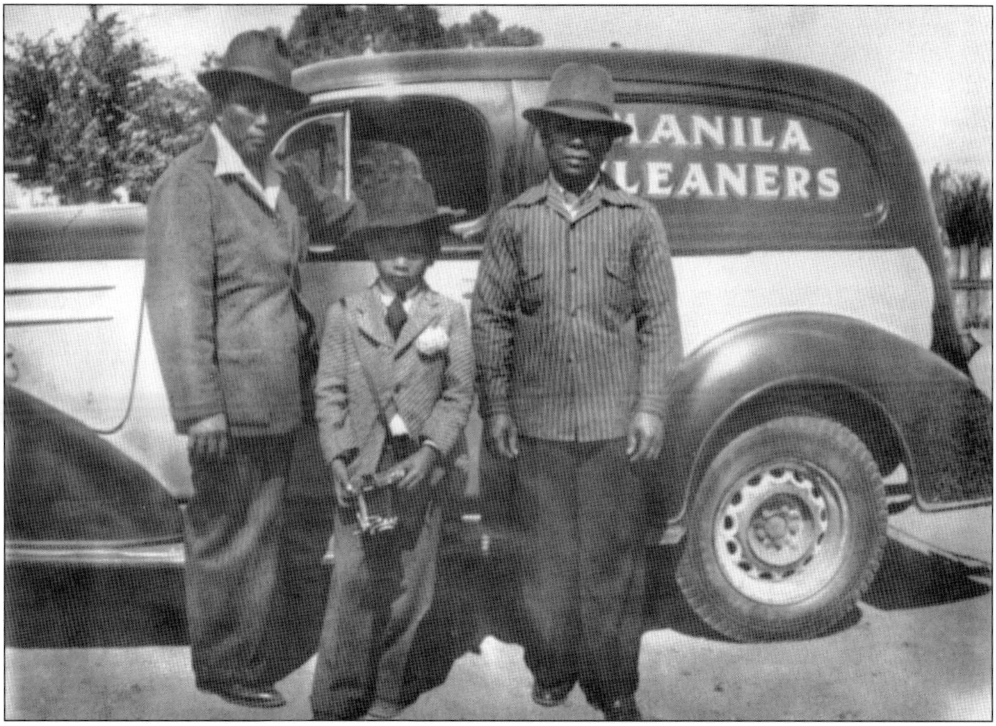

Because of the popularity of the McIntosh suit—and in the 1940s, the zoot suit—Filipino tailoring and dry cleaning businesses could always find clientele in Stockton. The Manila Cleaners did brisk business in Stockton from the 1930s onwards. From left to right are Andy Barrangan, Clemente Morales Jr., and an unidentified friend. (Courtesy of Vicky Ramos McElyea.)

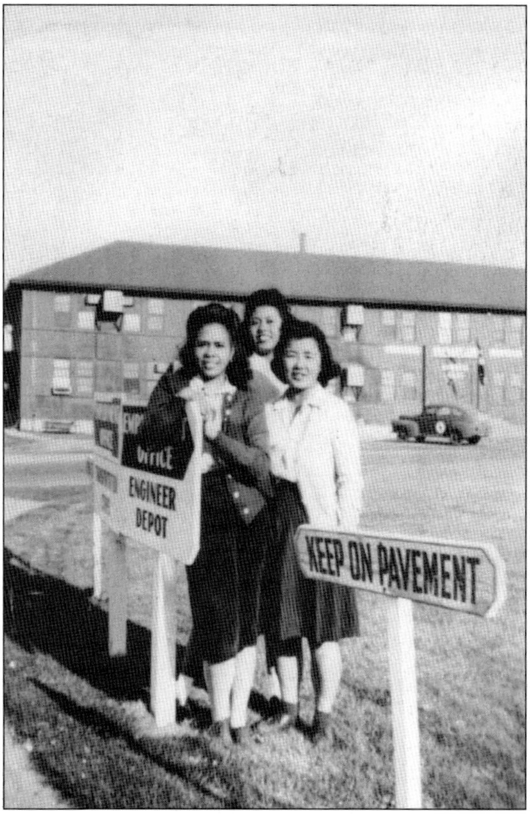

Beginning in World War II until the present, Filipinos have worked at the Sharpe Army Depot. Here, from left to right, Teofila Sarmiento, an unidentified friend, and Angelina Bantillo (Magdael) pose for a photograph after they found jobs at the depot during World War II. Angelina Magdael retired from the depot after almost four decades of service. (Courtesy of the Magdael family.)

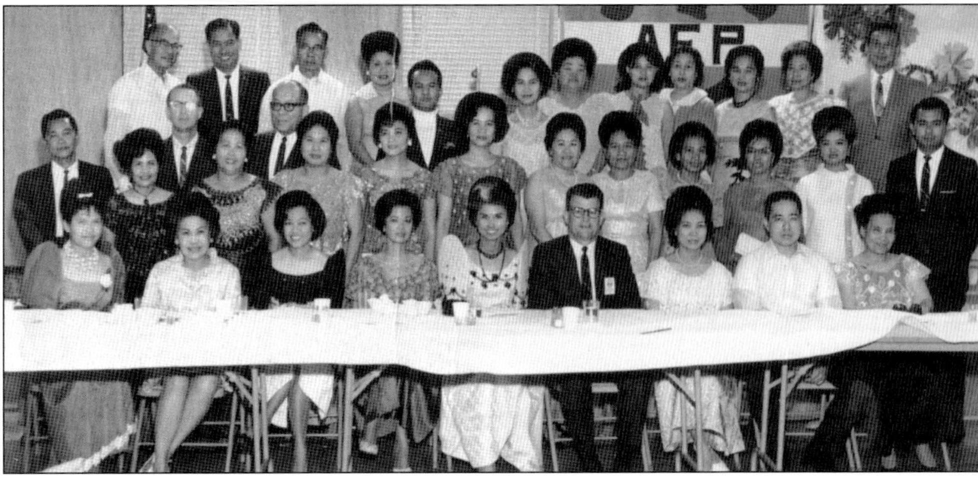

Formed in 1968, the Association of Filipino Professionals (AFP) organization reflected the immigration of Filipino professionals to Stockton after World War II, as well as a new environment in which earlier immigrants and their children could at last use their educations and skills. From left to right are (first row) Anna Pena, Jean Adlao, Evelyn Gwariz, Estela Pinga, Pres. Priscilla G. Magpale, Vice Mayor Mike Ivanhoe, Del T. Perez, Alan Perez, and Dr. Rose Guinto; (second row) Dr. Ernie Mabalon, Eufemia Macahilas, Concepcion Bohulano, Jaty Jusa, Purificacion Favis, Dr. Ismaela Carpio, Angie Mabalot, Irudita Ambuyat, Virginia J. Navarro, Josie T. Regio, Elvira Patacsil, and Ray Paular; (third row) Tom Jusa, John Leitch, Dr. Narciso Lapuz, Pete Adlaro, Delfin Bohulano Sr., Juanita Leitch, engineer Amor Paraso, Zoilo Cabal, Eliza Moscoso, Angelita Cruz, Mary Inosanto, Flora Mata, Catalina dela Cruz, and Vidal Mata. (Courtesy of Virginia Navarro.)

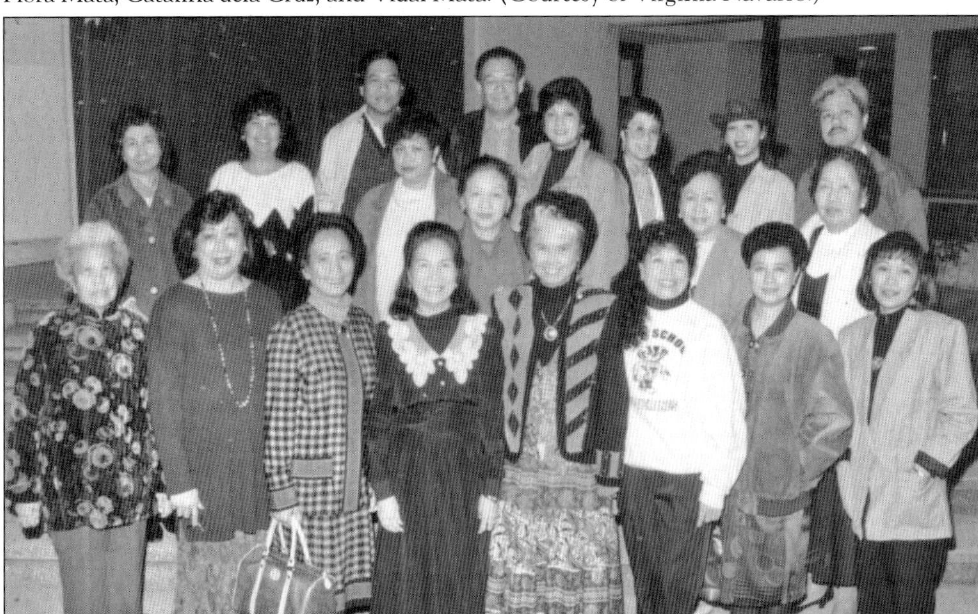

The AFP became the Association of Filipino American Educators. Here Stockton's K-12 and college educators found companionship and support and offered scholarships to local students. Priscilla Magpale (center, in the striped vest) had become Stockton's first non-white principal, and many Filipinos were teaching at local schools and colleges. (Courtesy of Virginia Navarro.)

After World War II, Susanna Monton met and married Fructuoso Y. Monton, who had been in Stockton since 1926, and immigrated to Stockton, where she worked as a nurse. Many Filipina nurses and other professionals began immigrating to the area after World War II. In addition, second- and third-generation Filipinos were attending college and becoming nurses, doctors, engineers, and other professionals. (Courtesy of Sharon Monton Robinson.)

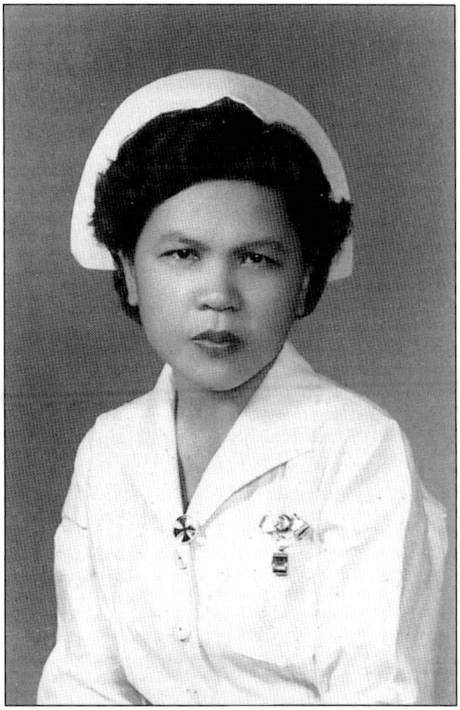

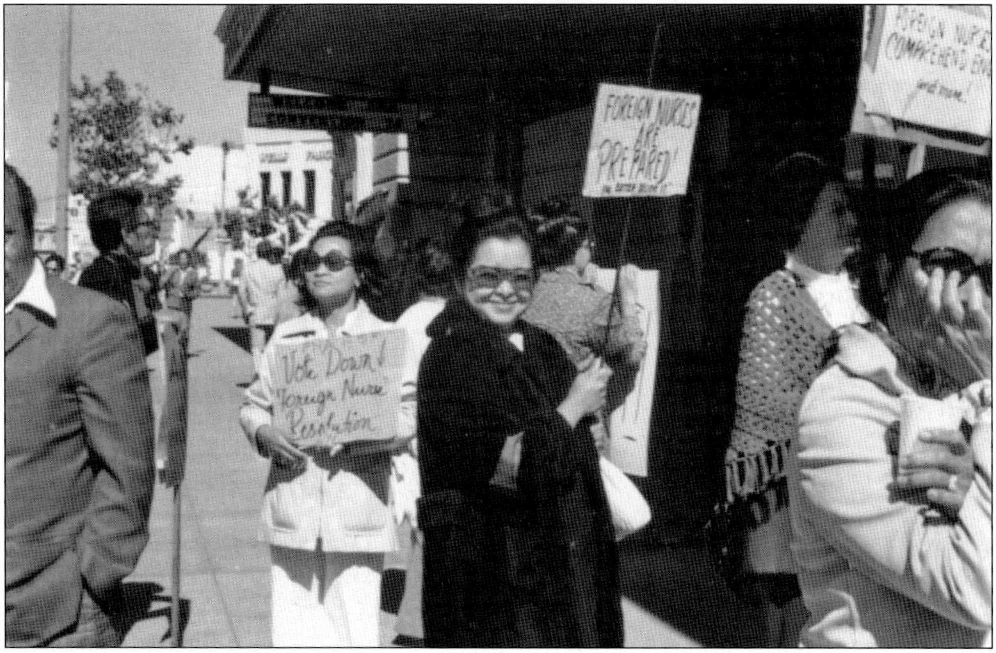

In June 1974, Stockton nurses Nady Saqueton, R.N., (in black) and Grace Tolentino, R.N., traveled to San Francisco to protest an American Nurses Association (ANA) resolution that would end visa preferences for immigrant nurses and require foreign-trained nurses to undergo extra training at that organization's San Francisco conference. With the resolution, ANA had targeted Filipina nurses, who had been recruited by hospitals into the United States in large numbers after 1965. (Courtesy of Carolina Saqueton Luces.)

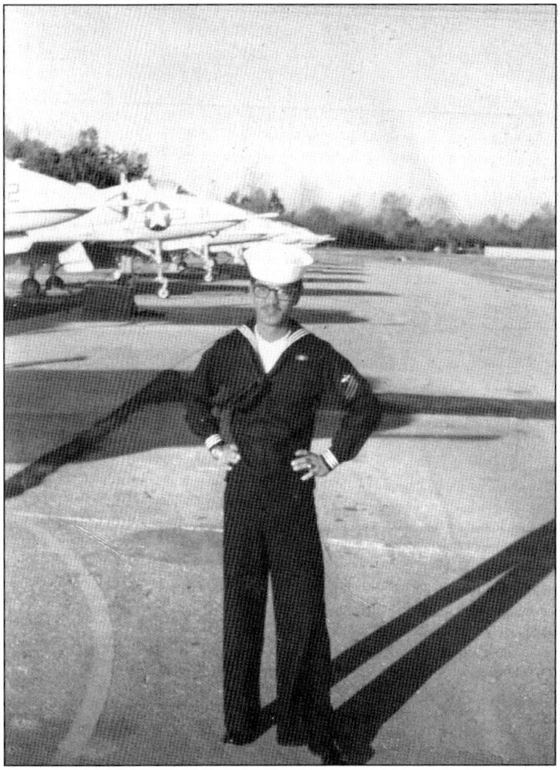

Many young Filipinos found their calling in the military. Here Stockton native Christopher Mateo pauses for a photograph during his aviation training at the Naval Air Technical Training Center in Memphis, Tennessee, in 1973. Stockton has sent hundreds of its Filipino sons and daughters into every branch of the military. (Courtesy of Christopher Mateo.)

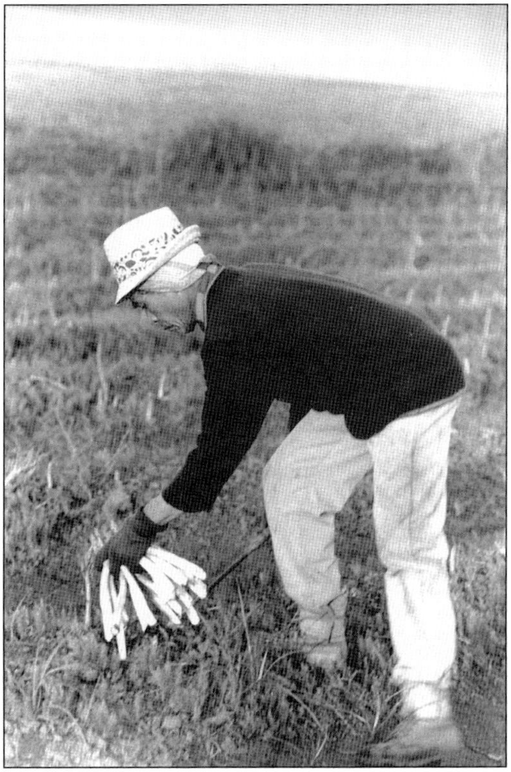

Filipinos continued to work in the fields well into their 70s and 80s. Here Mauro Villadores cuts asparagus on Bacon Island in the 1970s. (Photograph by James Villadores, courtesy of the Villadores family.)

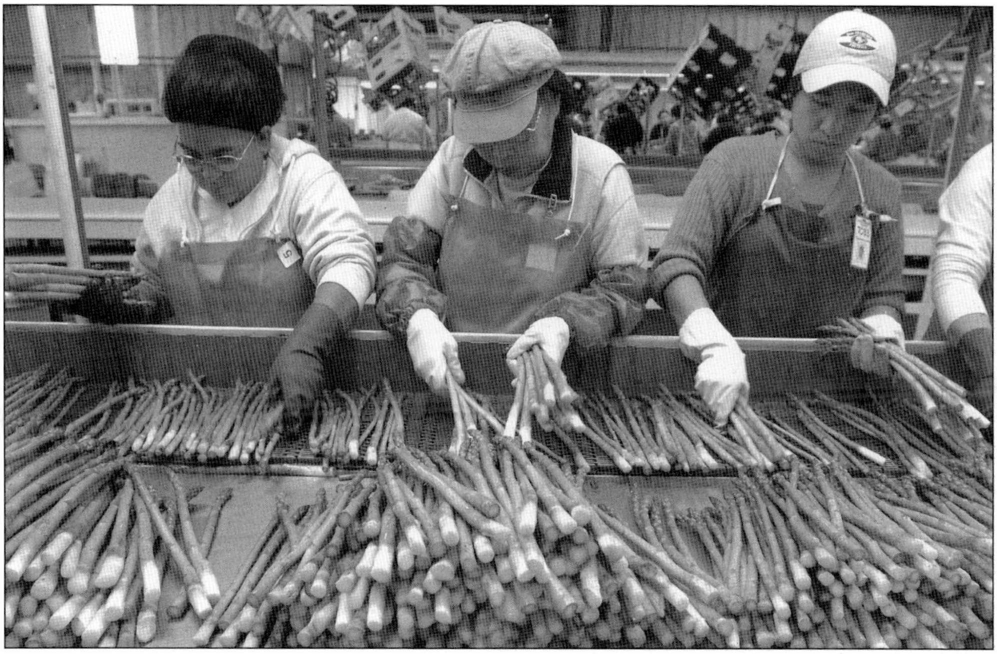

Filipino workers are still engaged in the multi-million-dollar asparagus industry of the San Joaquin Delta. Here, from left to right, Hortensia Macario, Cristita Riego, and Inocensia Garaza sort asparagus for King's Crown Packaging in Stockton in late April 2007. (Photograph by Michael McCollum, courtesy of the *Record.*)

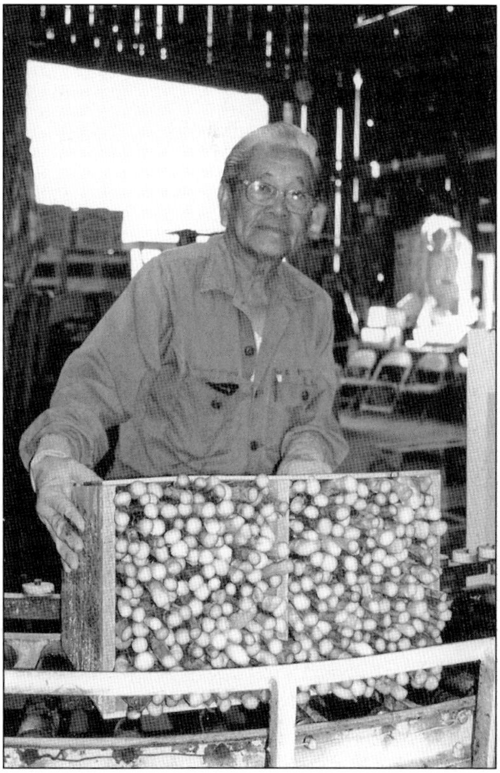

Though trained as a medical doctor, Ernesto T. Mabalon worked all over the Delta from the moment he arrived in Stockton in 1963, working in grapes, peaches, pruning, and asparagus until his death in 2005. He was a passionate community leader and served as president of the Filipino community, as supreme minister of the Legionarios del Trabajo, and in leadership positions in many other local organizations. He worked as a contractor and supervisor for the Yamada Brothers asparagus farm in Stockton, shown here in March 2004. (Photograph by and courtesy of Tony Somera.)

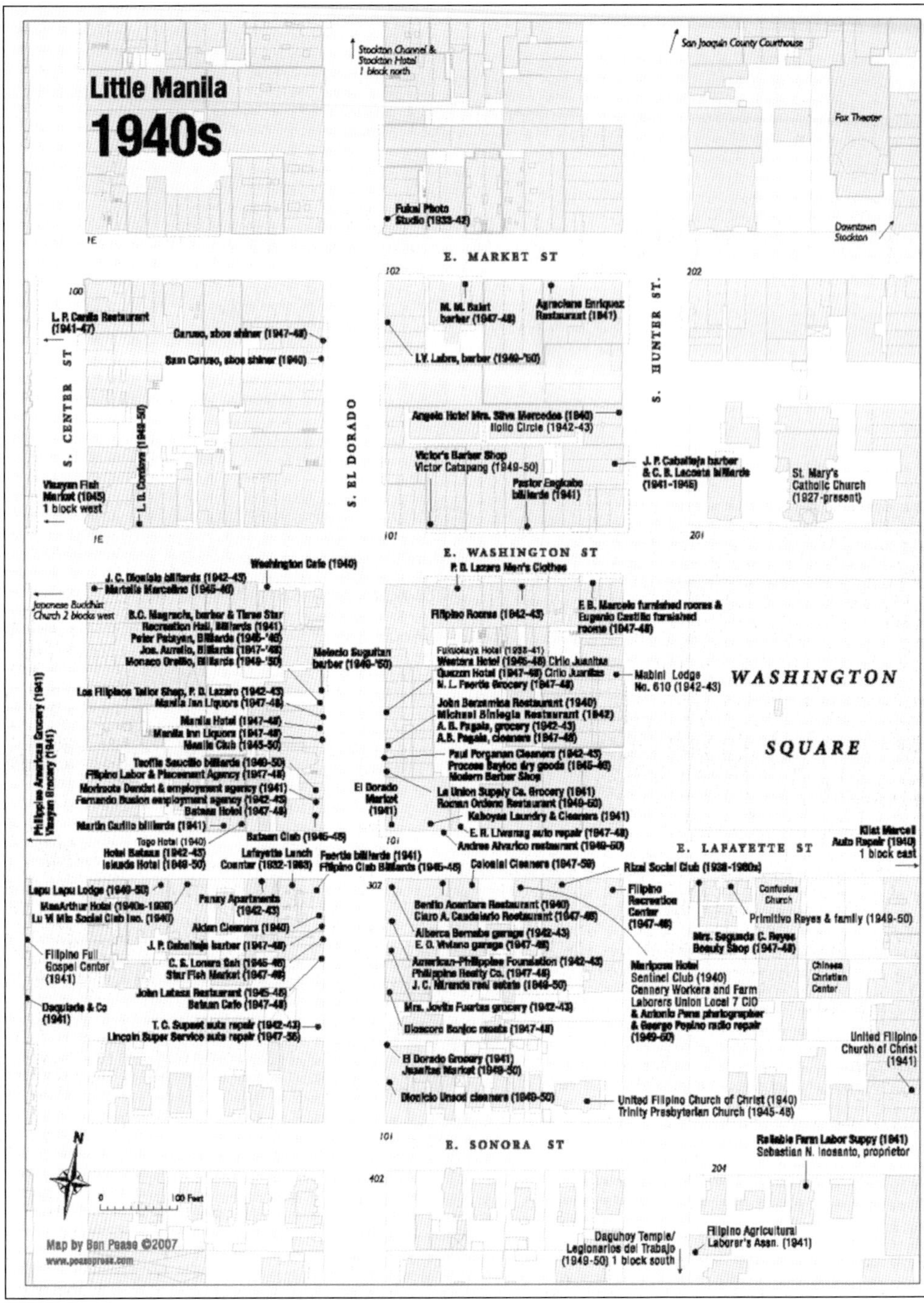

This map shows how Little Manila mushroomed during and after World War II, when Japanese Americans were incarcerated in internment camps and Filipino entrepreneurs took over their empty storefronts. The Filipino population swelled because of new immigration and the Filipino American postwar baby boom. Addresses and dates were taken from city directories. (Courtesy of Ben Pease.)

Three

PUTTING DOWN ROOTS
LIFE IN LITTLE MANILA

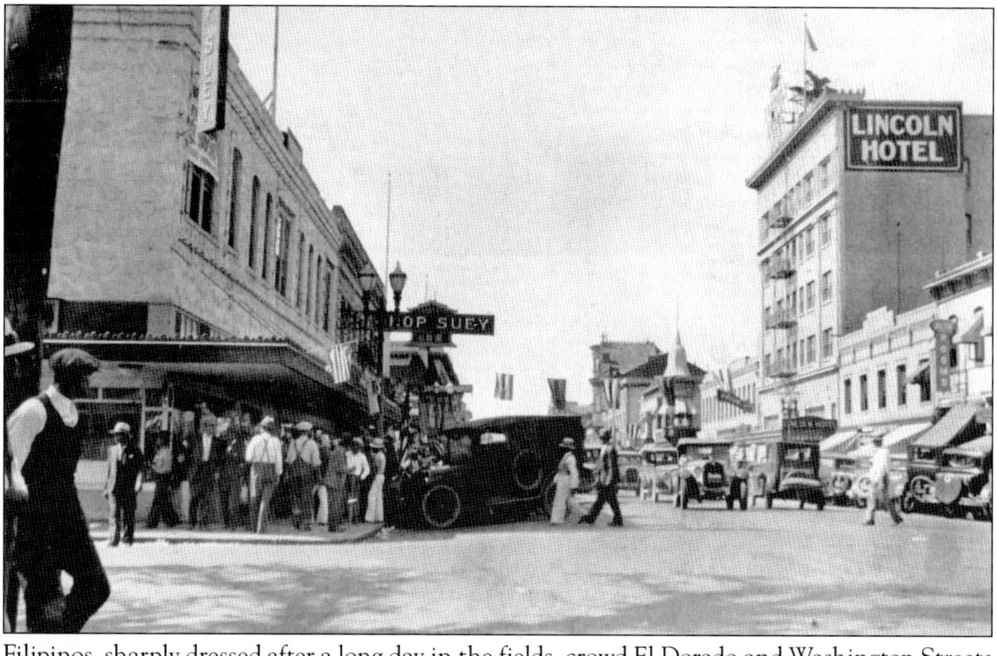

Filipinos, sharply dressed after a long day in the fields, crowd El Dorado and Washington Streets in the late 1920s. Filipinos gathered at El Dorado Street because they found that the only neighborhood that would welcome them was near Chinatown and Nihonmachi (Japantown). The neighborhood soon grew to six blocks. Little Manila thrived from the 1920s to the 1970s. Entrepreneurs opened restaurants, grocery stores, churches, beauty salons, barbershops, pool halls, card rooms, meeting halls, gas stations, rec halls, movie theaters, ice cream shops, candy stores, labor union headquarters, dry cleaning stores, photography studios, newspapers, clothing stores, and dance halls. These sites served multiple purposes; businesses could also serve as social gathering centers, informal banks and post offices, and labor recruitment sites. In the 1950s and 1960s, redevelopment projects and the Crosstown Freeway destroyed much of Chinatown, Nihonmachi, and Little Manila. However, the neighborhood held on, with old-timers still walking its streets and living in its remaining hotels well into the 1990s. (Photograph by Frank Mancao, courtesy of FANHS National.)

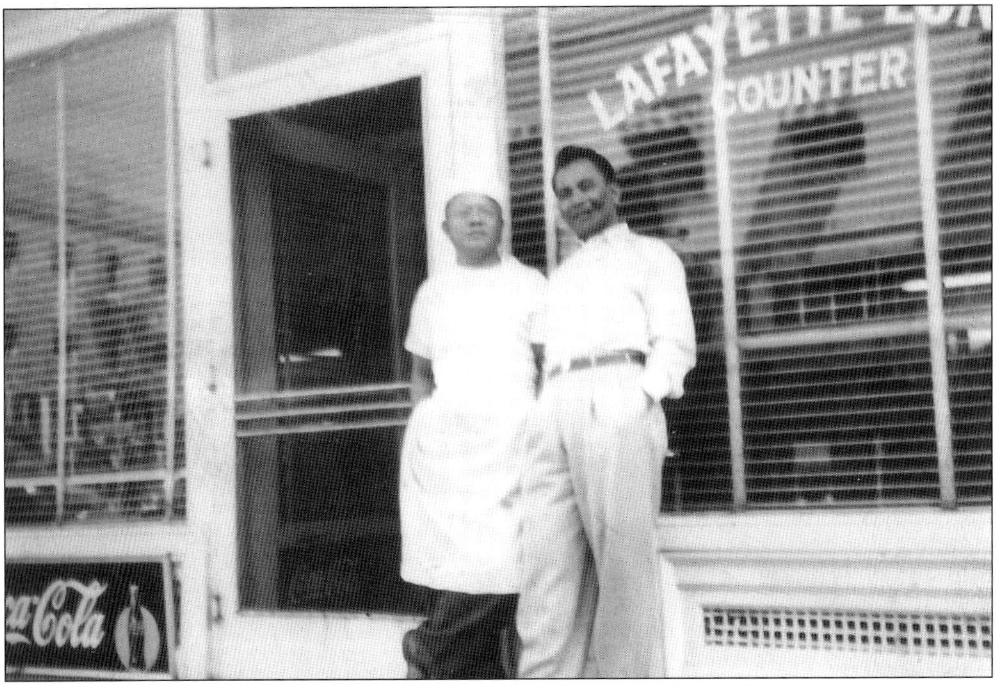

From 1931 to the 1980s, Pablo Mabalon (on left) served heaping plates of hotcakes, diniguan, and adobo to three generations at his popular Lafayette Lunch Counter at 50 East Lafayette Street. Because of his kindness to fellow Filipinos who couldn't pay for their food during lean times, some old-timers called him "Mr. Little Manila." (Courtesy of the Mabalon family collection.)

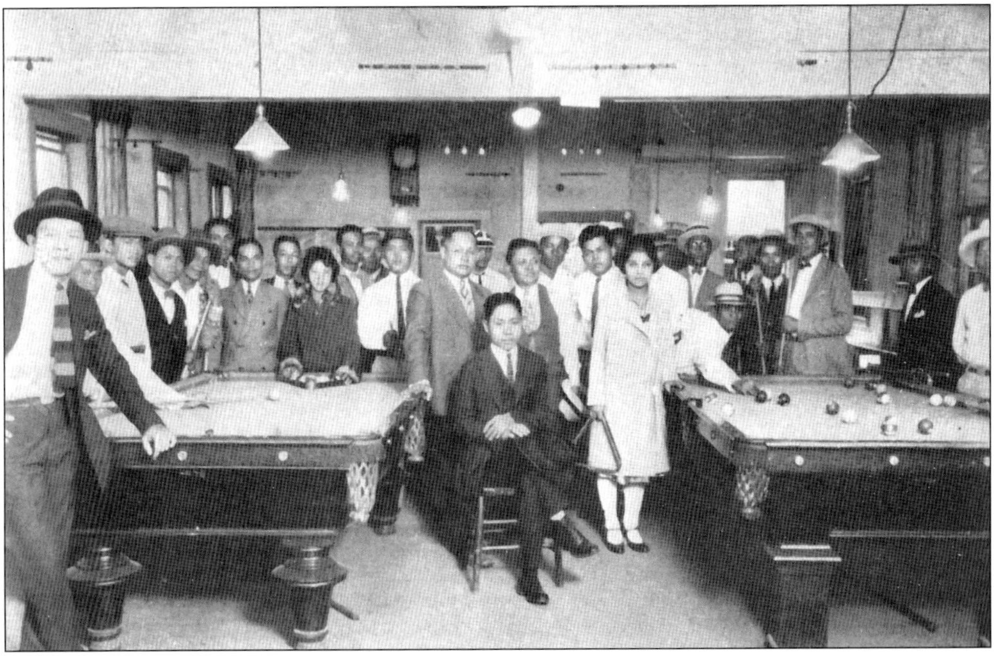

Some of the first Filipino businesses in the burgeoning Little Manila district were pool halls. Labor recruiters often found workers in the halls. Here locals gather in a photograph taken by local Filipino photographer John Y. Billones in the 1920s. (Courtesy of FANHS Stockton.)

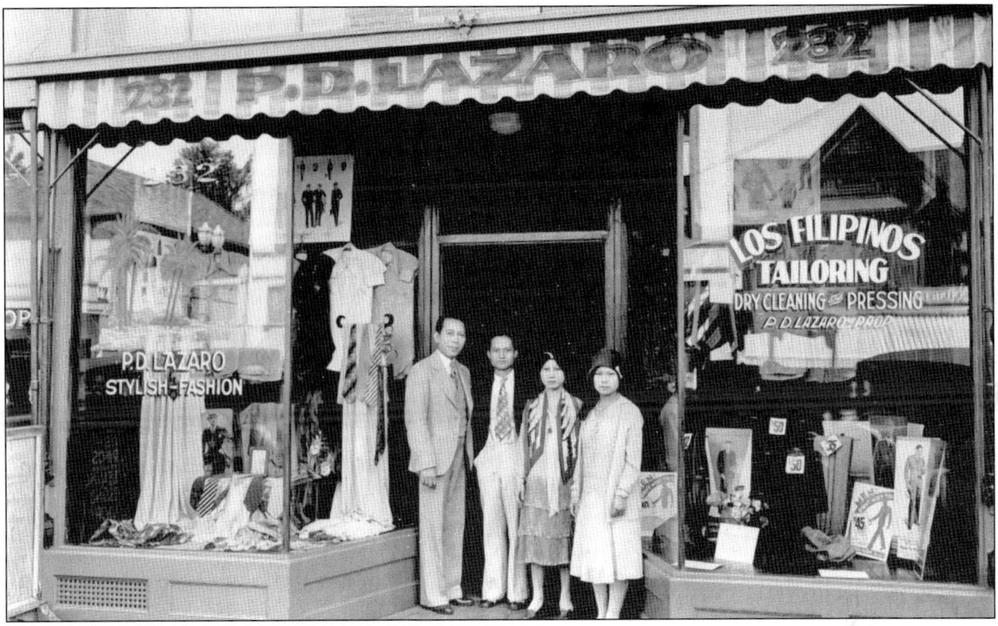

At 232 El Dorado Street, the Lazaro family owned the Los Filipinos Tailoring Shop, shown here in the early 1930s. Placido Lazaro (on left), his wife, Juliana (third from left), and their daughter, Asuncion Guevarra (Nicolas), in white dress, hailed from Iloilo, Panay. The Pinoy and Pinay penchant for sharp suits and beautiful Filipina dresses kept the shop bustling. (Courtesy of FANHS National.)

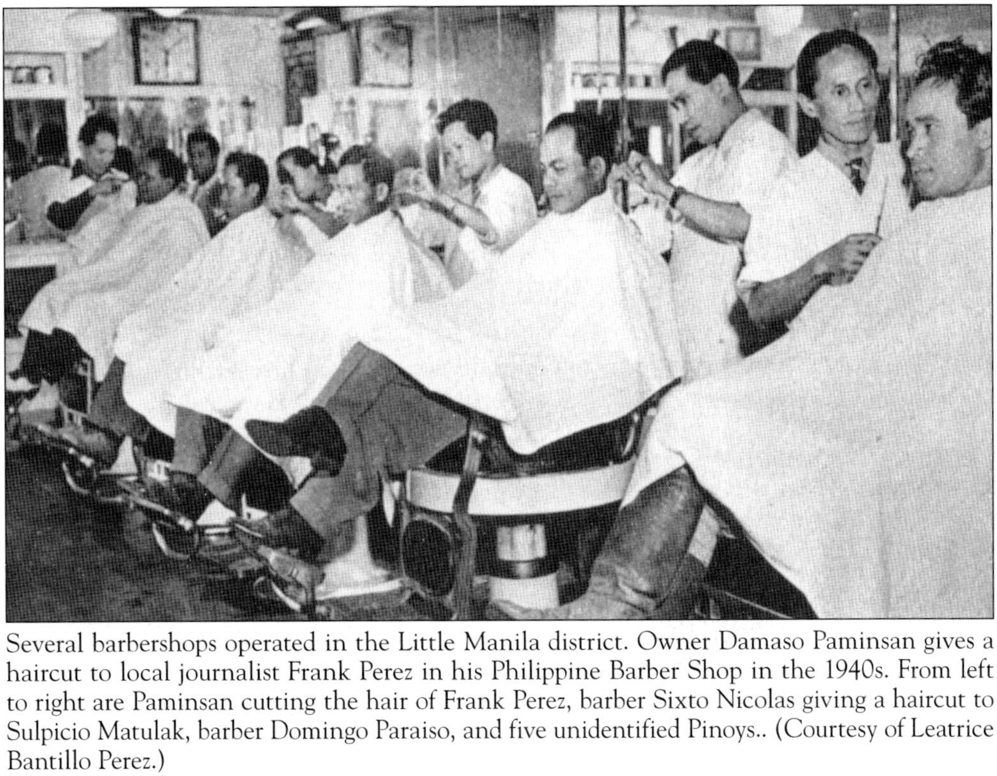

Several barbershops operated in the Little Manila district. Owner Damaso Paminsan gives a haircut to local journalist Frank Perez in his Philippine Barber Shop in the 1940s. From left to right are Paminsan cutting the hair of Frank Perez, barber Sixto Nicolas giving a haircut to Sulpicio Matulak, barber Domingo Paraiso, and five unidentified Pinoys.. (Courtesy of Leatrice Bantillo Perez.)

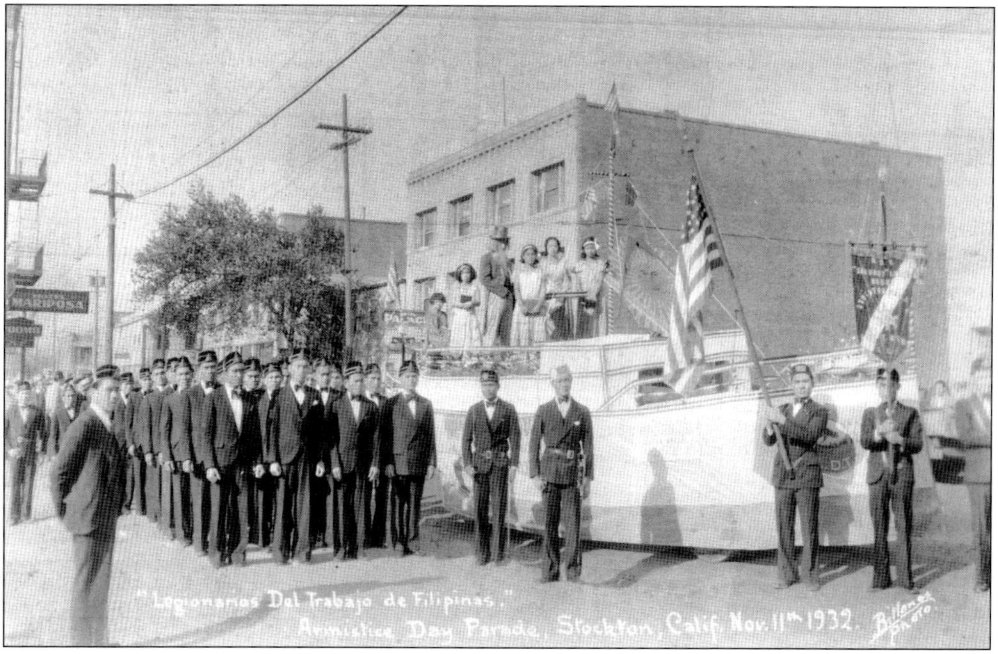

Legionarios del Trabajo members line up for the Armistice Day Parade in 1932 on Lafayette Street in Little Manila. The Mariposa Hotel is on the left. (Photograph by John Billones, courtesy of Tony Somera.)

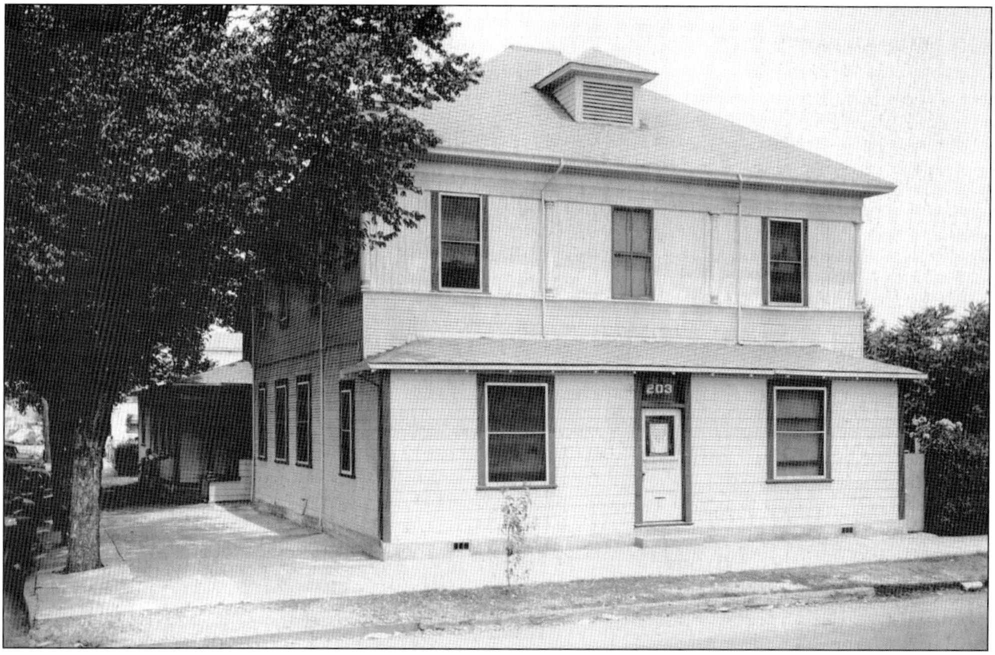

The Daguhoy Lodge of the Legionarios del Trabajo purchased this building at 203 East Hazelton Avenue just south of Little Manila in 1937. The building served as a meeting hall and space for families to congregate. Filipino Stocktonians have fond memories of holiday celebrations and other events in the building, which was named a historic landmark by the City of Stockton in 2003. (Courtesy of Tony Somera.)

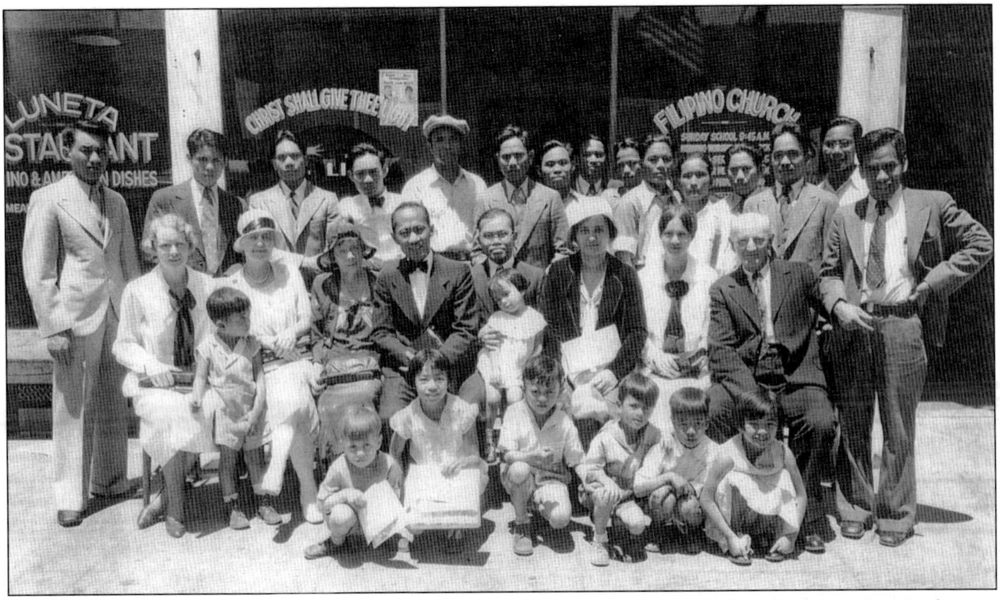

Filipino families gather in front of the Lighthouse Mission, a Protestant church, at 111 East Lafayette Street in the late 1920s. The mission offered spiritual and moral support for Filipino immigrants and families. From left to right are (first row) unidentified, Alice Bantillo (Buenavista), Fidel Villaruz, Benny Villaruz, Anastasio "Bo" Bantillo Jr., and Angelina Bantillo (Madgael); (second row) unidentified, Richard Villaruz, three unidentified, Primo Villaruz Sr., Henrietta Villaruz (Diangson), Rita H. Villaruz, Mabel Erickson, and unidentified; (third row) Rev. Vicente Zambra.

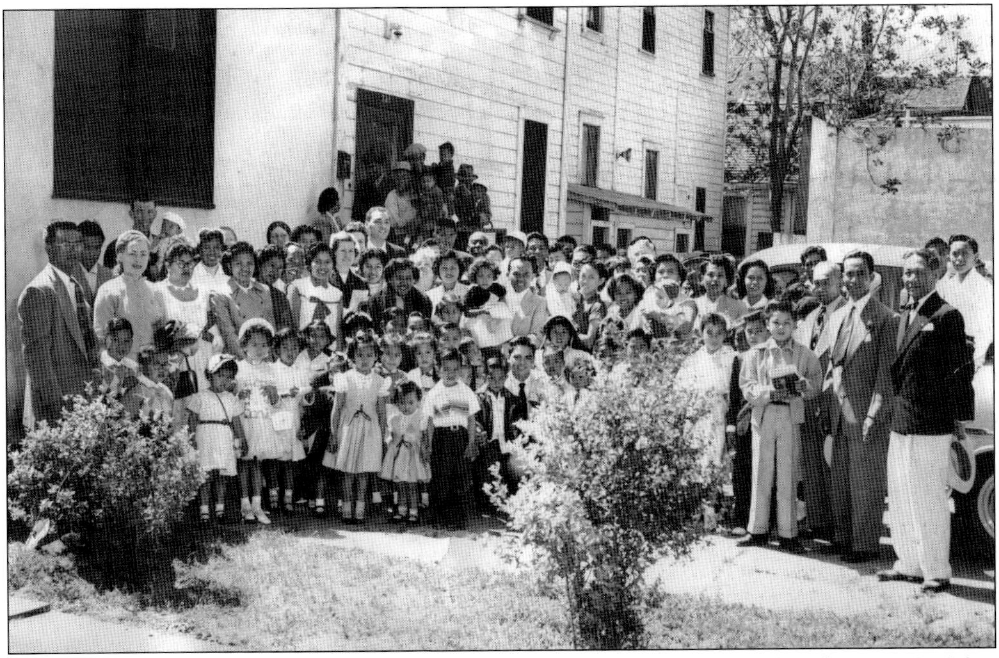

Members of the Lighthouse Mission formed the Trinity Presbyterian Church in 1942. After spending many years on Lafayette Street, members of the church secured a building at 341 South Hunter Street, where they were led by Rev. Maurice Legare until his untimely death in 1954. This photograph was taken in the late 1950s. (Courtesy of the Magdael family.)

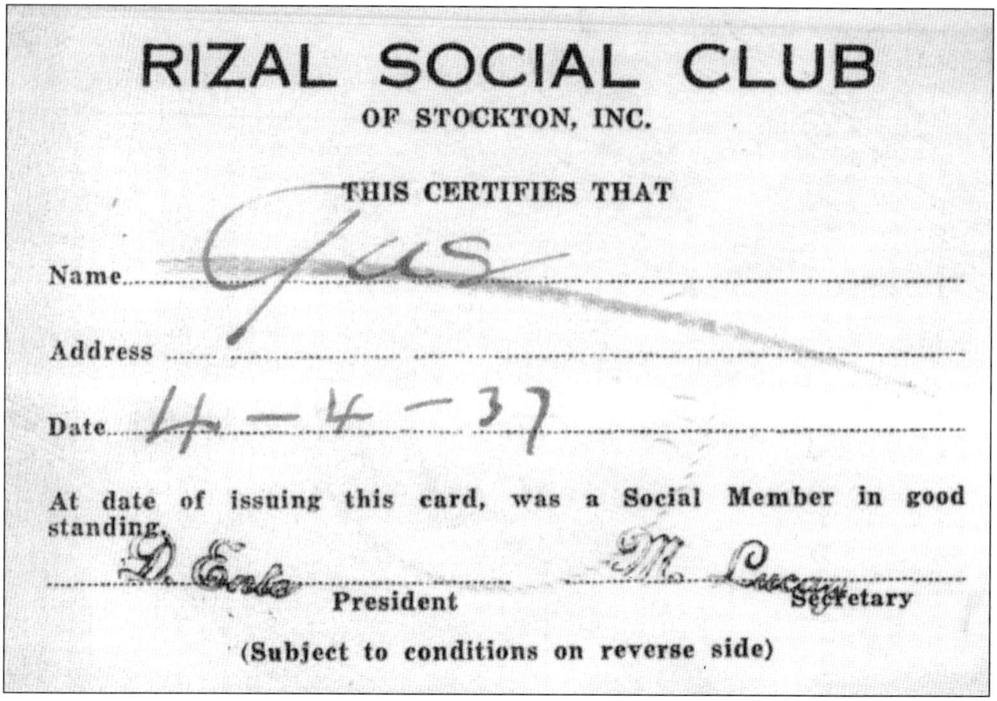

RIZAL SOCIAL CLUB

OF STOCKTON, INC.

THIS CERTIFIES THAT

Name: Gus

Address

Date: 4-4-37

At date of issuing this card, was a Social Member in good standing.

President

Secretary

(Subject to conditions on reverse side)

From the 1920s to the 1950s, dance halls drew hundreds of Pinoys and other Stockton residents every night. Filipinos were known for their sharp suits, excellent jazz bands, and dancing expertise. This is a membership card for the exclusive Rizal Social Club. (Courtesy of Nelson Nagai.)

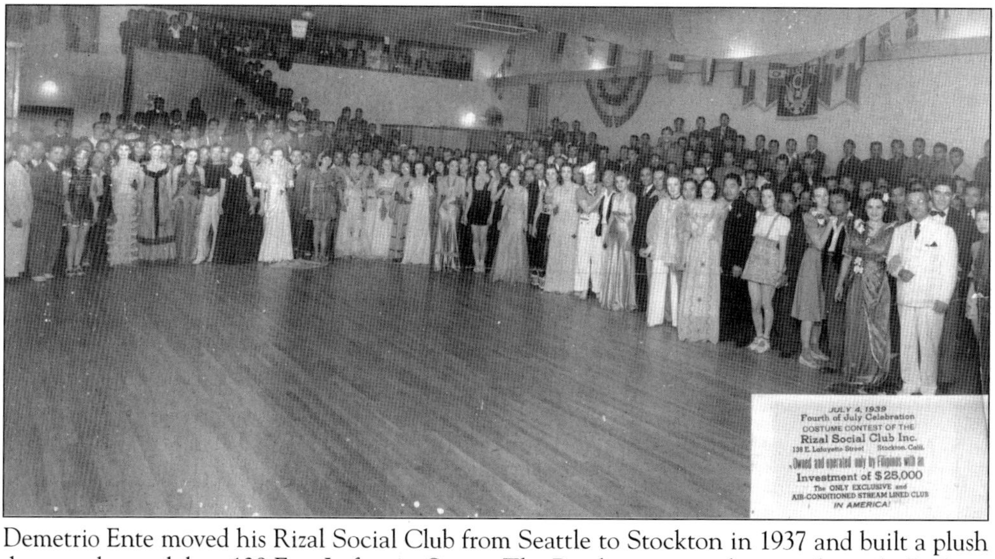

Demetrio Ente moved his Rizal Social Club from Seattle to Stockton in 1937 and built a plush deco moderne club at 138 East Lafayette Street. The Rizal was a popular taxi-dance hall where patrons bought tickets to dance with women. In the 1950s, it became a community hall and then, in the 1960s, a boxing gym. Here clubgoers celebrate Fourth of July 1938 with a costume contest. (Courtesy of the Filipino Oral History Project, Inc.)

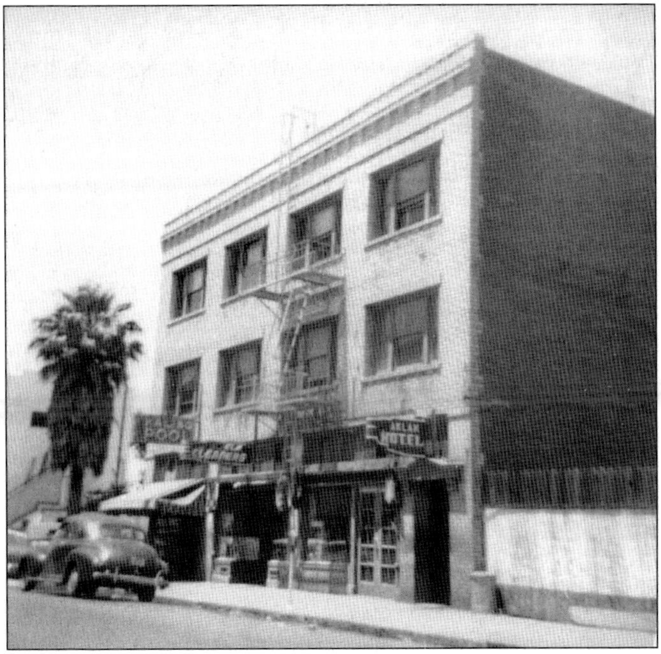

The Kalibo Pool Hall and Aklan Hotel, at 25 and 31 West Lafayette Street, served the large numbers of Stockton Filipinos who traced their roots to Aklan province, on Panay, and its provincial capital, Kalibo. This photograph was taken in the 1960s before the Crosstown Freeway demolished both buildings. As few Japanese-leased hotels reopened after the war, the Aklan Hotel, owned by Pablo Mabalon, was another Filipino-owned boarding hotel that provided low-cost housing. (Courtesy of Ernesto T. Mabalon.)

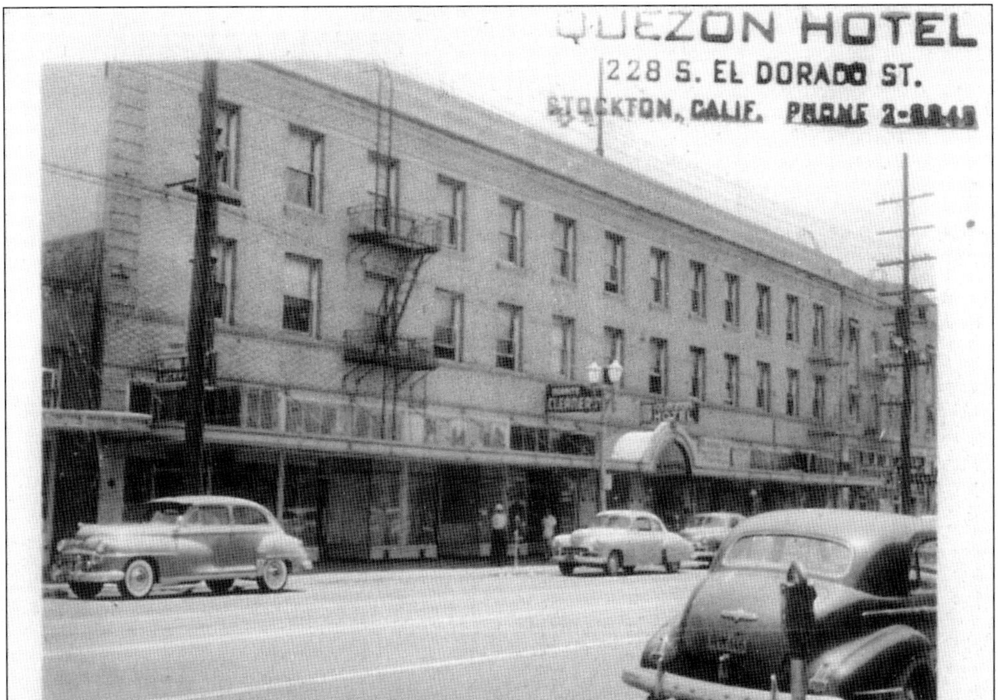

Before World War II, most residential hotels in the Chinatown/Little Manila/Nihonmachi area were leased and managed by Japanese Americans. During World War II, Filipinos took over neighborhood hotels and renamed them to reflect wartime American and Filipino patriotism. The Juanitas family ran the Quezon Hotel, named after Manuel Quezon, president of the Philippine Commonwealth during World War II. (Courtesy FANHS Stockton.)

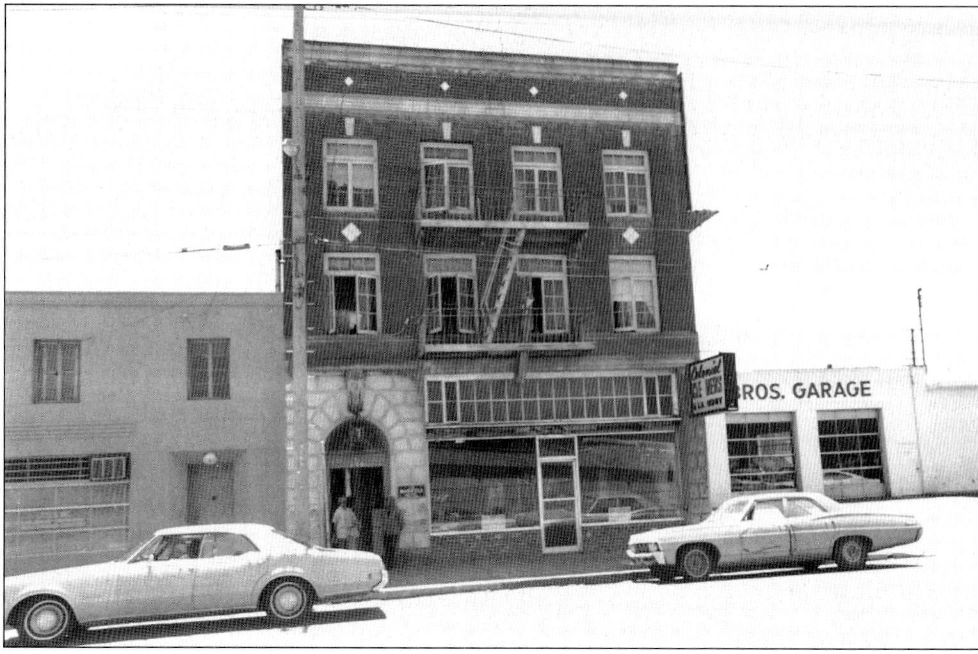

The Lapineg family owned the Mariposa Hotel at 130 East Lafayette Street during the early 1940s. Felisa Lapineg was a skilled midwife, and many babies were born at the hotel during their tenure there from the 1930s to the 1950s. Their daughter, Irene Edralin, remembers a close-knit community on that block of Little Manila. Here she returns to the hotel with her uncle Frank Lapineg in 1985. Next door is the Rizal Social Club. (Courtesy of Irene Plaza Edralin.)

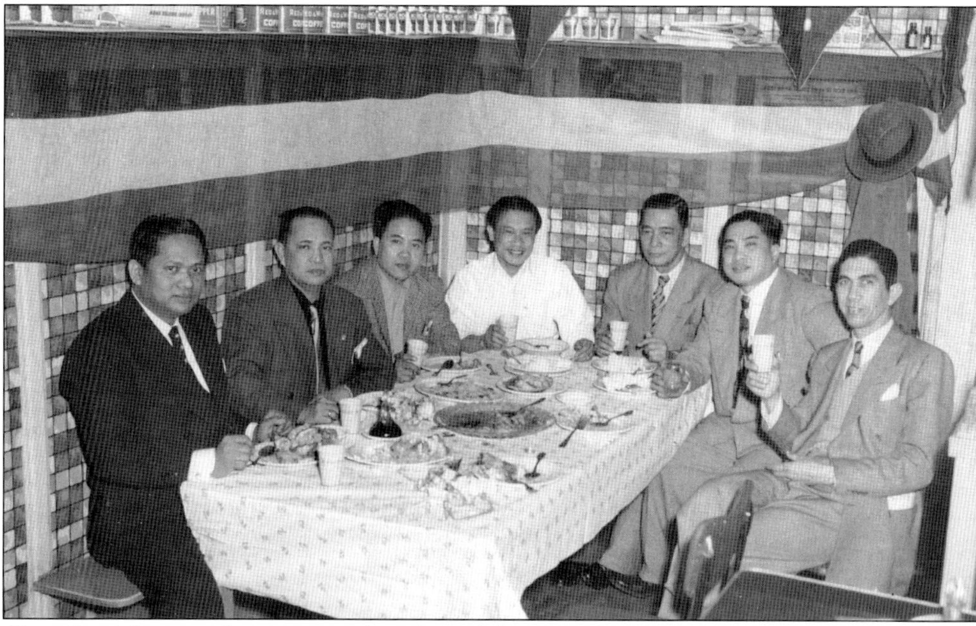

Claro Candelario, in the center in white, hosted the Consul General Benigno Pidlaon at his Luzon Café at 112 Lafayette Street in 1951. The restaurant and Candelario are featured in Carlos Bulosan's novel *America Is in the Heart*; in the novel, a Claro, a political activist, comforts Carlos with food and political education at the restaurant. (Courtesy of Angelina Candelario Novolezo.)

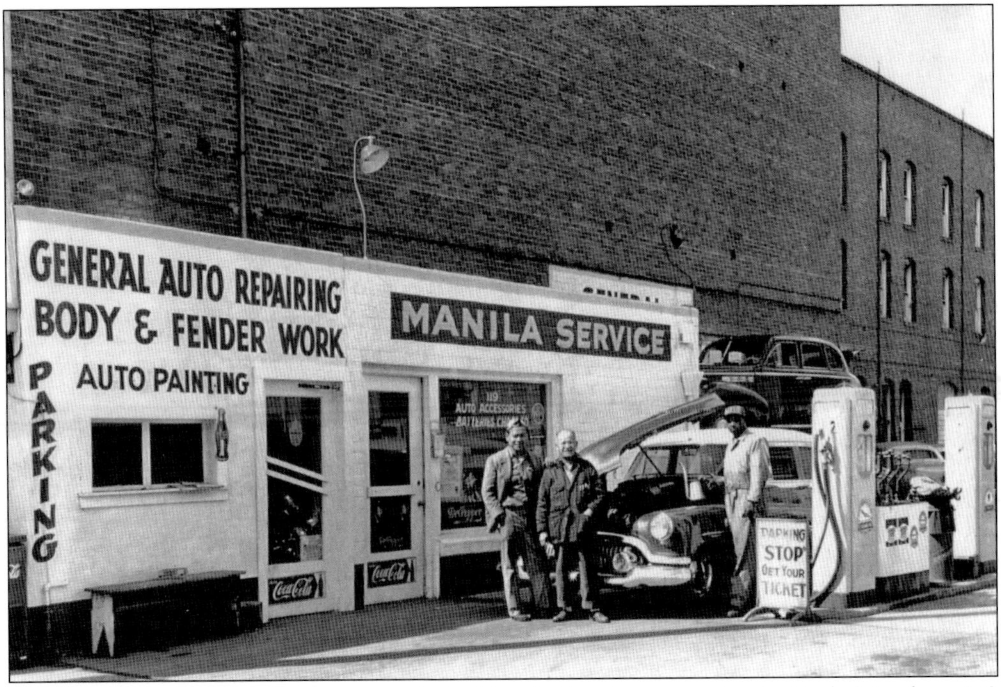

Albert Liwanag and his family operated the Manila Service gas station in Little Manila at 119 East Lafayette Street in the 1940s and 1950s. It was one of several Filipino-owned service stations in the district. (Courtesy of Helen Liwanag.)

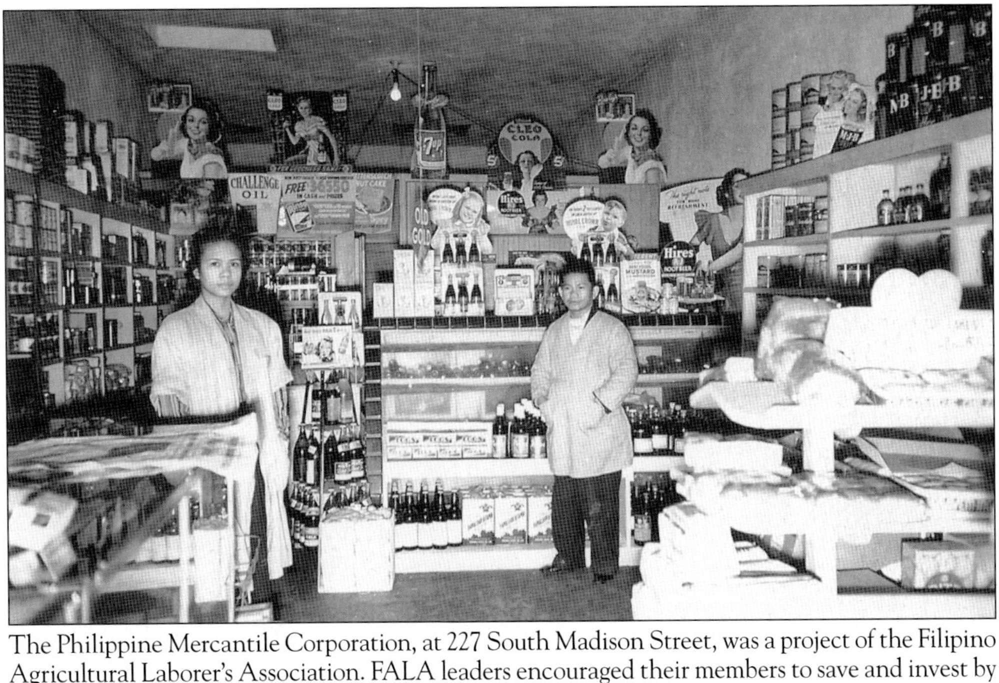

The Philippine Mercantile Corporation, at 227 South Madison Street, was a project of the Filipino Agricultural Laborer's Association. FALA leaders encouraged their members to save and invest by buying shares in the corporation instead of pouring their wages into gambling, pool, and dance halls. On the left is Teofila Sarmiento who worked at the Philippine Mercantile Corporation. (Courtesy of Rosaline Dickinson.)

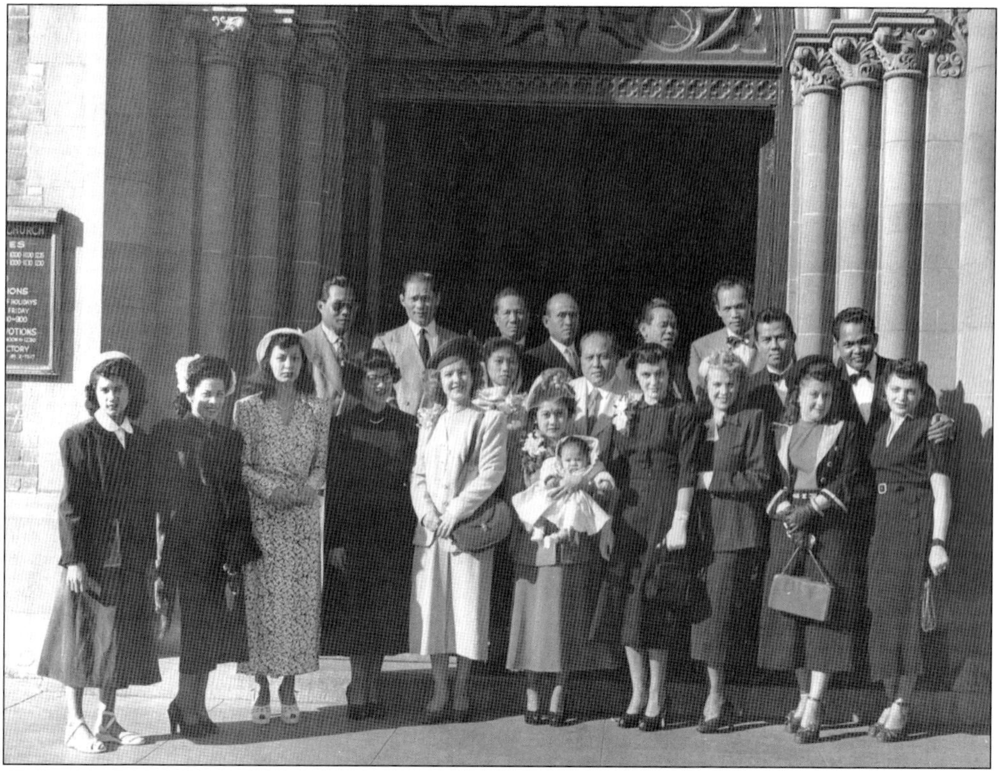

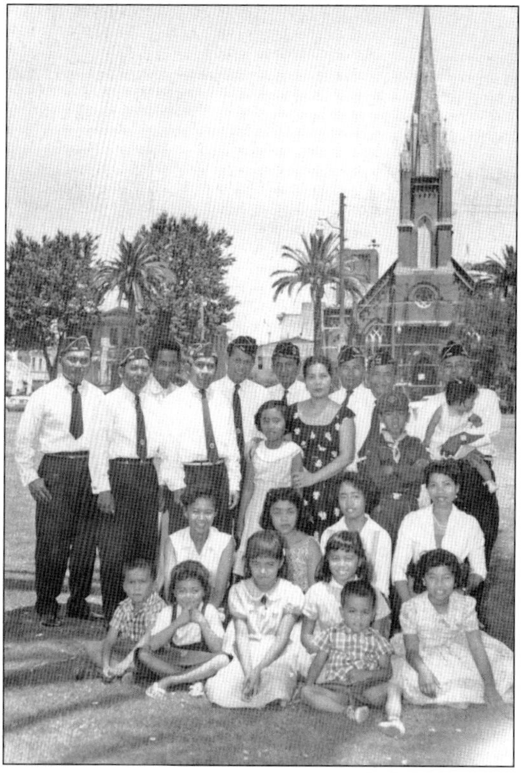

Beverly Castillo (Engkabo) is baptized at St. Mary's Catholic Church in 1949. Located near Little Manila, the church, one of the oldest in California, played an important spiritual role for Stockton's Catholic Filipinos. (Courtesy of Beverly Engkabo.)

World War II veterans, members of the newly created Manuel A. Roxas Post of the American Legion, gather with their families at Washington Square Park in the late 1950s. The post was named after the first president of the Philippine Republic. From left to right are (first row) Ernest Cabañero, Laura Cabañero, Aurora Cabañero, Laurena Cabañero, Leo Cabañero, and Connie Sajulan; (second row) Teri Cabanero, Nora Alcala, Alma Alcala, and Conching Sajulan; (third row includes) unidentified, Martin Atad, Sid Samporna, Fred Yurong Sr., Rory Alcala, three unidentified, Atanasio Alcala, Ala Simeon Alcala, Lucresio Cabañero, and Irene Cabañero. (Courtesy of Laurena Cabañero.)

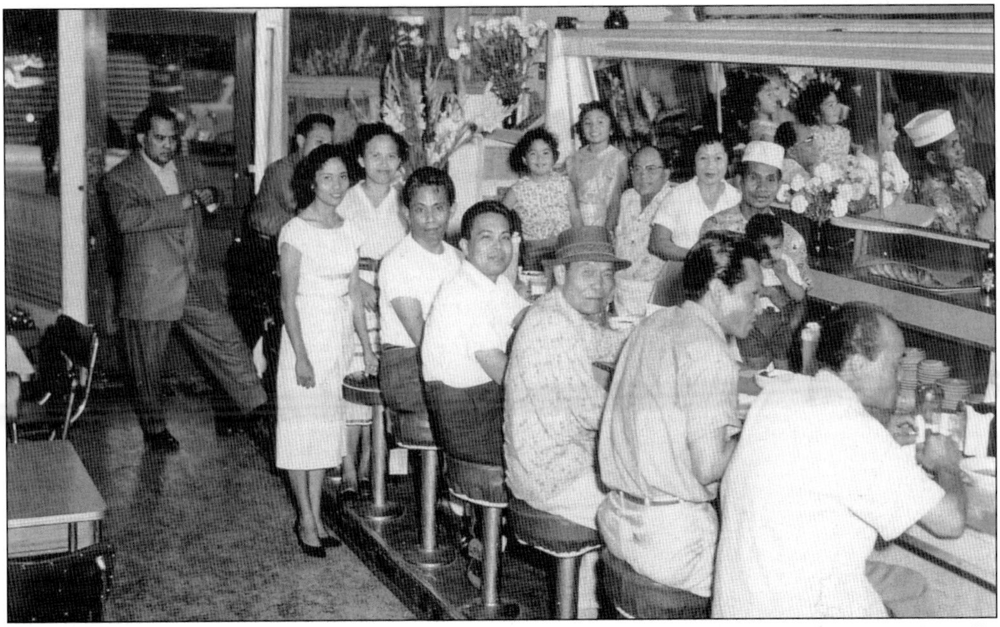

Restaurants proliferated in Little Manila, especially after World War II. Hortensia Castillo opened Horten's Café at 112 East Lafayette Street in the 1950s. From left to right are (in front of the counter) Steve Cabayan, two unidentified, Helen Pena, and five unidentified; (behind the counter) Evelyn Castillo (Zulueta), Beverly Castillo (Engkabo), John Castillo, Hortensia Castillo, cook "Benny." (Courtesy of Beverly Engkabo.)

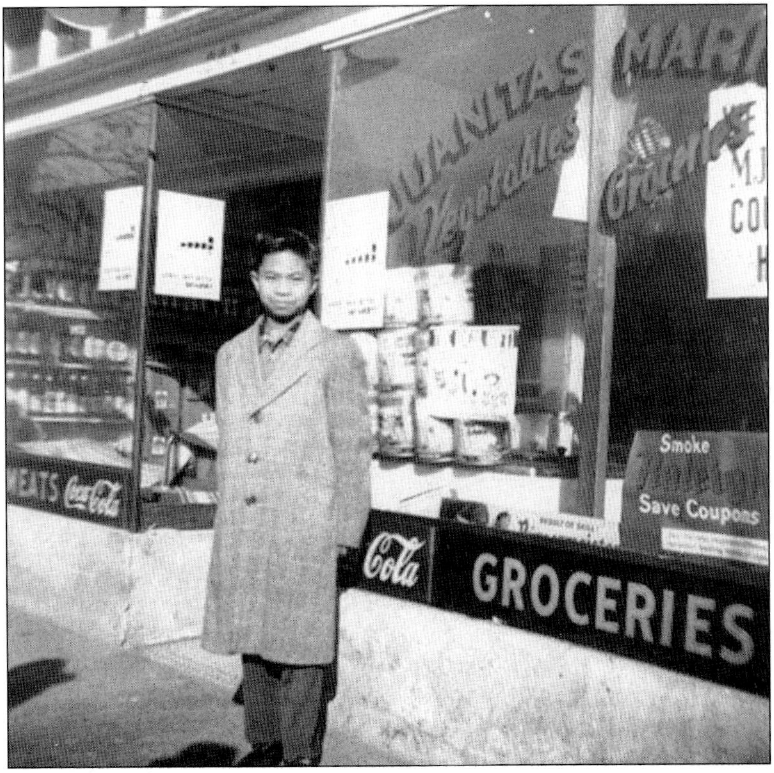

Cyril Juanitas Jr. stands in front of his family's grocery in the 1950s. The Juanitas family owned several businesses in Little Manila, including the Juanitas Grocery at 342 South El Dorado Street. Prior to World War II, Japanese grocers had dominated the area. (Courtesy of FANHS Stockton.)

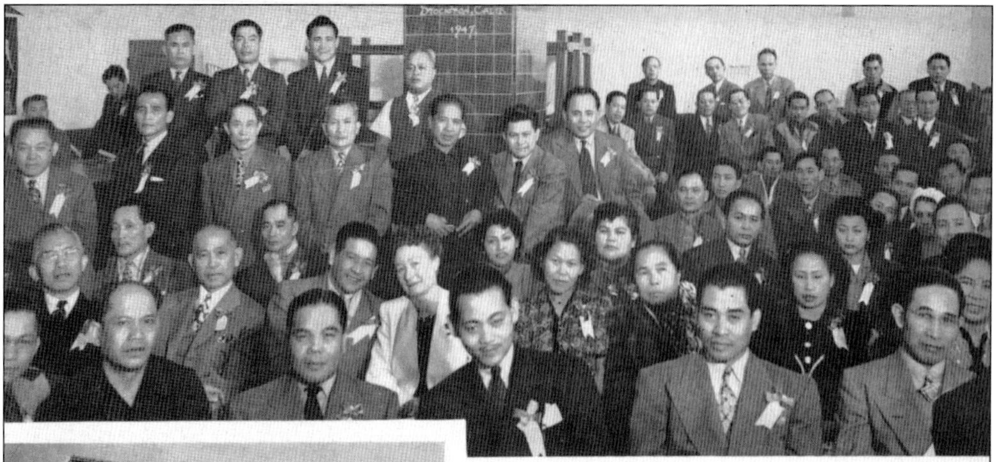

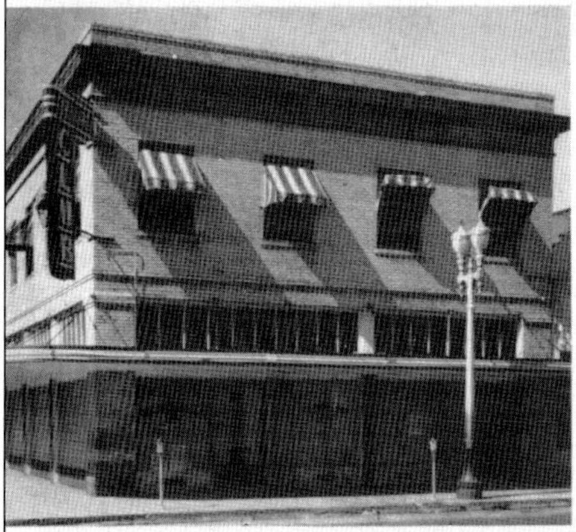

$1,000,000.00 Bataan-Manila Enterprises

1. President . . . . Mr. Teofilo P. Suasillo
2. Vice-President and General Manager . . . . . Mr. Deming Y. Asensi
3. Secretary . . . . Mr. Fructuoso Y. Monton
4. Assistant Secretary . . . . Mr. Olympio R. Manubag
5. Treasurer . . . . Mr. Lucio A. Tanzo
6. Assistant Treasurer . . . . Mr. Teodulo R. Lagura
7. Cashier . . . . Mr. Esteban A. Mira
8. General Bookkeeper . . . . Mr. Consurcio Bernido
9. Assistant Bookkeeper . . . . Mr. Esteban S. Idao
10. Auditor . . . . Mr. Anastasio Asunsion
11. Floor Manager—Bataan Club . . . . Mr. Angel Galindo
12. Floor Manager—Bataan Club . . . . Mr. Ted Tumol
13. Floor Manager—Manila Club . . . . Mr. Roque Navales
14. Floor Manager—Manila Club . . . . Mr. Buddy Rendon

Bataan Enterprise Building

Bataan Enterprise includes: Bataan Hotel, Bataan Cigar Stand, Bataan Pool Hall, and Bataan Club.

MANILA STOCKHOLDERS

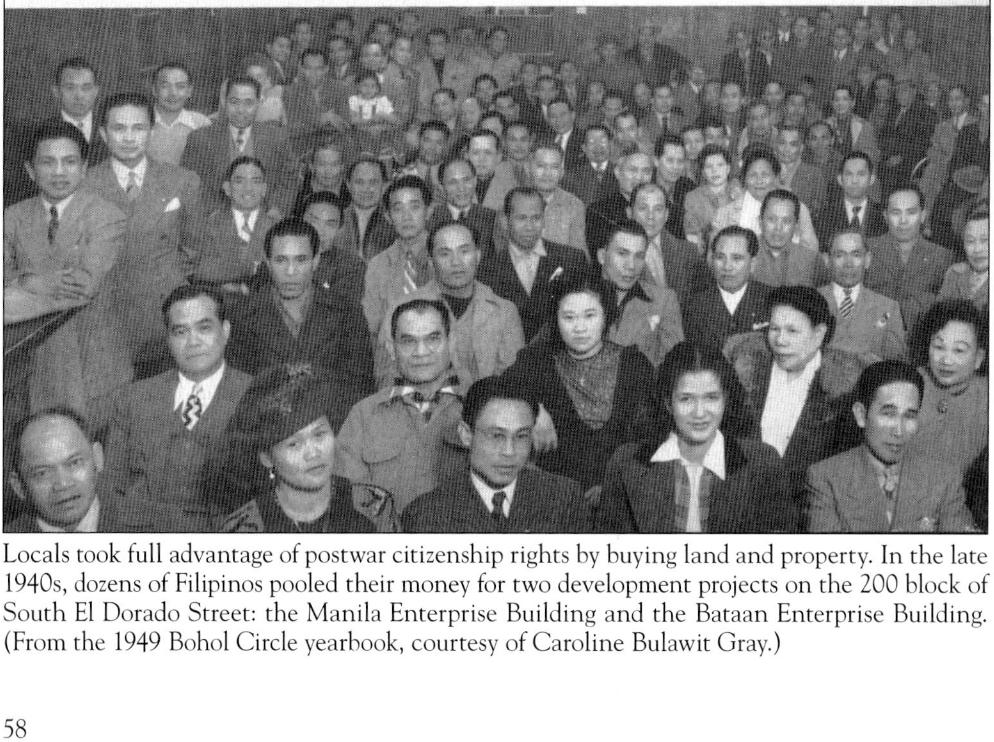

Locals took full advantage of postwar citizenship rights by buying land and property. In the late 1940s, dozens of Filipinos pooled their money for two development projects on the 200 block of South El Dorado Street: the Manila Enterprise Building and the Bataan Enterprise Building. (From the 1949 Bohol Circle yearbook, courtesy of Caroline Bulawit Gray.)

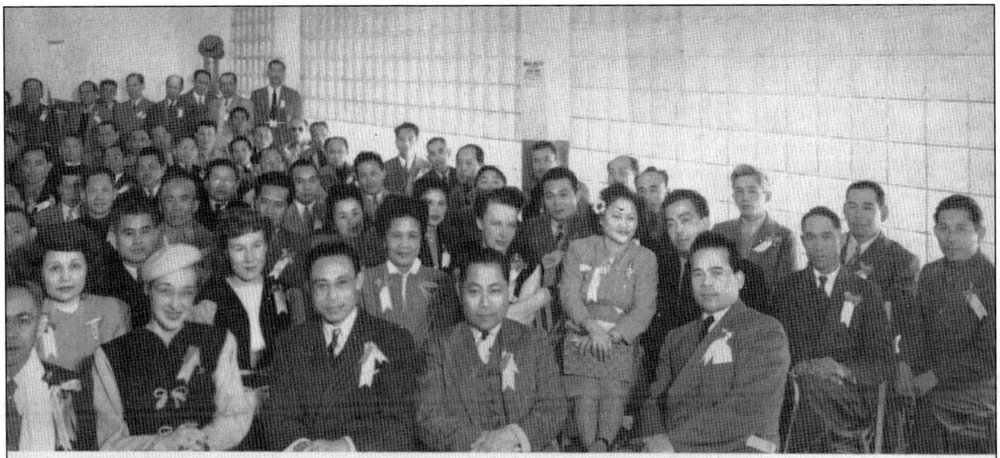

BATAAN STOCKHOLDERS CONVENTION

Bataan-Manila Enterprises, Inc., Stockton, California, U. S. A.

The Bataan-Manila Enterprises is a million dollar business located in Stockton, California. It is the largest business of its kind owned and operated by Filipinos in the United States. The two buildings owned by the Enterprise occupy two-thirds of the 200 block of South El Dorado St. in Stockton.

The Corporation is the mecca of Filipinos in the United States. It is frequented as a vacation and recreation spot by Filipinos all over the country. Friends from different parts of the United States may meet each other at the Bataan Club or the Manila Club. It is located in the central heart of the San Joaquin Valley in California, one of the most active agricultural centers in America, where crops are harvested during all four seasons of the year.

The Stockholders of the Bataan-Manila Enterprises, Inc., pictured above, invite all Filipinos living in America or visiting America to visit their headquarters in Stockton whenever possible and enjoy the hospitality of the many recreational services at their disposal.

BOARD OF DIRECTORS

Mr. Teofilo P. Suasillo . . . . *Chairman*
Mr. Deming Y. Asensi . . . . *Member*
Mr. Nemesio Tiempo . . . . *Member*
Mr. F. A. Mancao . . . . *Member*
Mr. Ted Market . . . . *Member*

FIRST ANNUAL CONVENTION

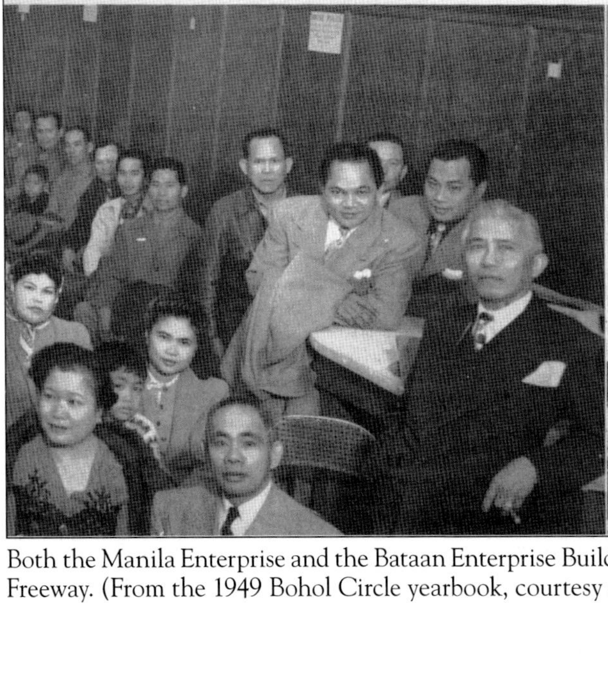

Manila Enterprise Building

Manila Enterprise includes: Manila Hotel, Manila Inn, Manila Bar, Manila Cigar Stand (by E. S. IDAO Agency), Manila Club.

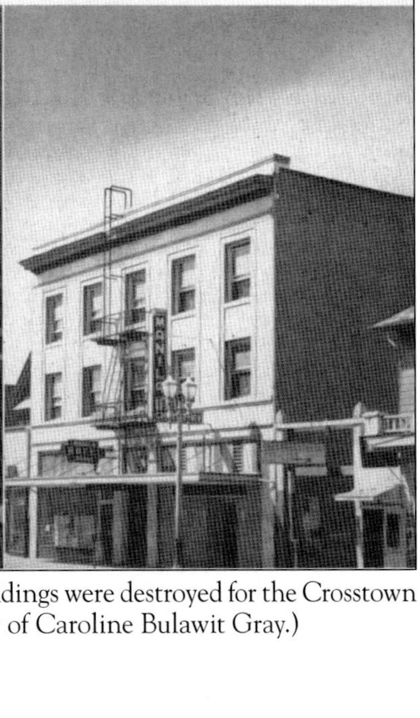

Both the Manila Enterprise and the Bataan Enterprise Buildings were destroyed for the Crosstown Freeway. (From the 1949 Bohol Circle yearbook, courtesy of Caroline Bulawit Gray.)

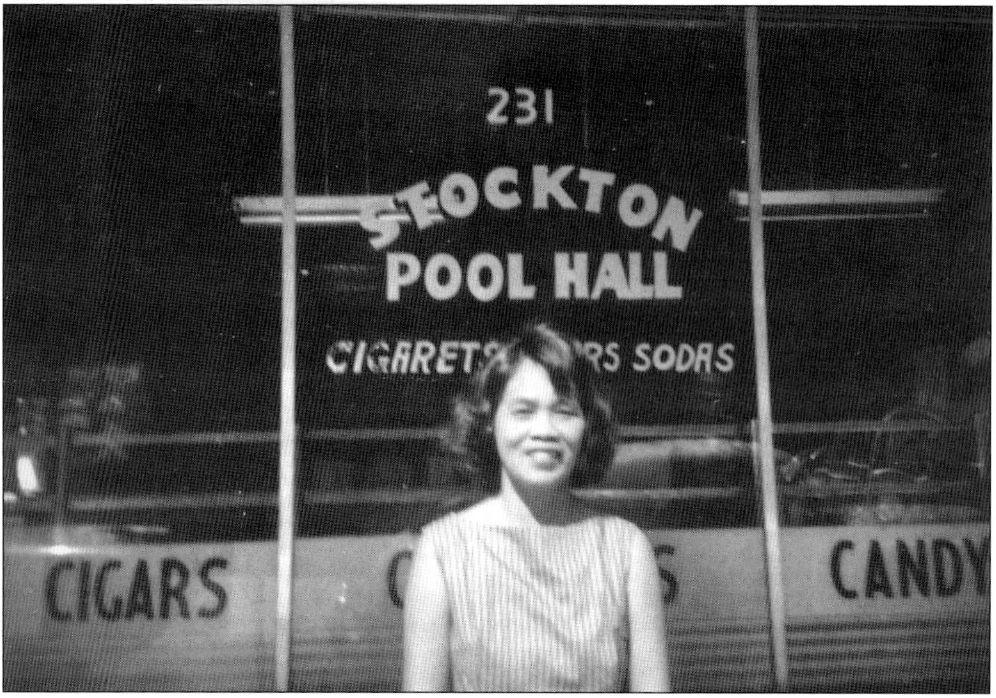

Carmen Saldevar was a schoolteacher in her native Ilocos Norte when she met and married her husband, Fernando, a barber who owned the New Deal Barbershop (Frenando is pictured below, with their son Fernando Jr.). She operated the popular Stockton Pool Hall but was relocated to Washington Street (shown above) during redevelopment. (Courtesy of Fernando Saldevar.)

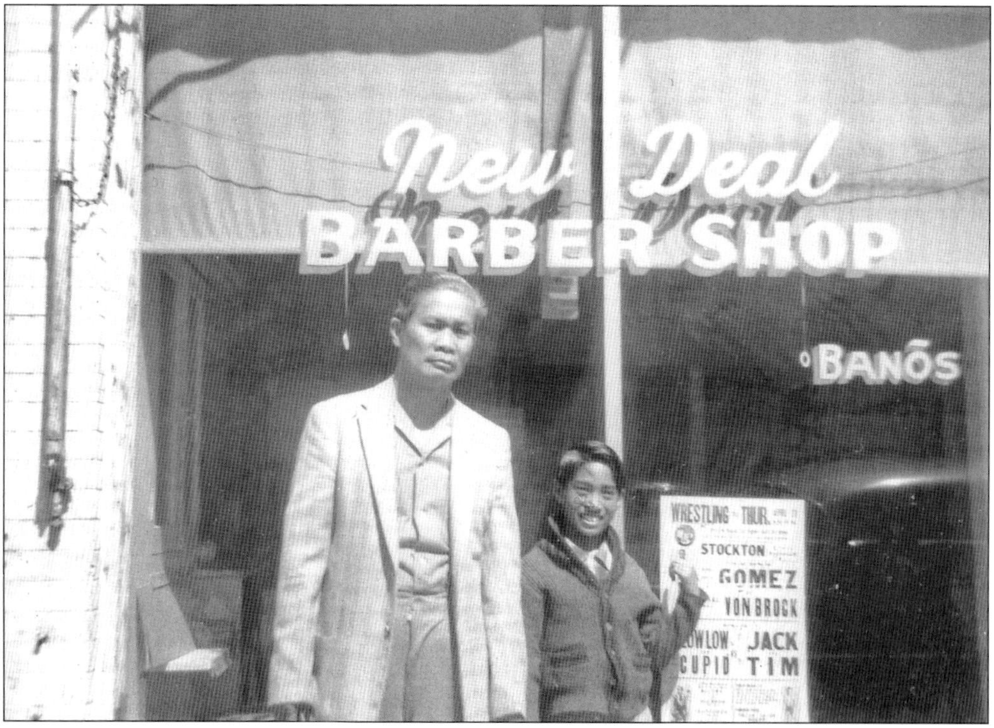

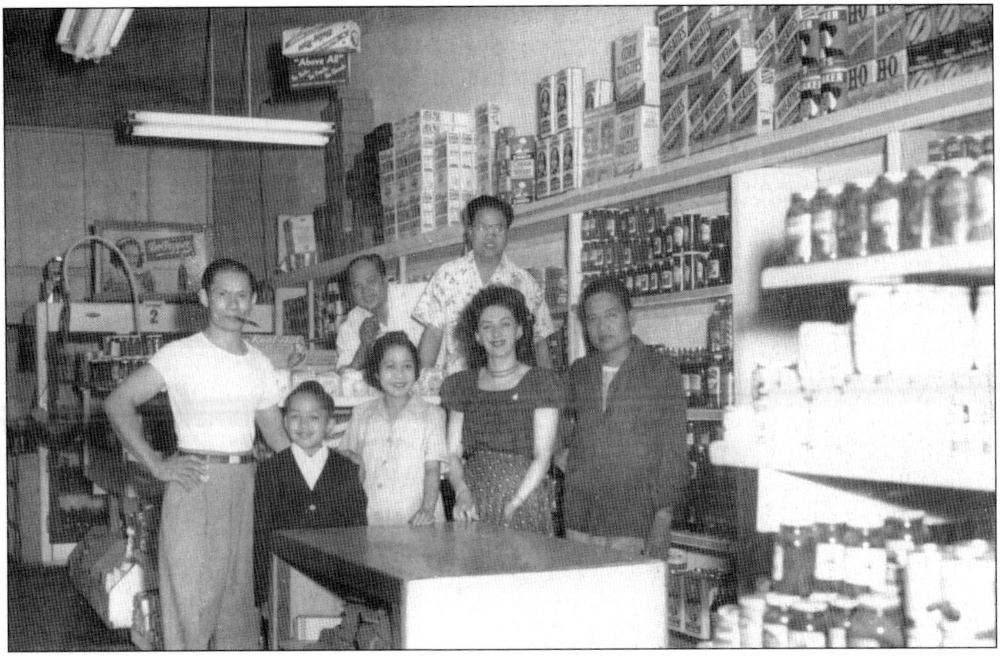

The Castillo family ran a grocery store at the Mariposa Hotel, shown above, before opening John's Family Market at 113 East Lafayette Street in the 1950s. Below, From left to right, are Hortensia Castillo, John Castillo (holding unidentified child), Beverly Castillo, and three unidentified friends. (Courtesy of Beverly Engkabo.)

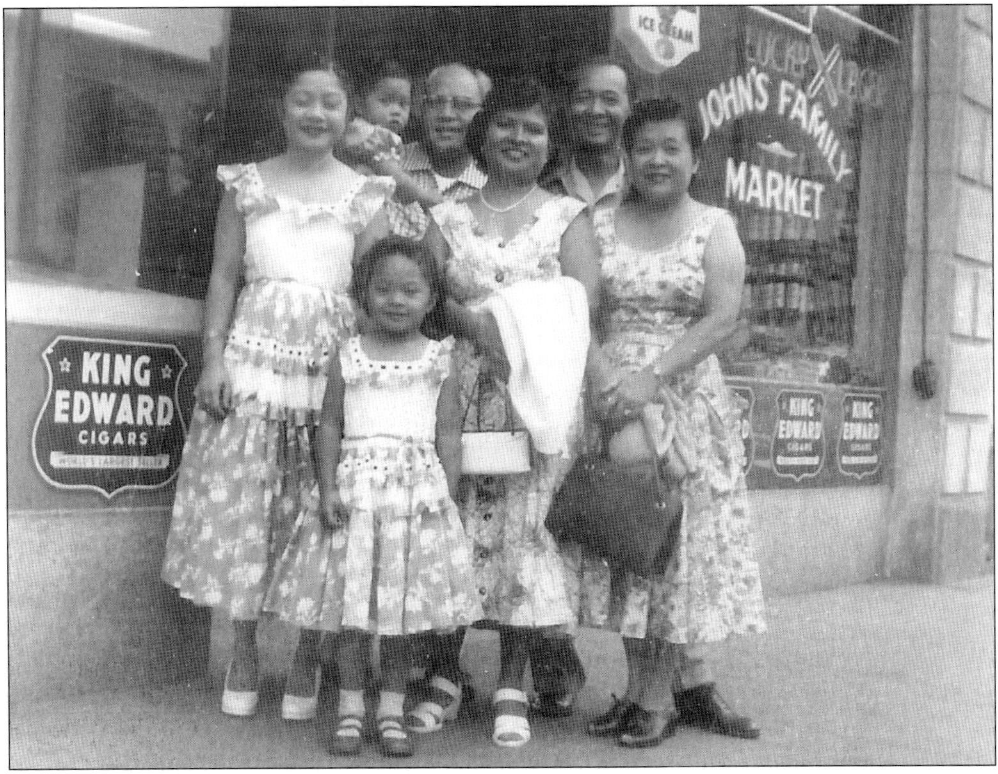

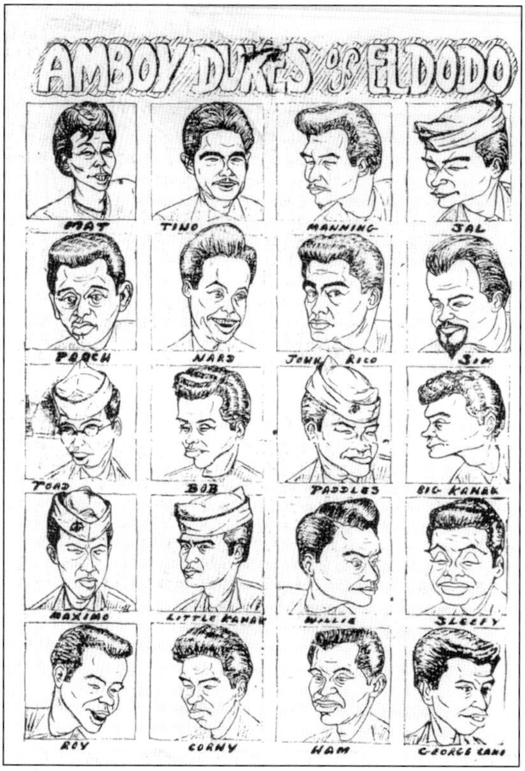

In his cartoon "Amboy Dukes of El Dodo," published in San Francisco's *Liwanag* anthology in 1977, Stockton artist John Lanossa plays loving tribute to the American-born Pinoys who frequented the streets of Little Manila, among them "Sleepy," "Toad," "Paddles," and "Little Kanak." (Courtesy of FANHS Stockton.)

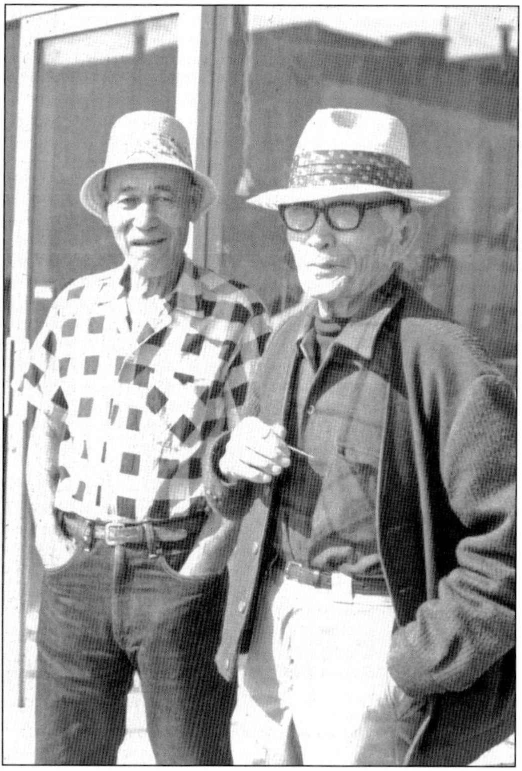

Redevelopment and the Crosstown Freeway demolitions still couldn't completely displace the Filipino old-timers who, for decades, had called Little Manila home. Here Manong Johnny (in front) and a friend pose on Washington Street in the 1970s. (Photograph by and courtesy of Laurena Cabañero.)

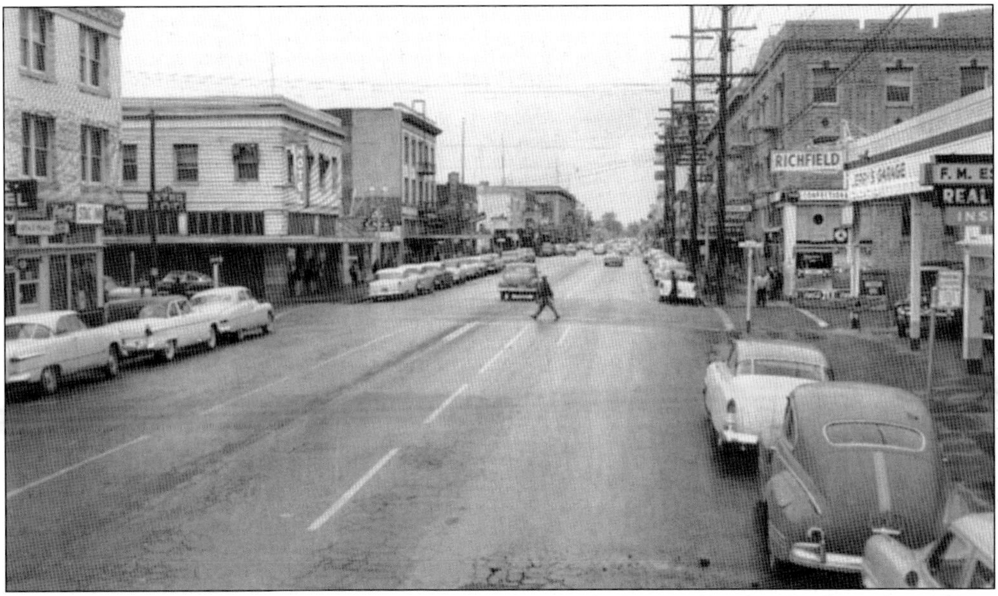

The intersection of El Dorado and Lafayette Streets was the heart of Little Manila in the 1950s, a decade before much of it was destroyed for redevelopment and the Crosstown Freeway. The West End Redevelopment Project demolished nine downtown blocks in the 1950s, destroying much of Chinatown, Nihonmachi, and the northern end of Little Manila. (Courtesy of the Bank of Stockton Photo Collection.)

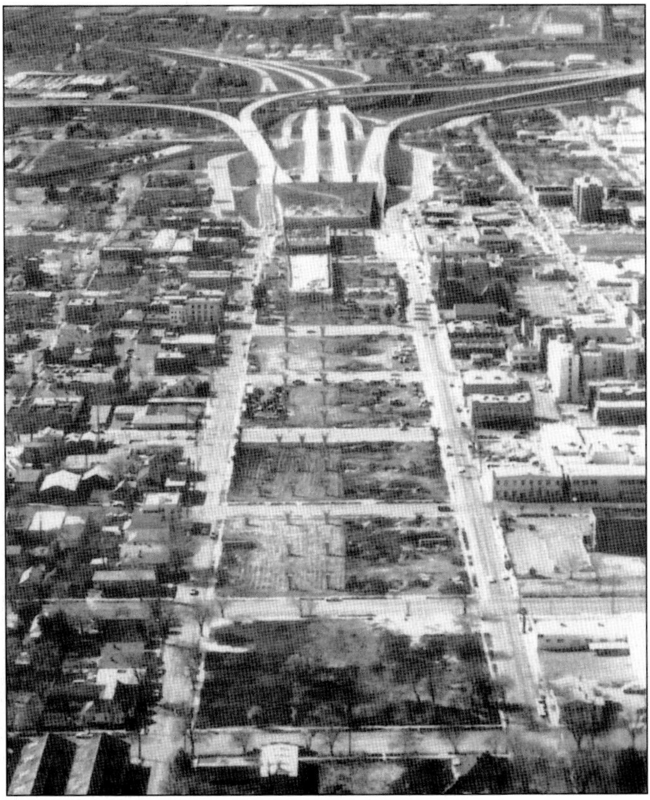

When the Crosstown Freeway was plotted onto downtown Stockton, many Stockton residents challenged the planned route, arguing that less displacement and destruction would occur if it was only relocated several blocks south. Freeway planners remained steadfast to their plan of demolition of several dozen city blocks. Here the freeway creeps along Lafayette and Washington Streets in the 1970s. In the left-hand corner is what remained of Little Manila after the demolitions: about two blocks. Thousands of people lost homes, churches, and businesses. (Courtesy of FANHS Stockton.)

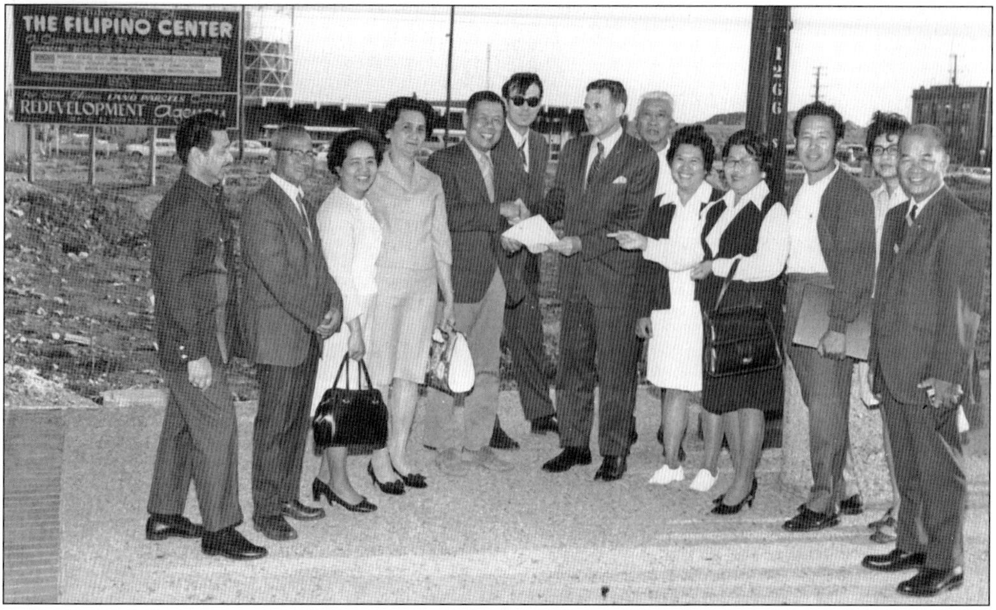

In the late 1960s, the Associated Filipino Organizations (AFO), a consortium of Filipino organizations, rallied the community behind a low-income housing and retail complex to house displaced old-timers and businesses. By tapping into the spirit of civil rights and federal funding for affordable urban housing, the group was successful. Here the AFO board celebrates the July 1971 ground breaking for the Filipino Center at 6 West Main Street. Leaders of the project were Ted Lapuz and Jose Bernardo. From left to right are Ramon Roxas, Fausto Rabaca, Maxine Yurong, Illuminada Unson, Ted Lapuz, Dave ? (building architect), Congressman John McFall, Rosauro Daclan, Naty Jusa, Concepcion M. Bohulano, Jose Bernardo, Carmen Carido (Griggs), and Tom Jusa. (Courtesy of Concepcion M. Bohulano.)

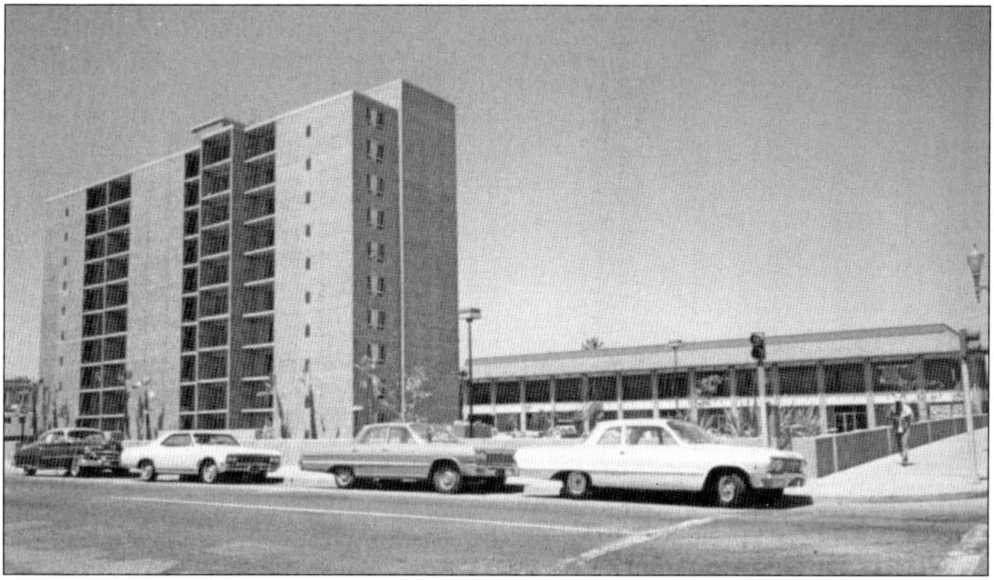

Celebratory postcards of the Filipino Center were published to commemorate the opening in 1972, which was celebrated with a barrio fiesta. The plaza's annual fiesta, held the second weekend of August, commemorates the plaza's opening. (Courtesy of Concepcion M. Bohulano.)

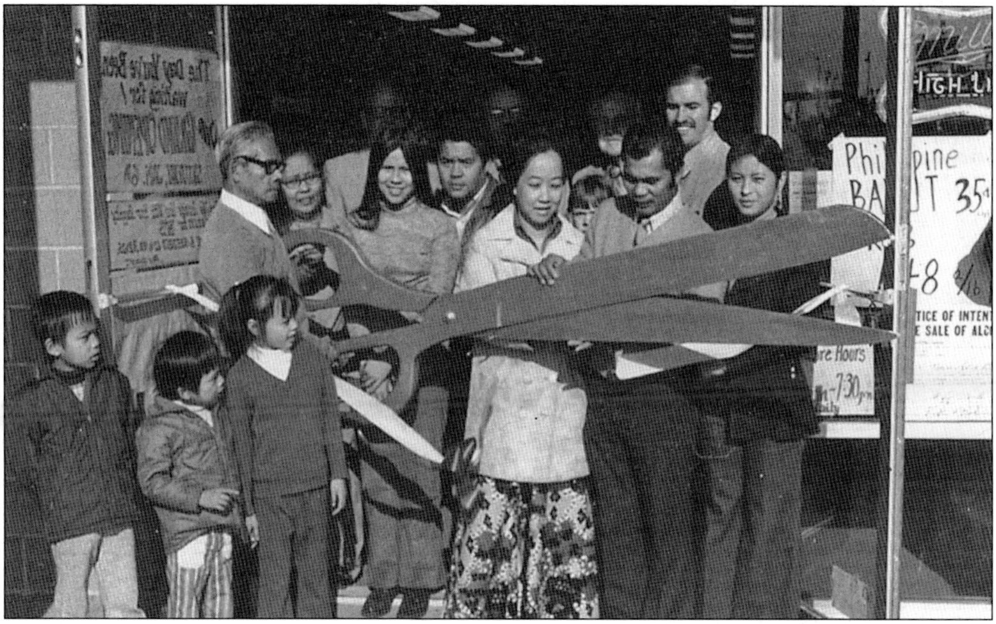

The B&G Market was one of the first businesses to open in the Filipino Center complex. Here the Bohulano and Giva families cut the ribbon on their Filipino grocery store in 1972. From left to right are Joey M. Giva, Dale M. Giva, Rosie M. Giva, Delfin Bohulano Sr., Concepcion M. Bohulano, Adeline Bohulano, Delfin Bohulano Jr., Bernie Giva, Narcy Giva, and Virginia Bohulano. (Courtesy Bernie M. Giva.)

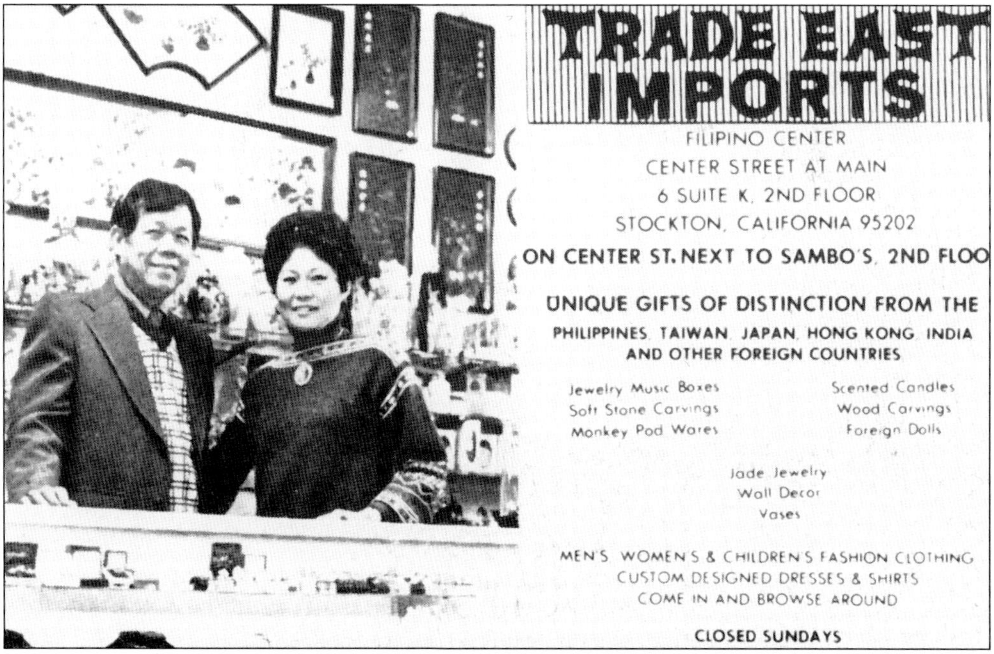

For 26 years, Ted (left) and Africa Lapuz operated the largest store for Philippine-crafted décor and clothing, Trade East Imports, in the Filipino Plaza and then on Main Street in downtown. They also owned the Karomata Restaurant and the Vinta Cocktail Lounge in the Filipino Center (now Plaza). (Courtesy of FANHS Stockton.)

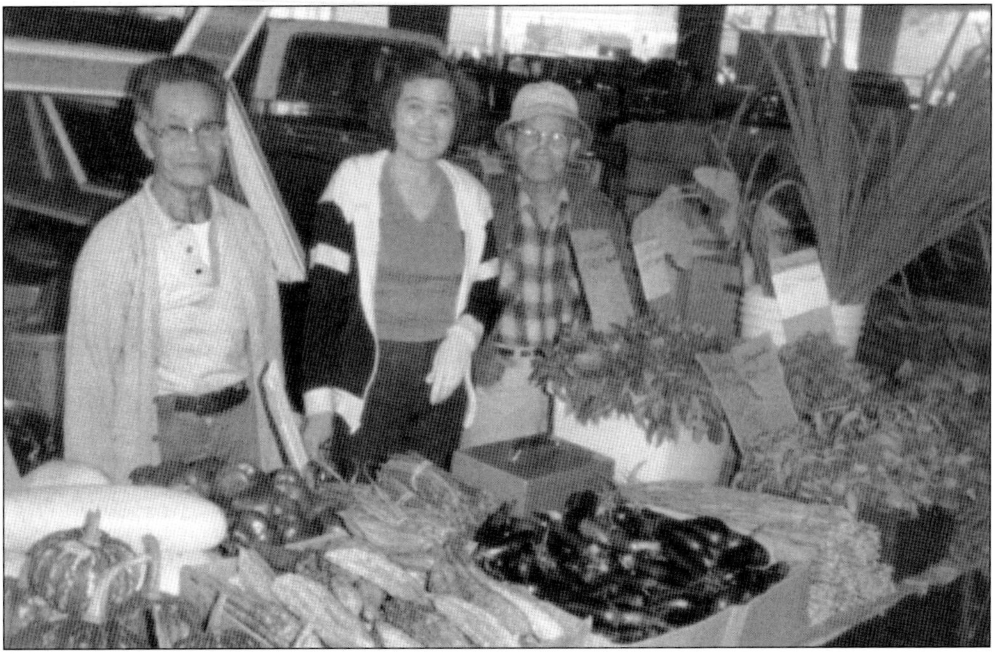

Simon, Leonila, and Eusebio Aynaga, former grocery store owners in Little Manila, are at their booth at the Farmer's Market in 1984. Every Saturday, the Farmer's Market, co-conceived by local Filipino farmer Cecil Bonzo, is held under the Crosstown Freeway near Little Manila. Today the market is lauded as one of the country's first and best farmer's markets. (Courtesy of Betty Aynaga.)

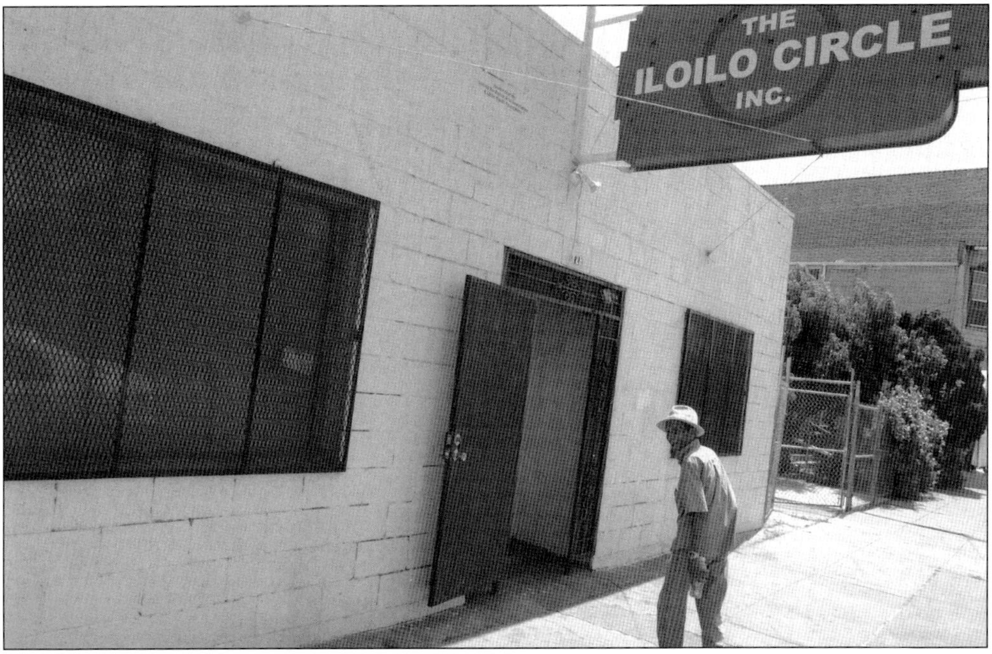

The Iloilo Circle, a mutual aid association, bought this building at 128 Sonora Street in the 1960s. The home is used to house elderly members and still serves as a lively gathering spot for cards and conversation in Little Manila. Here a local visits the building in June 2007. (Photograph by Calixtro Romias, courtesy of the *Record*.)

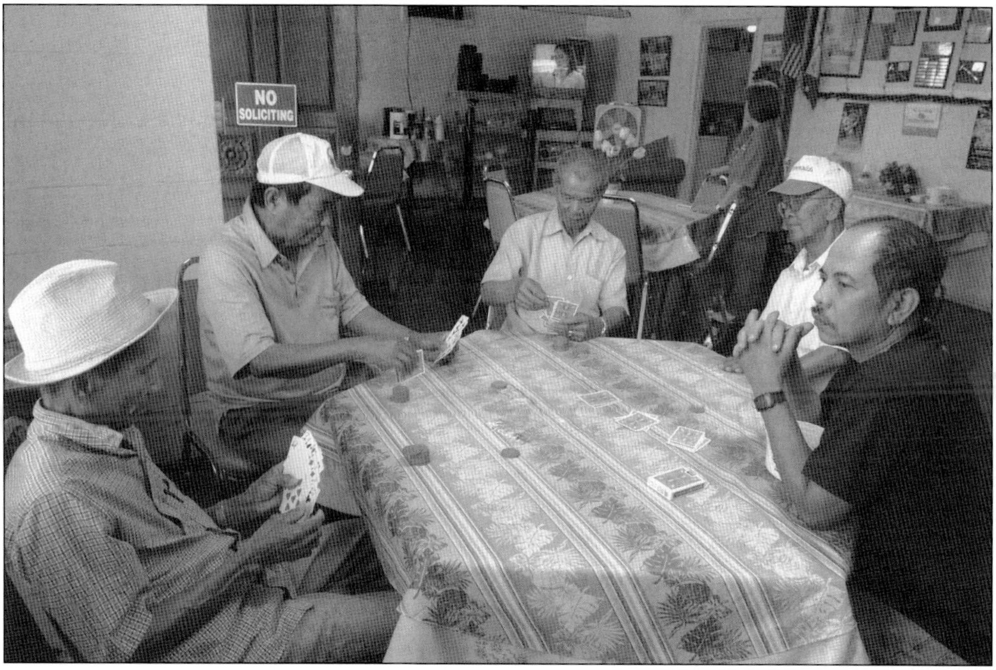

Filipinos still gather in Little Manila every day. Here residents play cards in the Iloilo Circle in June 2007. (Photograph by Calixtro Romias, courtesy of the *Record*.)

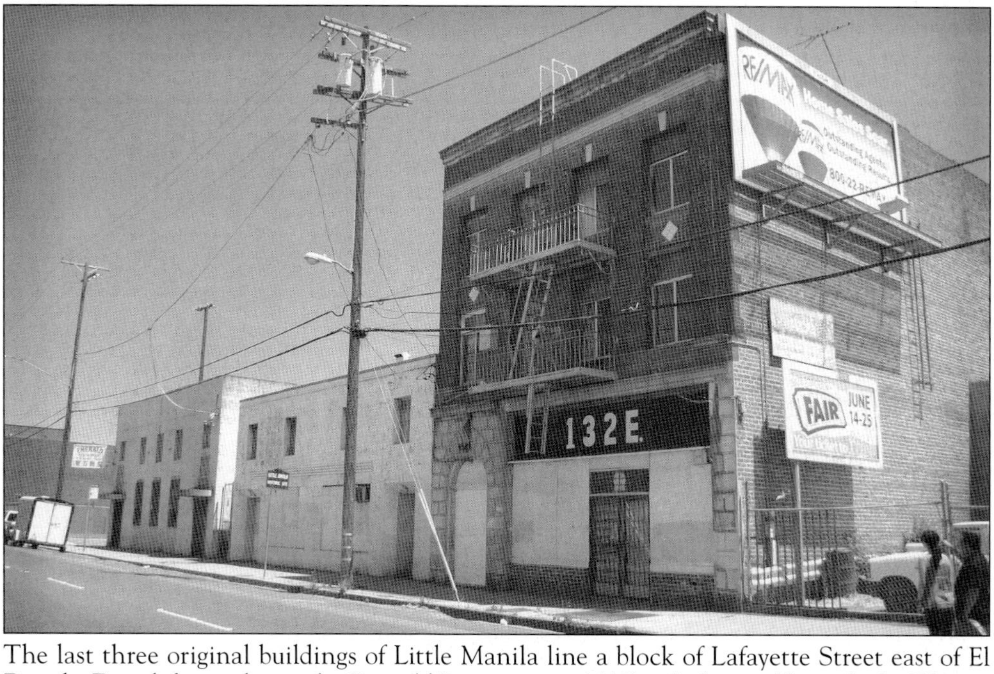

The last three original buildings of Little Manila line a block of Lafayette Street east of El Dorado. From left to right are the Emerald Restaurant at 144 East Lafayette (formerly the Filipino Recreation Center/AF of L Hall), the Rizal Social Club at 138 East Lafayette Street, and the Mariposa Hotel at 130/132 East Lafayette Street. At the time of construction, each of the buildings was considered plush and modern by Stockton standards. (Photograph by Dillon Delvo, courtesy of the Little Manila Foundation.)

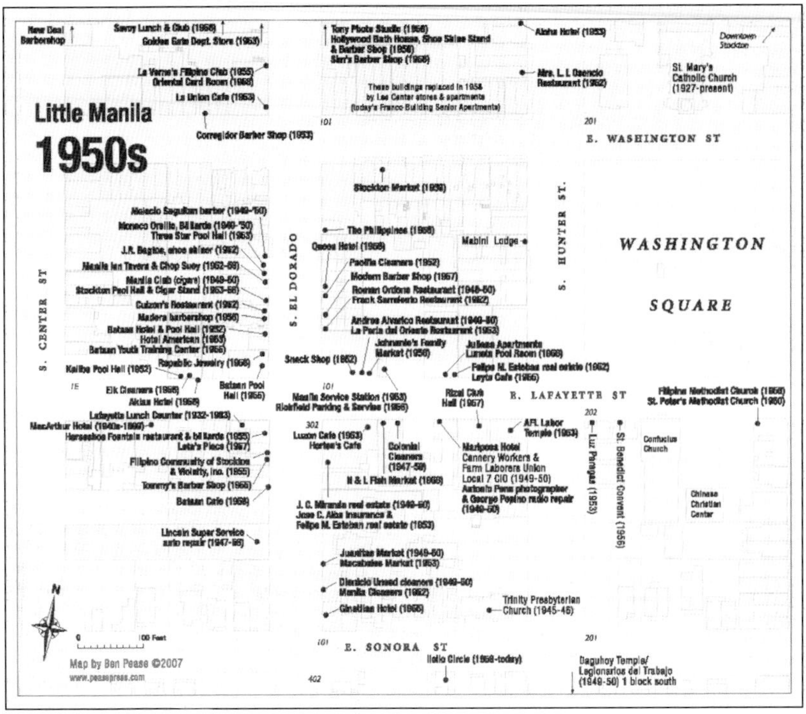

This map of Little Manila in the 1950s shows many businesses, but pressure on the district from the West End Redevelopment Project is evident. (Courtesy of Ben Pease.)

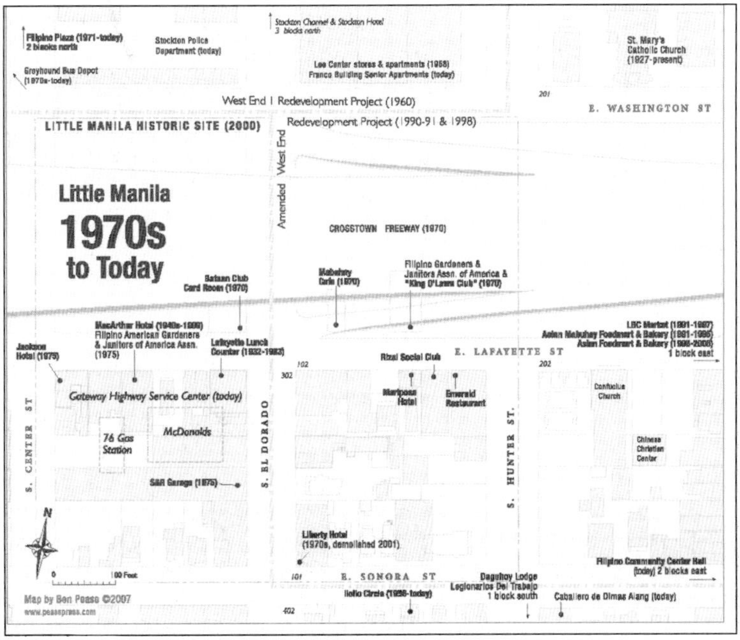

This map of Little Manila shows the district from 1970 to today. The West End Redevelopment Project and the Crosstown Freeway destroyed much of the neighborhood. The Gateway Redevelopment Project destroyed another block for a gas station and McDonalds. In 2000, the community campaigned to designate the Little Manila Historic Site. (Courtesy of Ben Pease.)

Four

Filipino American Generations

Families and Youth

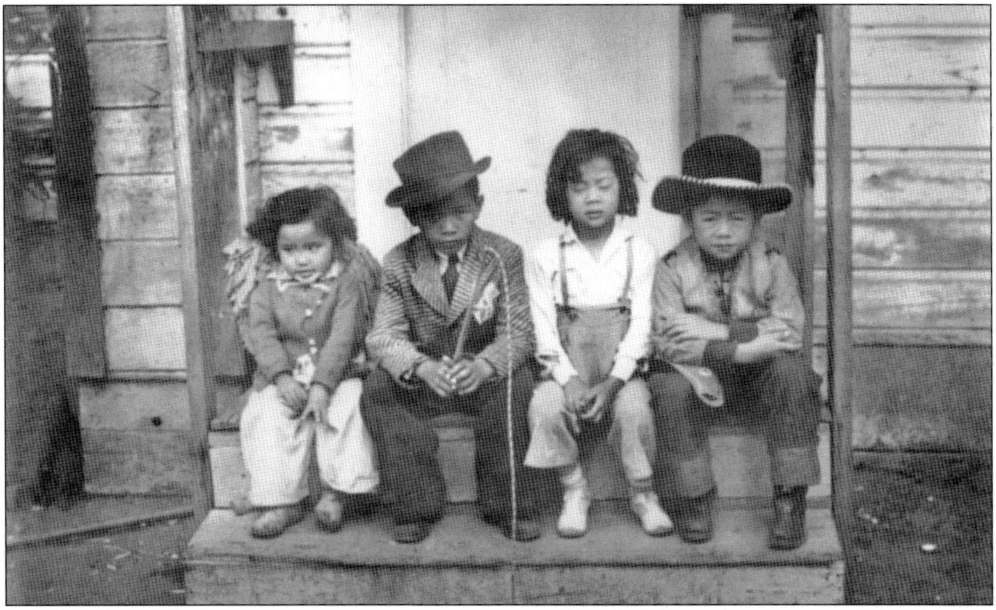

A skilled tailor made Clemente Morales Jr.'s kid-size McIntosh suit to match his father's and uncle's. He is pictured with friends near Stockton. Because they were a rarity in the early, mostly male community, Filipino children were cherished, because for most early immigrants, the sex ratio imbalance made marriage difficult, and anti-miscegenation law in California barred Filipinos from marrying whites. For Filipinos, "family" was any social unit that could include relatives, town mates, friends, godparents (*ninongs* and *ninangs*) and co-godparents (one's *comadres* and *compadres*), and coworkers. Several Filipino immigrant families settled in Stockton, and Filipino-white couples crossed state boundaries to marry in states like Arizona. Filipinos in Stockton have married spouses from other backgrounds and created a unique mixed heritage *mestiza/o* community. World War II created a Filipino baby boom as Filipino veterans brought back war brides from the Philippines and started families. Relaxed immigration laws and citizenship for Filipinos after World War II spurred family reunification. From the 1960s to the 1980s, many aging Filipino bachelors started families, creating tri-generational families. In the last four decades, the community has been revitalized by the arrival of thousands of new immigrants and their families, and the descendants of the pioneers are now in the fifth generation. (Courtesy of Vicky Ramos-McElyea.)

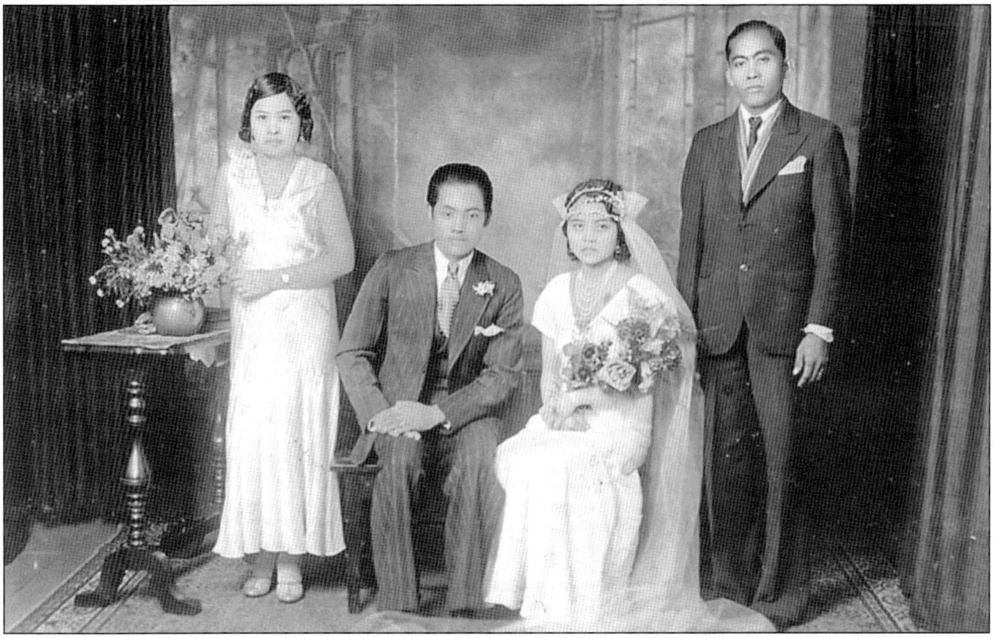

Camila Labor, who remembers that young, single Pinays were treated like "diamonds" and "queens" because they were so rare in the 1920s and 1930s, had several suitors, but she married Leon Carido in 1932. Carido hailed from Calape, Bohol, and Labor was a native of Hinundayan, Leyte. They became dedicated community leaders. (Courtesy of the Sharon Monton Robinson.)

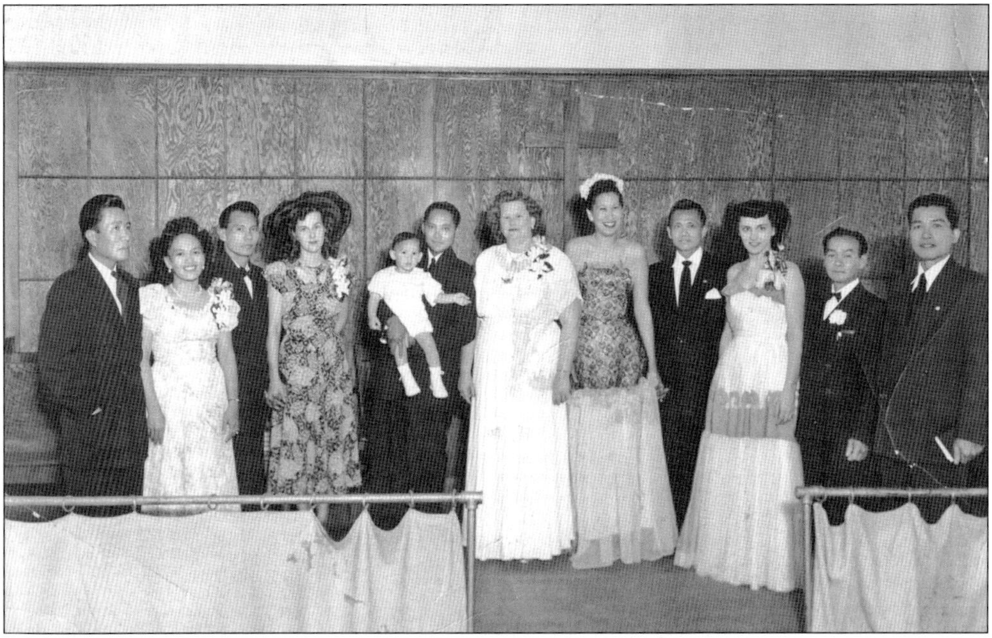

Mariano (holding Mariano Jr.) and Jessie Alcantra (to his right) had to get married in Seattle, Washington, because California anti-miscegenation laws barred Filipino-white marriages. They were married for 40 years. Here they baptized their son Mariano Jr. with friends at Trinity Presbyterian Church in the 1940s. Also present are Toni Alcantra (second from left), and next to Jessie, Louise Weaver. At the far right is Rev. Maurice Legare. (Courtesy of Susanne Alcantra.)

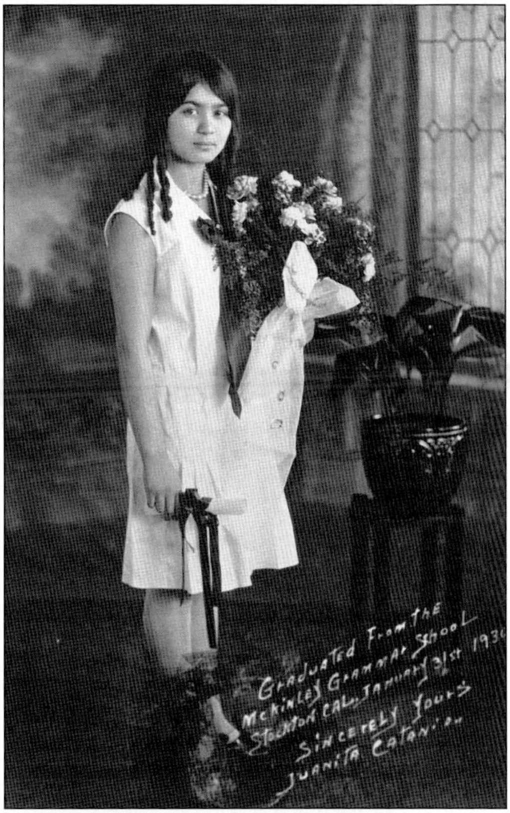

Second-generation Pinay Juanita Catanio (Baguio) takes a formal portrait with John Y. Billones to commemorate her graduation from McKinley Grammar School in 1930. The Catanios are a large family in Stockton. (Courtesy of Photographic Collections, Visual Communications.)

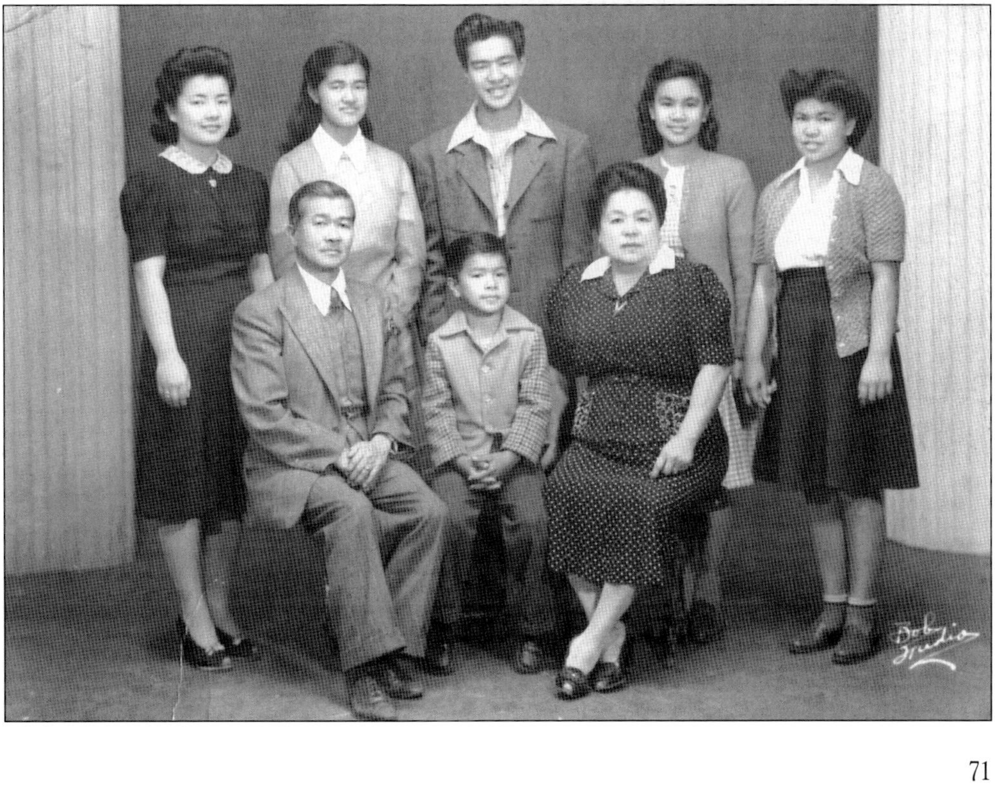

The Bantillo family gathered for a family portrait during World War II. From left to right are (seated) Anastasio Sr., Ernie, and Virgilia; (standing) Angelina, Norma, Anastasio "Bo" Jr., Leatrice, and Lily. After the portrait was taken, Bo left for the army and was killed in action. (Courtesy of the Mabalon family collection.)

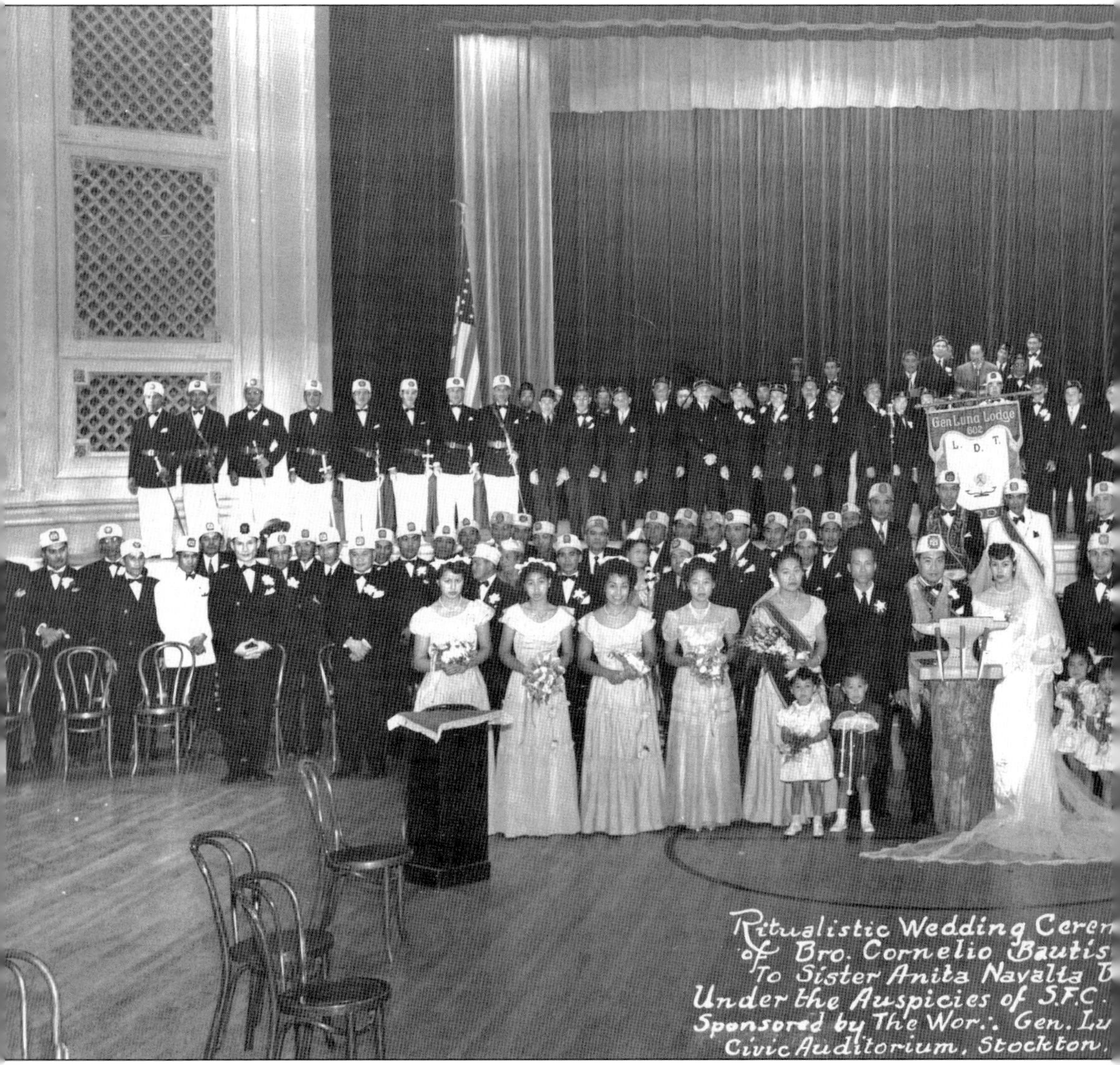
Gen Luna Lodge
602
L. D. T.
Ritualistic Wedding Ceren
of Bro. Cornelio Bautis
To Sister Anita Navalta B
Under the Auspicies of S.F.C.
Sponsored by The Wor.·. Gen. Lu
Civic Auditorium, Stockton.

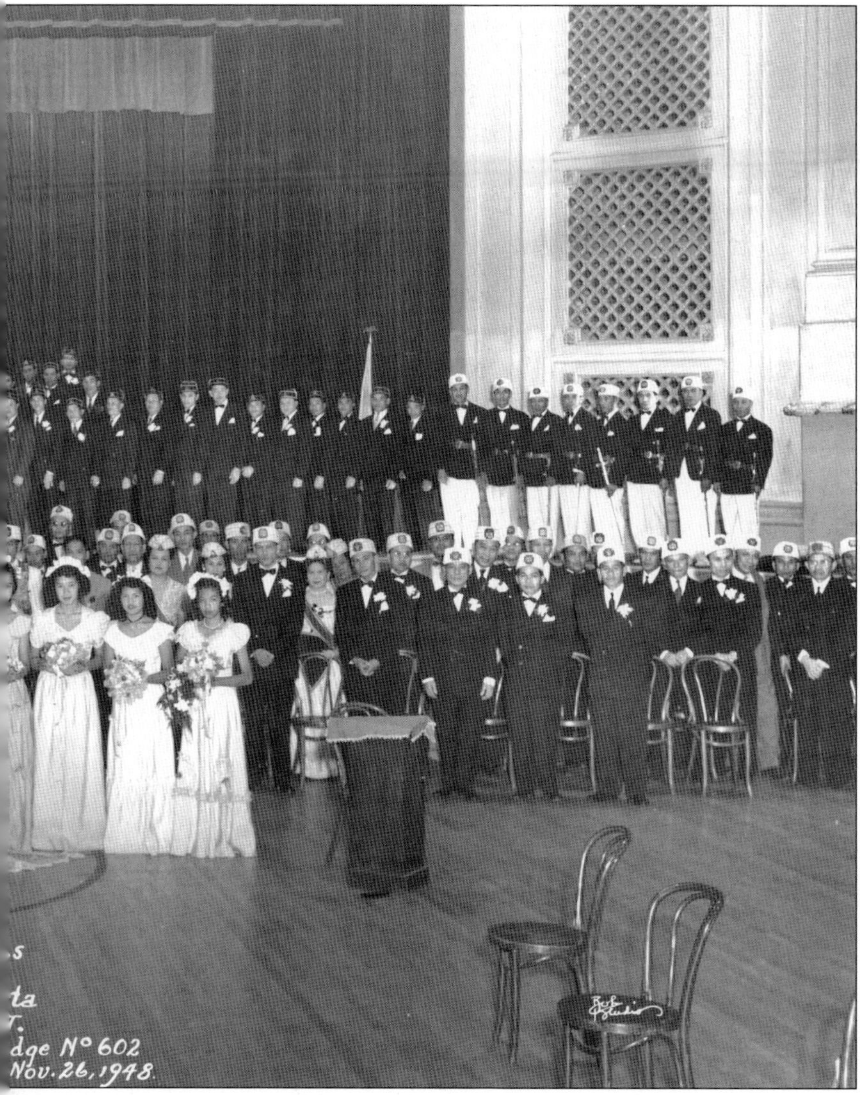

Second-generation *mestiza* Anita Navalta married Cornelio Bautista in an elaborate Luna Lodge No. 602, Legionarios del Trabajo wedding ceremony in the main hall of the Civic Auditorium in 1948. One's lodge was a surrogate family; lodges performed special rituals for christenings, weddings, and funerals. (Courtesy of Vicky Ramos McElyea.)

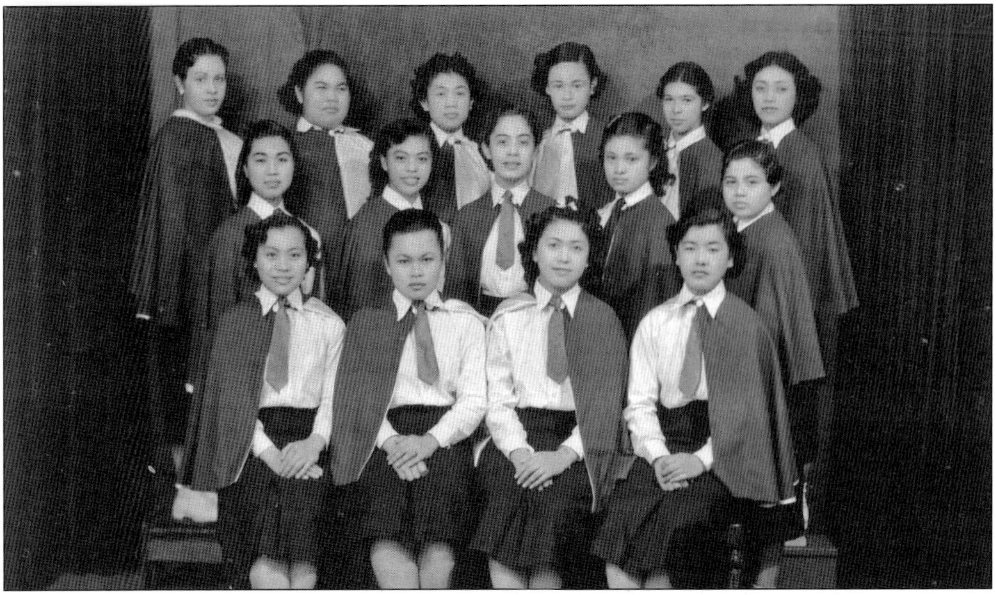

Second-generation daughters of Filipino pioneers organized the Filipina Society of America. From left to right are (first row) Colita Delgado (Luisen), Millie Mahumot, Trinedad Godinez, and Angelina Bantillo (Magdael); (second row) Neri Nunez, Trinidad Likong, Lucille Leybe, Delores Pasco, and Rita Leyble (Rallojay); (third row) Betty Leyble (Suarez), Eulalia "Dolly" Amen (Ragunton), Sally Godinez, Rosalie Flores, Pilar Padilla (Reynon), and Susanna Godinez (Fontanilla). (Courtesy of the Magdael family.)

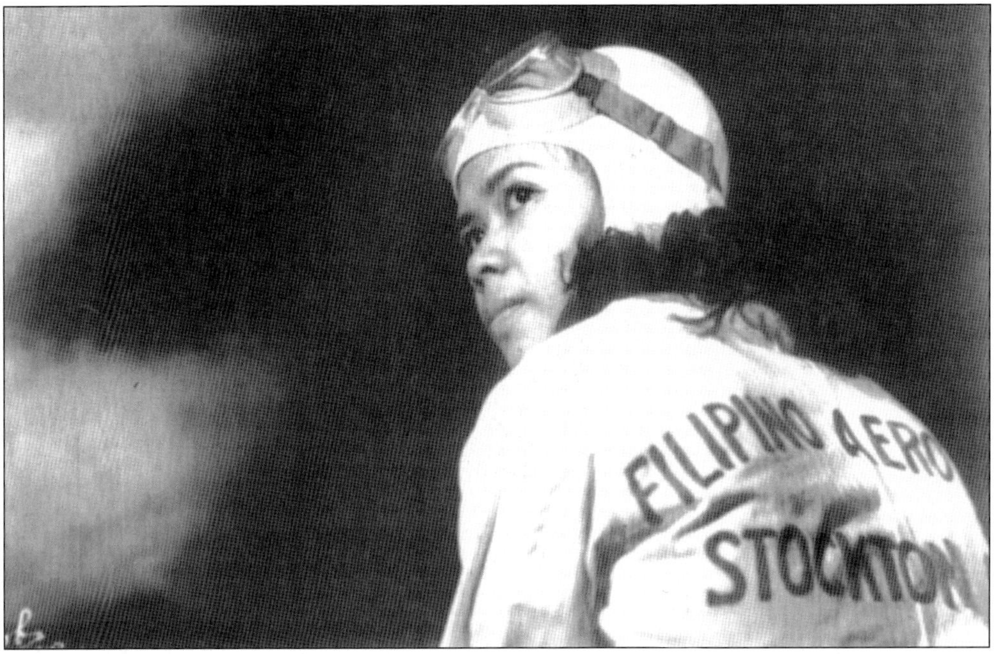

Teofila Sarmiento was an adventurous second-generation Pinay who was one of the only women in the Filipino Aero Club of Stockton in the late 1930s. She made her first long-distance flight, from Stockton to Oakland, on August 28, 1939, when she was only 19. (Courtesy of Rosaline Dickinson.)

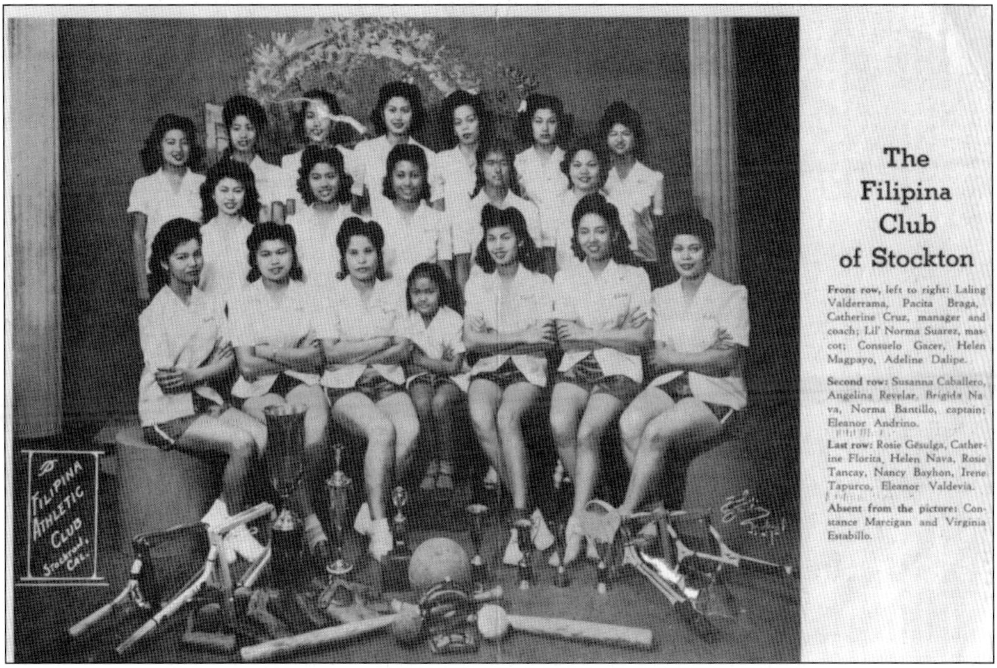

Second-generation Pinoys and Pinays formed their own sports organizations beginning in the 1930s, creating a large network of Filipino American sports clubs throughout the state that operated until the 1970s. The Filipina Athletic Club was formed in the late 1930s. (Courtesy of the Magdael family.)

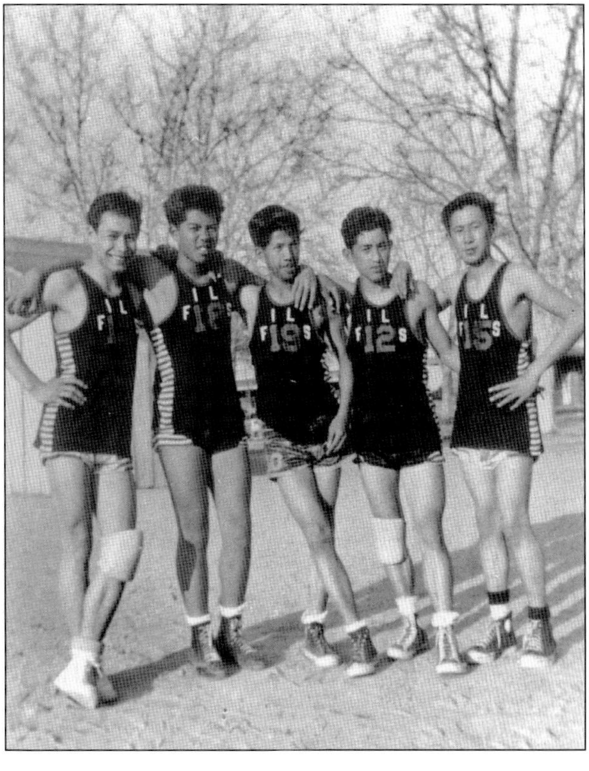

The Fils was a Stockton-based basketball club consisting of second-generation Pinoys in the 1940s. From left to right are Tino Fontanilla, George Orello, Joe Bucarizo, Ted Gabales, and George Ramirez. (Courtesy of Ted Gabales.)

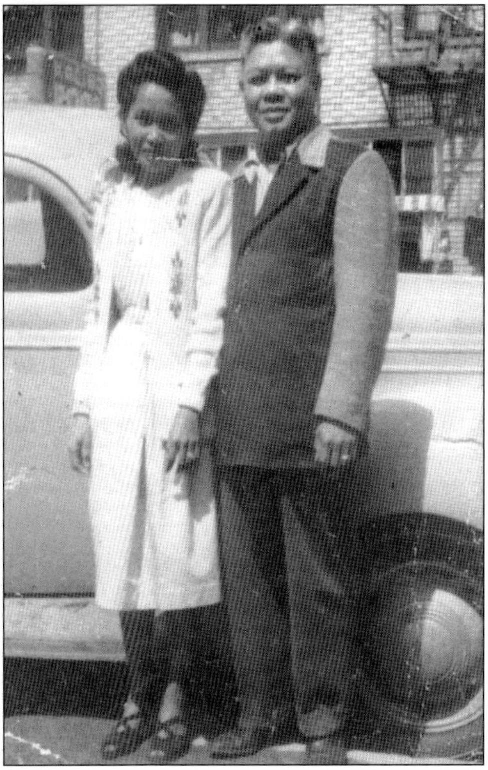

When Pablo Mabalon became a citizen, he immediately petitioned for his wife and three children to join him in Stockton. When Isabel Tirona Mabalon arrived in Stockton in 1947, she hadn't seen her husband, Pablo, since the day he left the Philippinesin 1929, approximately 17 years. It took several more decades for the entire family, including several Mabalon grandchildren, to come to Stockton. (Courtesy of Ernesto T. Mabalon.)

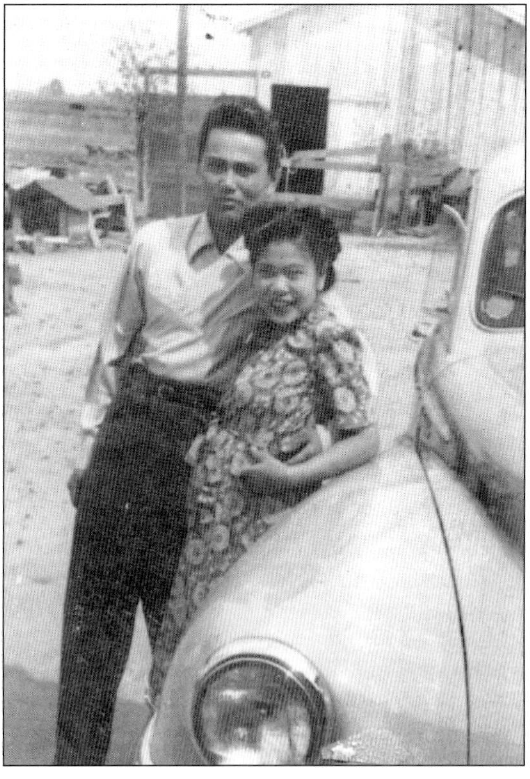

Sam Vallesteros Galicinao left Bacarra, Ilocos Norte, in 1930 to join his aunt and uncle, Lathrop farmers Margarita and Vicente Acoba. During military service in the Philippines, he fell in love with Lita, a girl from his hometown. They married on December 9, 1945, raised two daughters in Lathrop near Manila Road (shown here in 1949), and celebrated their 61st wedding anniversary before Sam's death in 2006. (Courtesy of Lita R. Galicinao.)

Prudencio and Adoracion Antaran attend a dance for the Mabini Lodge of the Legionarios del Trabajo in the late 1940s. The Antarans raised their family in Stockton. (Courtesy of Melissa Gust.)

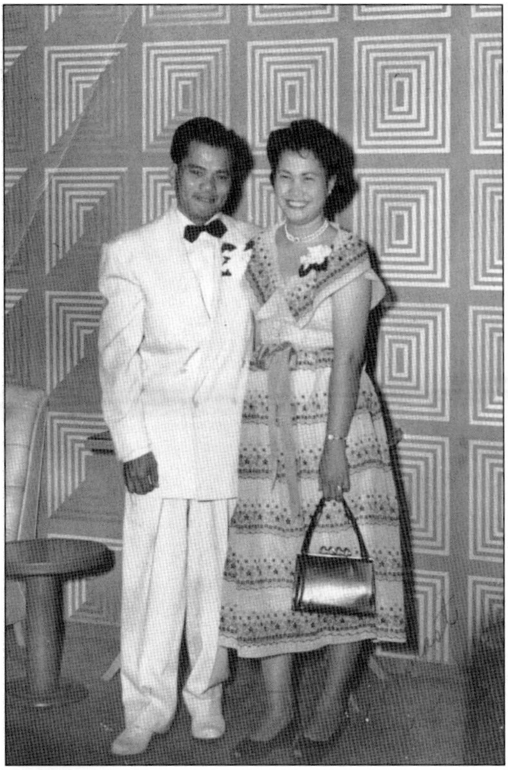

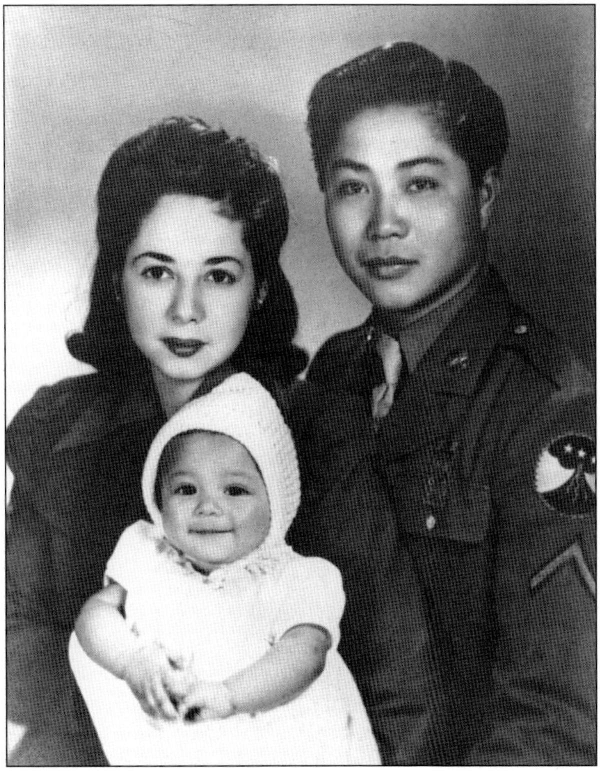

Gregorio "George," Esther, and baby Linda Alavazo, who was born in 1943, are shown here. A World War II veteran with the Filipino Infantry Regiments (his three-star patch is evidence of this), George was a decorated soldier who worked at the Defense Depot in Tracy until the end of his life. George and Esther raised 10 children and stepchildren in Stockton. (Courtesy of Linda A. Lazaro.)

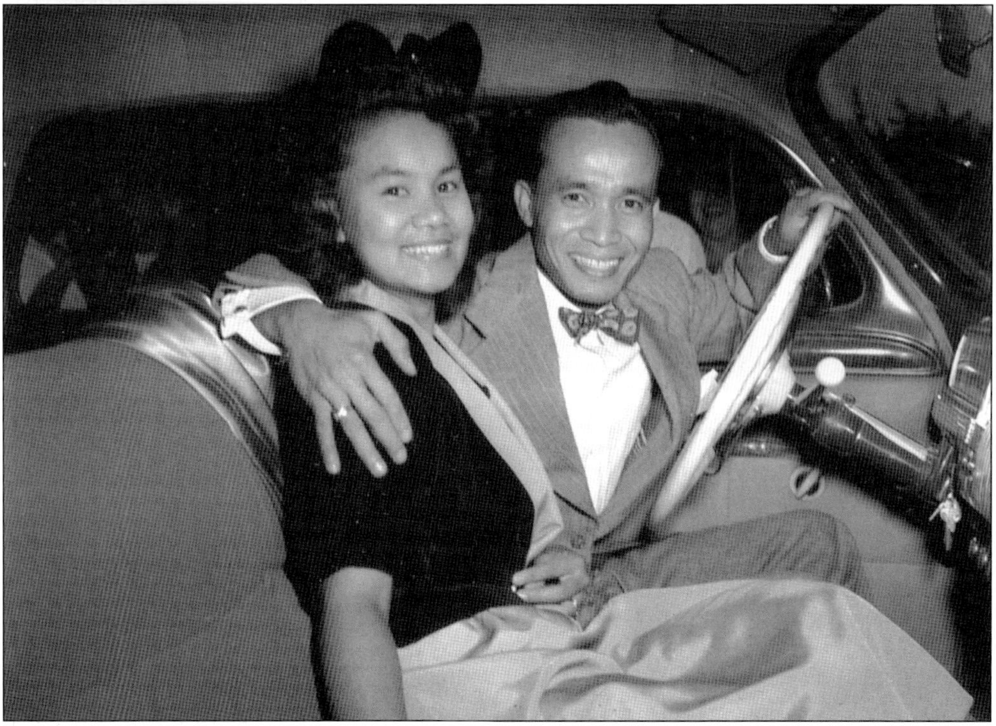

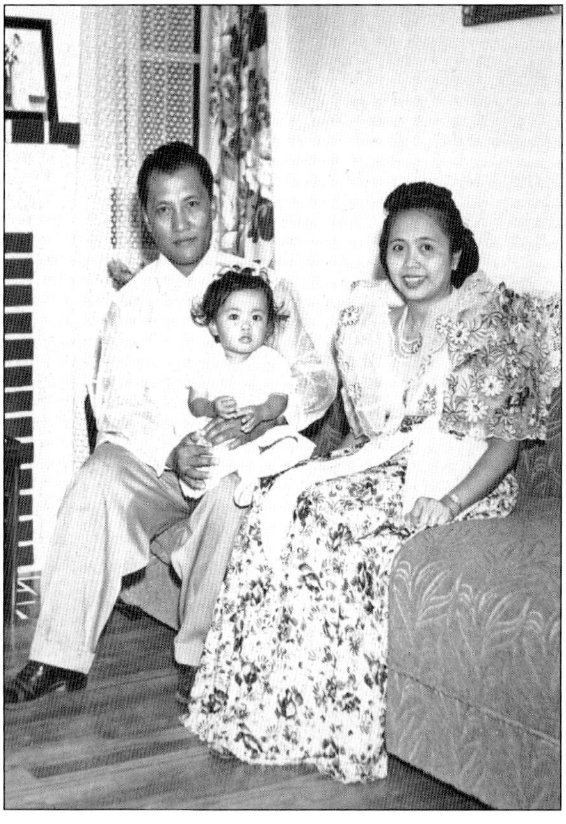

Leatrice Bantillo Perez and her husband, Frank Perez, leave for their honeymoon after their wedding on August 11, 1951. Leatrice came from a large Stockton family and was active in the Trinity Presbyterian Church; Frank was a prolific journalist who wrote for several newspapers well into the 1990s and was active in the Caballeros de Dimas Alang. (Courtesy of Leatrice B. Perez.)

The Agustin Tuliao family poses for a picture in 1949 at their home on East Anderson Street in Stockton. (Courtesy of Florence Quilantang.)

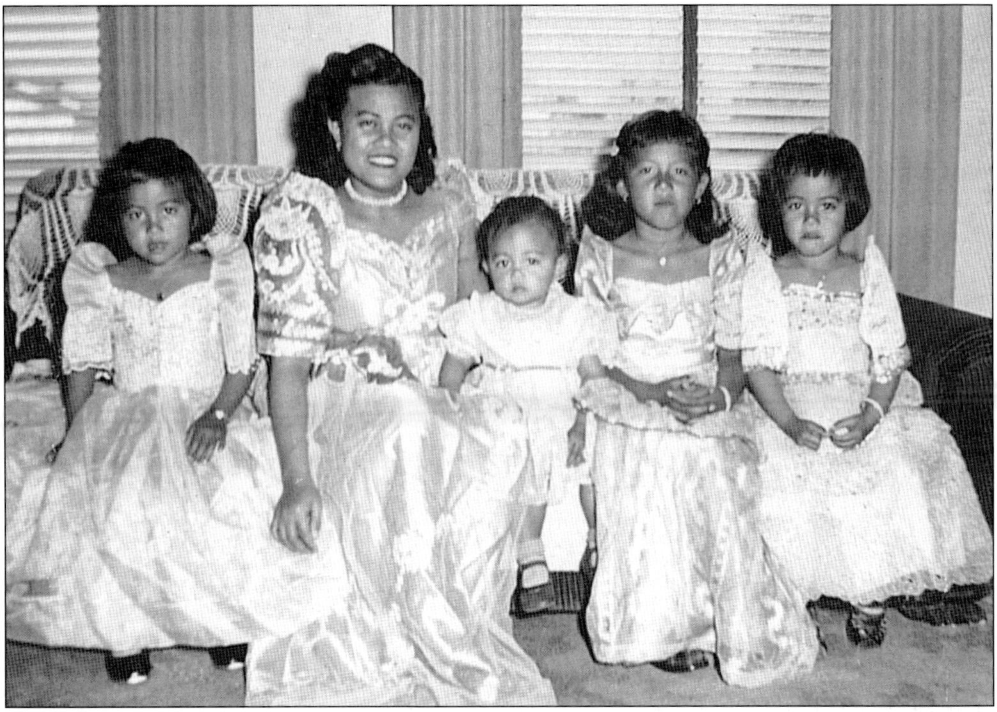

The Cabañero daughters pose in Filipina dress with their mother, Nene, in 1955. From left to right are Laurena, Nene, Laura, Teri, and Aurora. (Courtesy of Laurena Cabañero.)

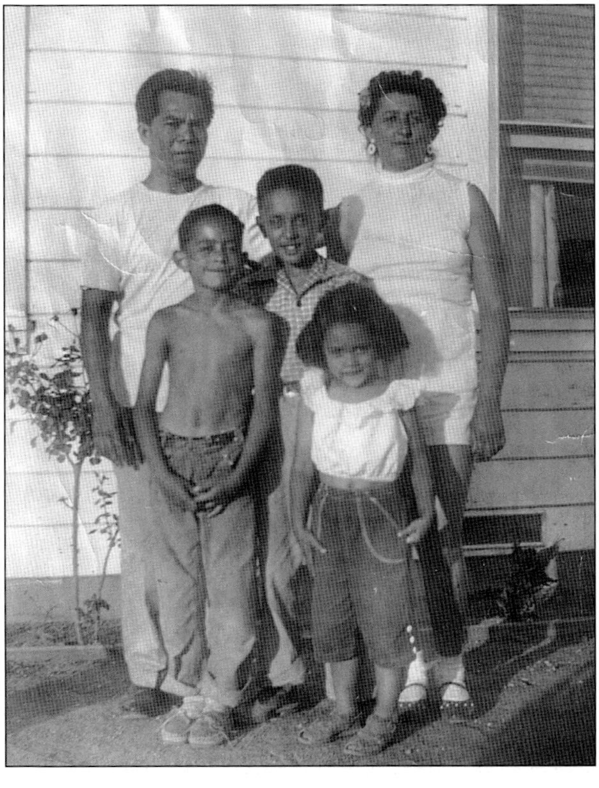

Marjorie Cabel married Vigan, Ilocos Sur, native Francisco Arcala Lagasca and had three children. When he passed away in 1954, she remarried Johnny Remocete and the family moved to Stockton. The Remocete-Lagasca family in 1956 is, from left to right (first row) Melvin, Frank, and Mary Lagasca; (second row) Graciano "Johnny" Remocete and Marjorie Remocete. (Courtesy of Mel Lagasca.)

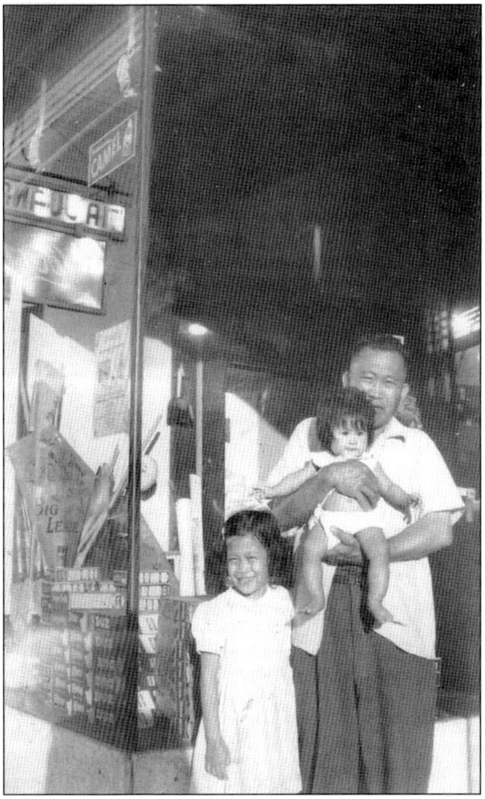

Inocencio Galedo stands in front of his Little Manila soda shop with his daughters Herminia and baby Lillian. (Courtesy of Remy Reyes.)

The Eddie and Luz (third row, first and second from left) Nieves extended clan are pictured at a family get-together in the 1950s. (Courtesy of Shirley Burnside.)

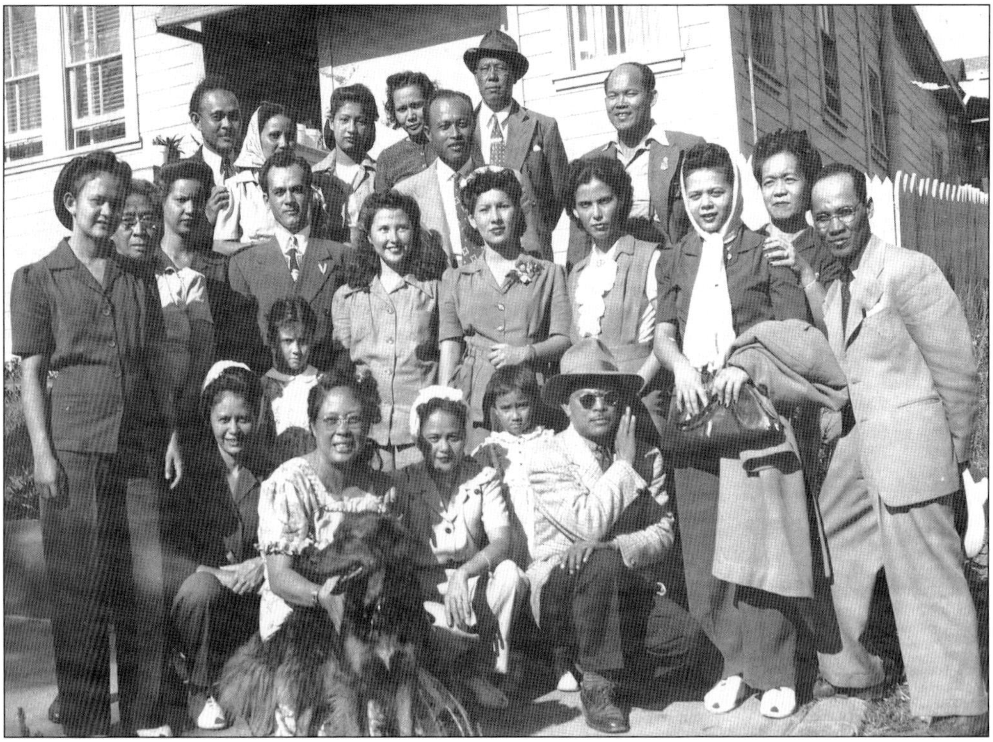

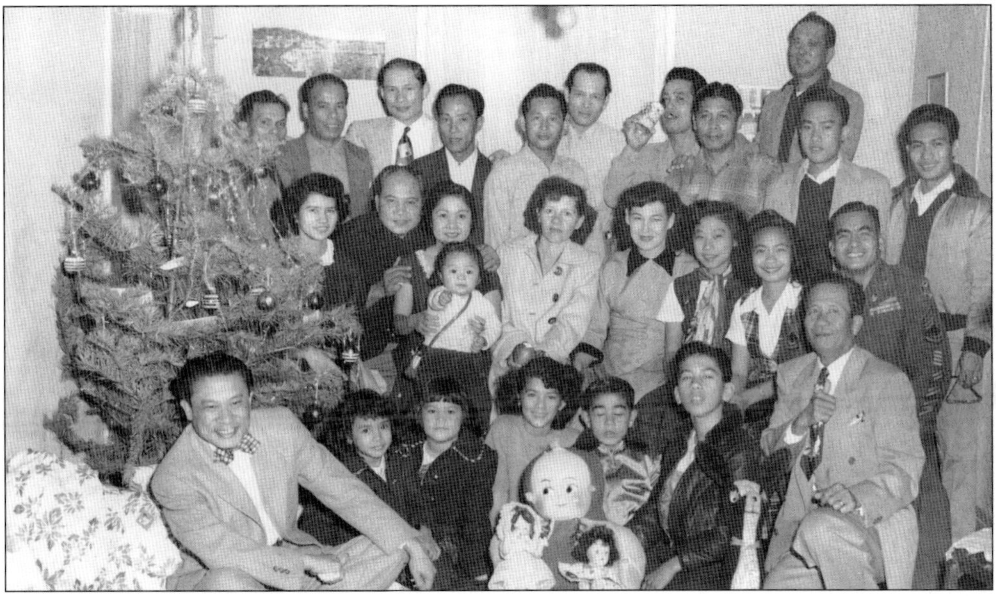

Christmas was a time for large celebrations with friends and family. This party took place in the 1950s. From left to right are (on floor) Claro Candelario, Riberal children, and Lauriano Bautista; (seated) Inez Riberal, John Castillo, Hortensia Castillo, Beverly Castillo, Adelo Riberal, "Lucky," Angelina Candelario, unidentified, and Vincente Villarta Sr.; (standing) Alex Riberal Sr., Sammy Noble, Joe Pacpaco, Manuel Novelozo, "Skippy," Felix Nera, unidentified, Segundo Bautista, unidentified, Antonio Novelozo, and Vincent Villarta Jr. (Courtesy of Beverly Engkabo.)

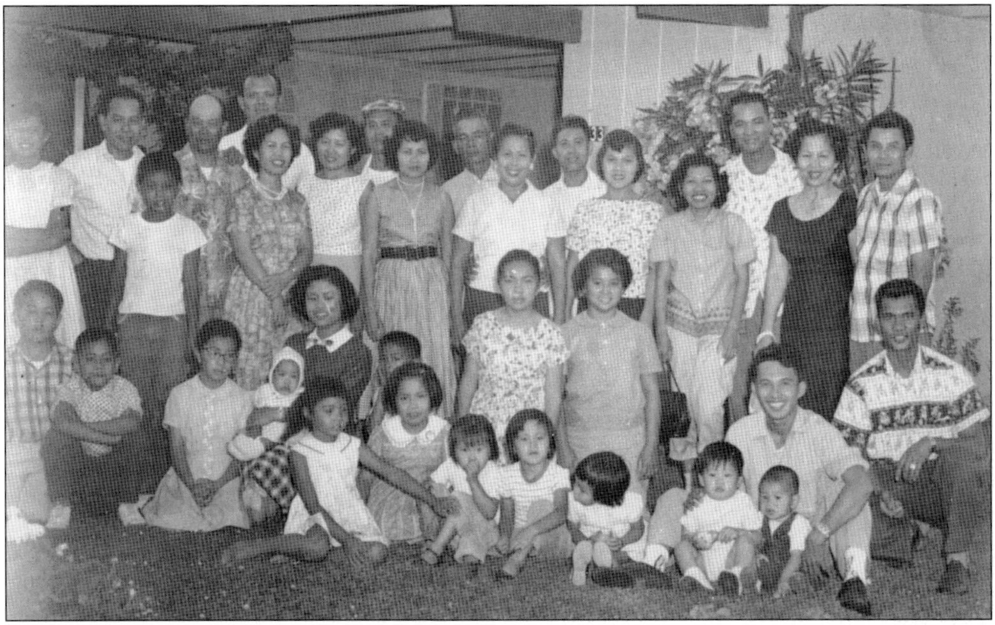

Every weekend was a house party in the 1950s and 1960s as Filipinos bought homes in South Stockton and as more relatives immigrated to the United States. At this celebration, the Bohulano family entertained the Cainap, Villegas, Jhao, and Rembulat families and other friends and relatives at their home at 633 Chicago Avenue in Lever Village in the early 1960s. (Courtesy of the Bohulano family collection.)

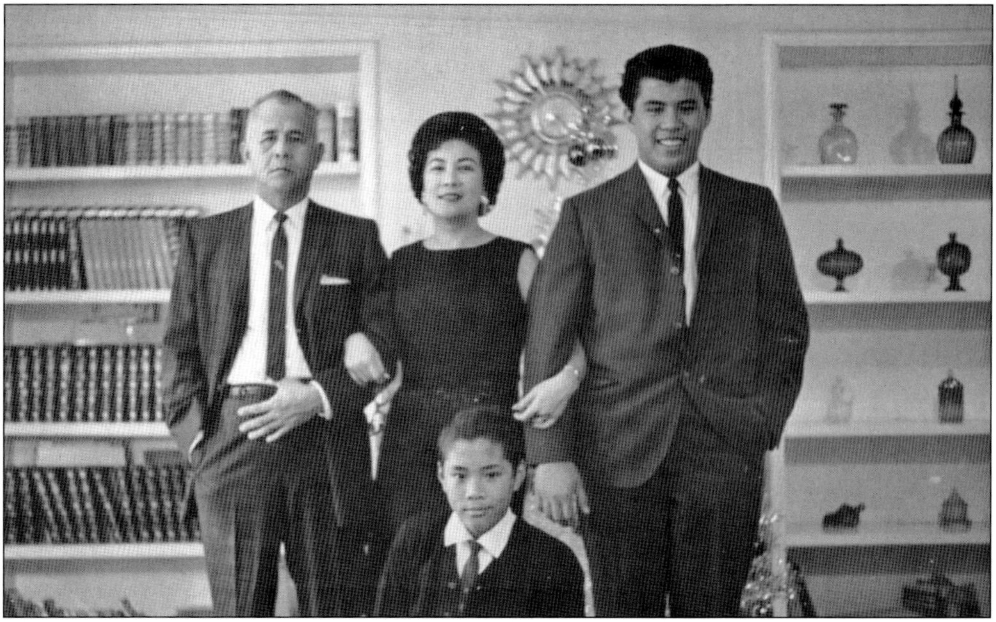

Juan "Johnny" C. Latosa and Purita Zurbito Latosa were community leaders. A respected labor contractor, Johnny Latosa was president of the Filipino Community of Stockton from the 1960s to the 1980s, and Purita was a leader with the Iloilo Circle. Here they are with their two sons in their Lodi home. Seated is Rene Latosa. Standing from left to right are Juan "Johnny" C. Latosa, Purita Latosa, and Eric Latosa. Rene is a renowned escrima master. (Courtesy of Rene Latosa.)

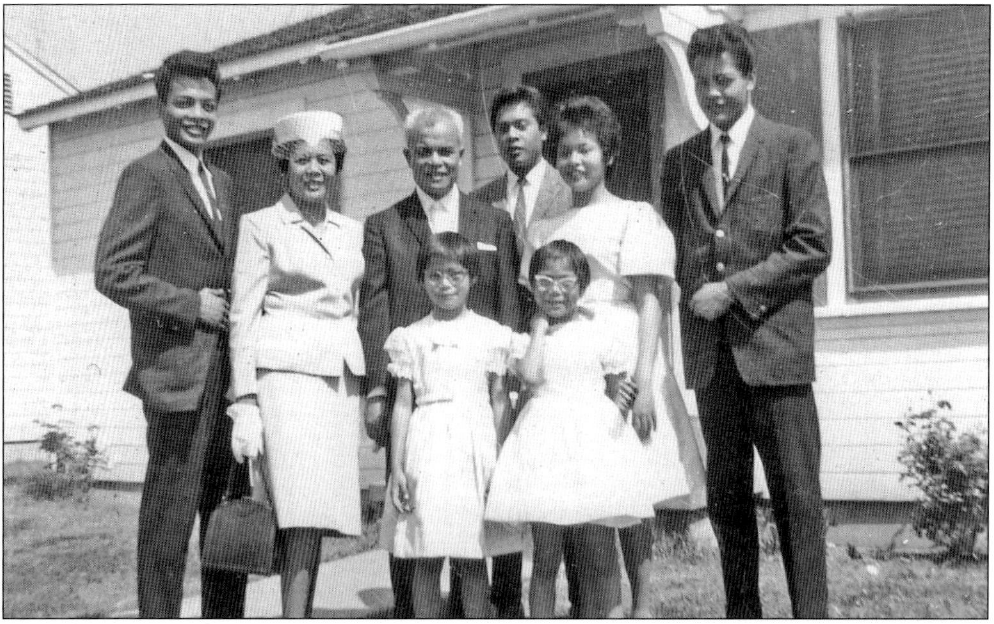

The Olamit family poses on Easter Sunday 1961. From left to right are (first row) Audrey and Eleanor Jr.; (second row) Albert, Eleanor Galvez Olamit, Eddie Olamit, Eddie Jr., Maria, and Victor. Eddie Olamit was a legendary community leader whose image is featured on a downtown mural of Stockton's greatest leaders. He and his wife, Eleanor, were very active in the community. (Courtesy of the Olamit family.)

Melbina and Ambrosio Macavinta were both natives of Numancia, Aklan. They pose here with their daughters, Melrose, Evelyn, and Dahlia, in Stockton in the 1960s. (Courtesy of Evelyn Oliveira.)

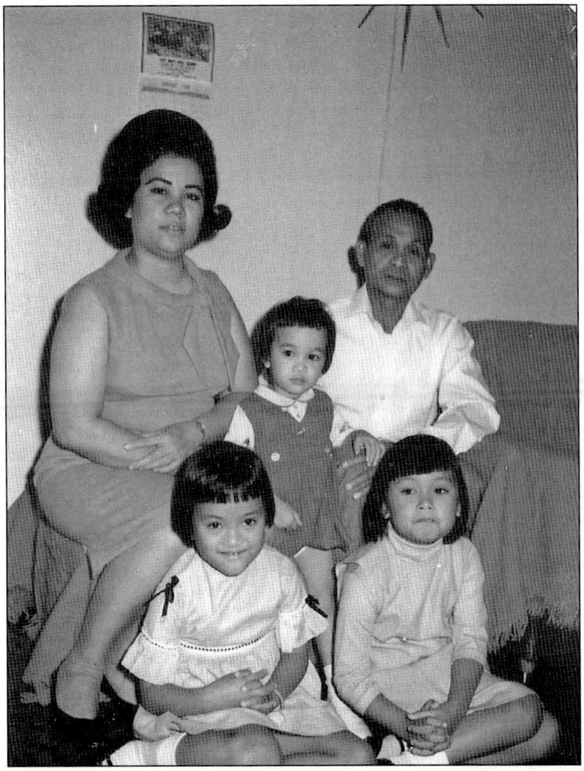

Cipriano "Rudy" Delvo fulfilled his wish for a wife and family when he met and married Regina Diola and they had a son, Dillon, in 1973, in the process creating a tri-generational family. A tri-generational family consists of parents who are of different generations. Filipino husbands are often 10–30 years older than their wives because few could marry before World War II because of the extreme sex ratio imbalance. (Courtesy of Dillon Delvo.)

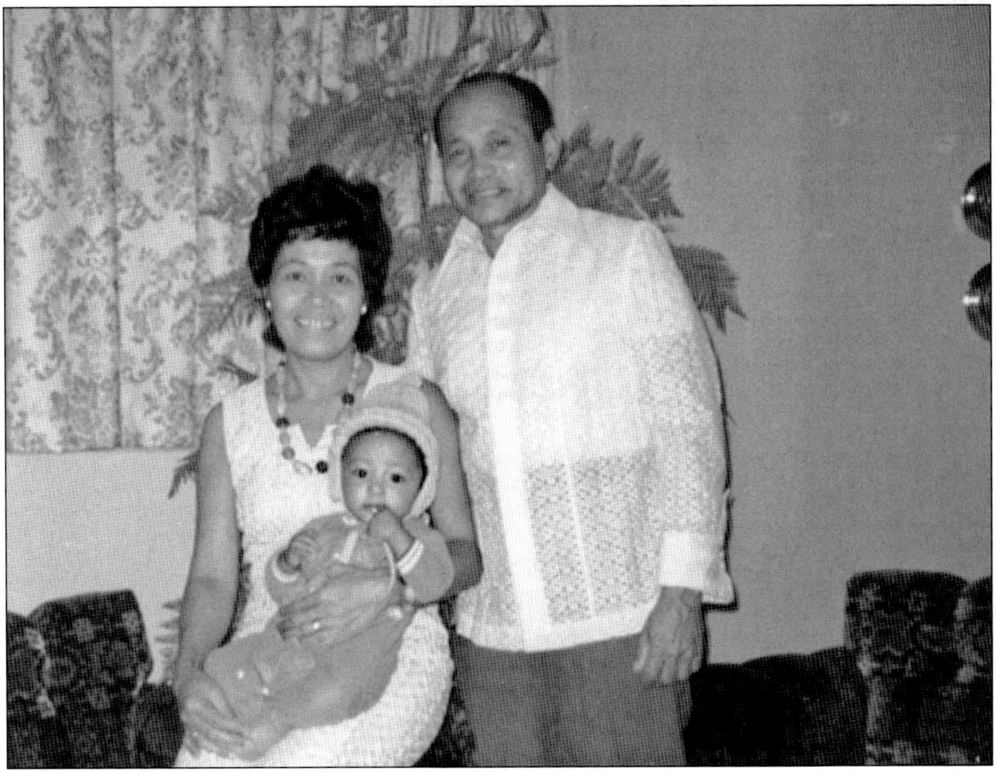

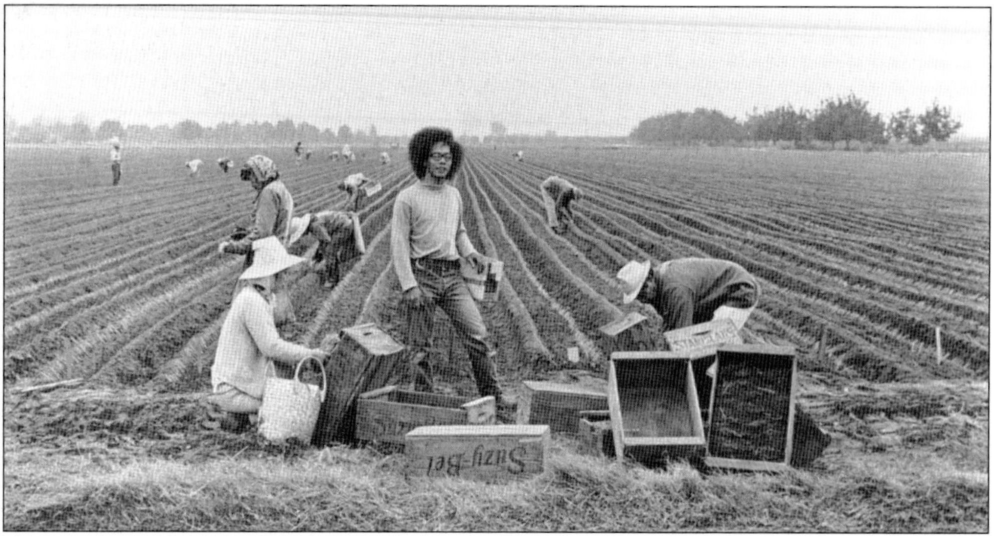

Many second- and third-generation Filipinos joined their families in the fields on school breaks. Here James Villadores (center, standing) works in the onions on the Delta in 1973. (Courtesy of Photographic Collections, Visual Communications.)

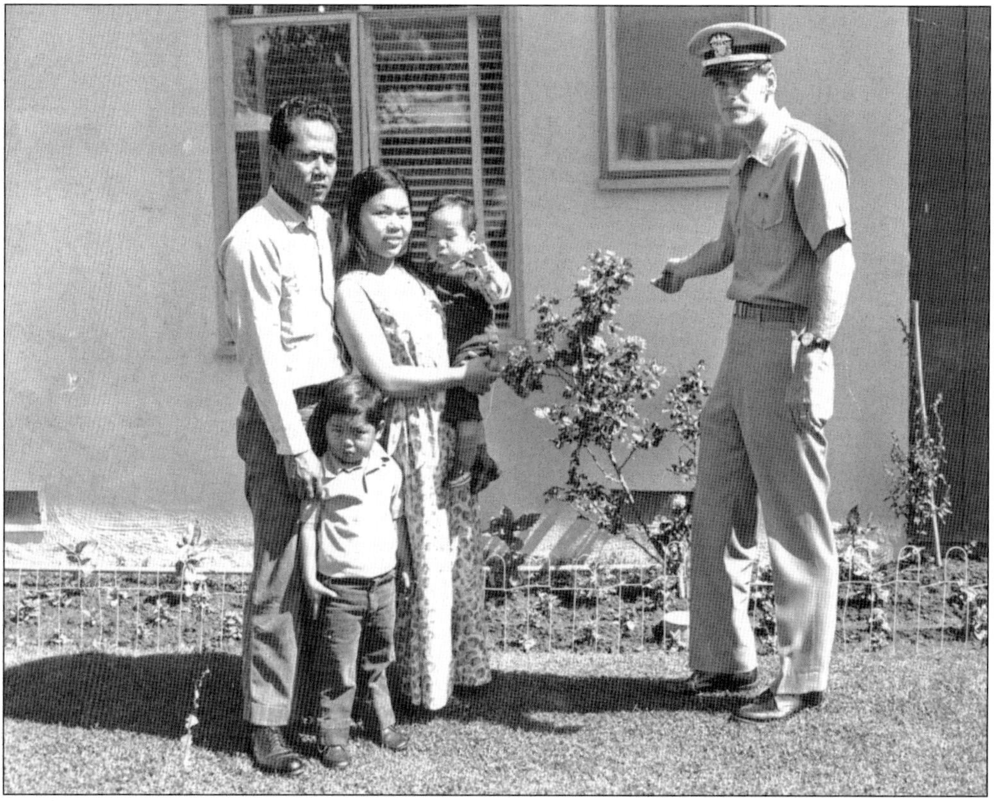

Edmundo and Elizabeth Espinueva are shown with their sons, Michael and Christopher, in front of their naval housing in Stockton after receiving the award for Best Yard in 1972. (Courtesy of Melanie Espinueva.)

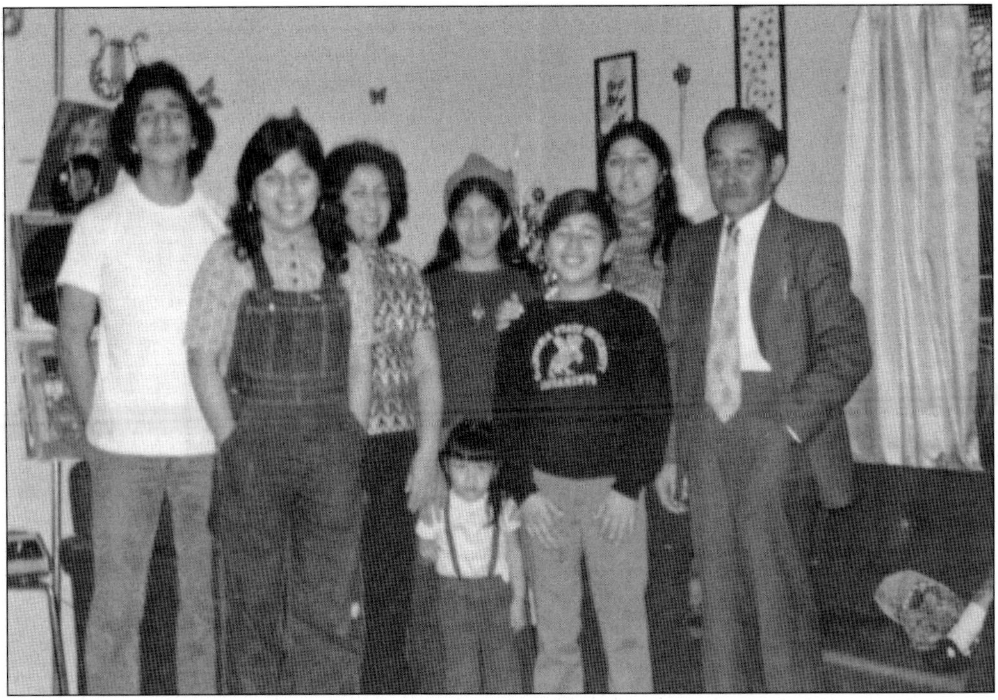

Philip Cornelio left Santa Cruz, Ilocos Sur, for Stockton in 1931. Here he celebrates Christmas with his family in 1972. (Courtesy of Myrna Elias.)

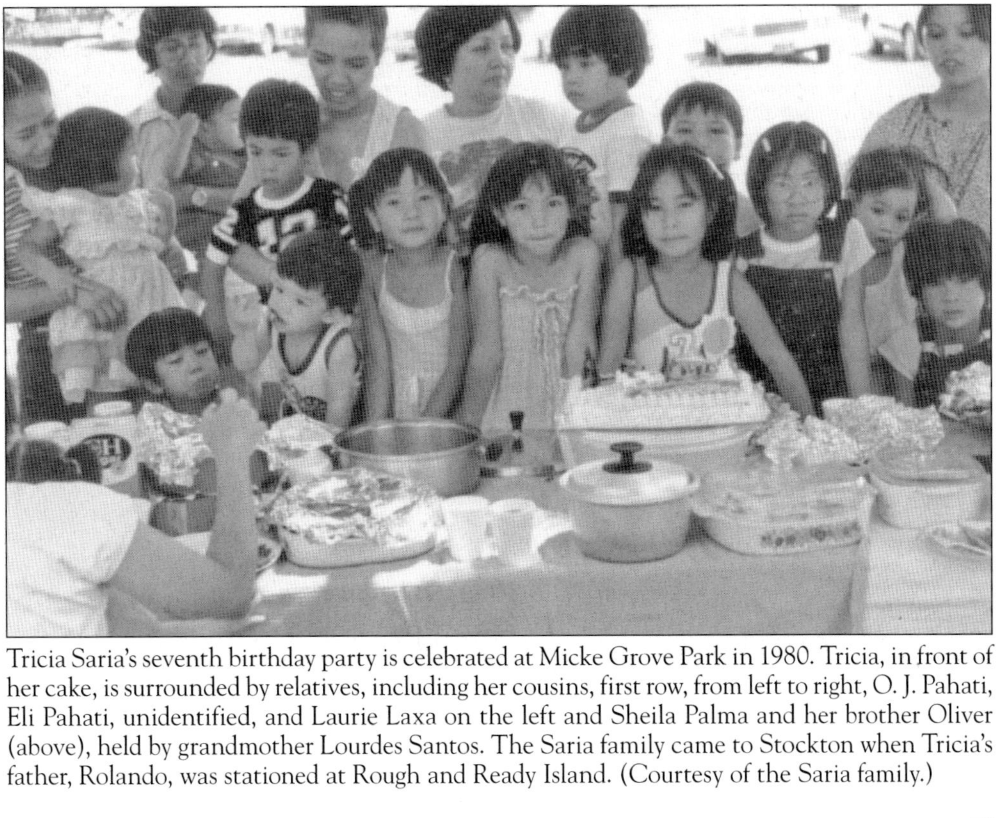

Tricia Saria's seventh birthday party is celebrated at Micke Grove Park in 1980. Tricia, in front of her cake, is surrounded by relatives, including her cousins, first row, from left to right, O. J. Pahati, Eli Pahati, unidentified, and Laurie Laxa on the left and Sheila Palma and her brother Oliver (above), held by grandmother Lourdes Santos. The Saria family came to Stockton when Tricia's father, Rolando, was stationed at Rough and Ready Island. (Courtesy of the Saria family.)

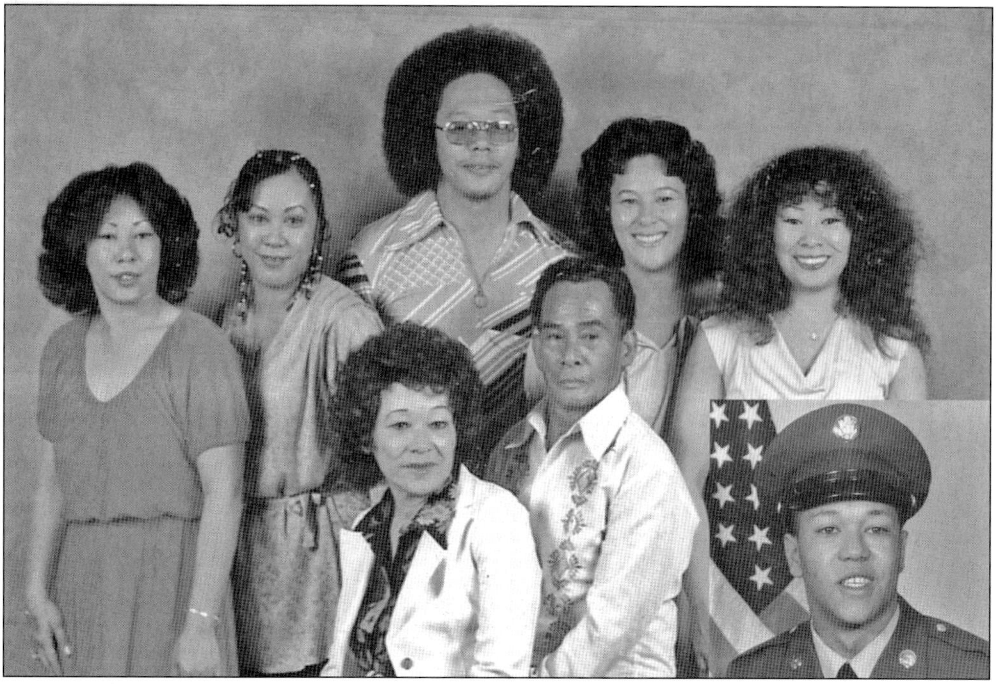

Clara and Mauro Villadores pose with five of their six children in the 1980s in Stockton. James Villadores (center, second row) became a community activist and photographer. (Courtesy of Clara Villadores.)

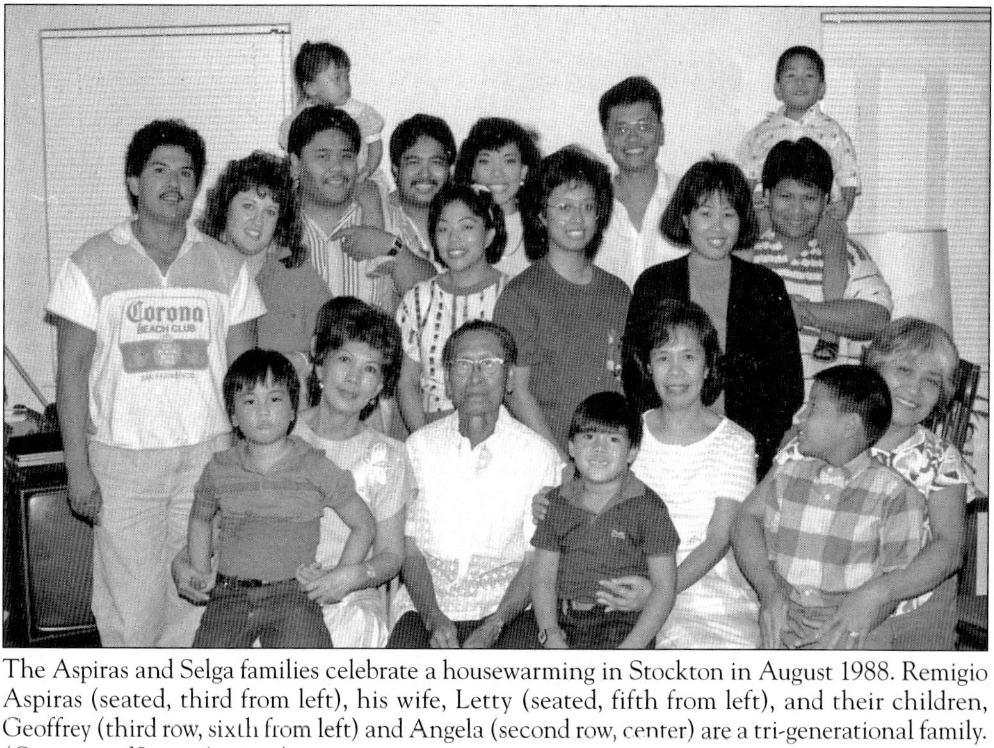

The Aspiras and Selga families celebrate a housewarming in Stockton in August 1988. Remigio Aspiras (seated, third from left), his wife, Letty (seated, fifth from left), and their children, Geoffrey (third row, sixth from left) and Angela (second row, center) are a tri-generational family. (Courtesy of Letty Aspiras.)

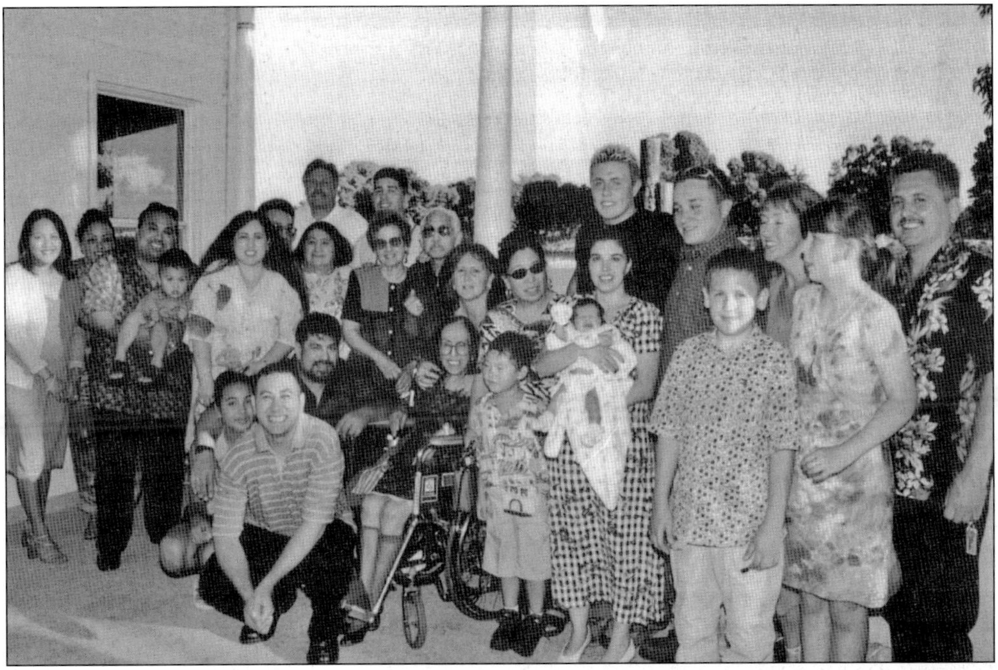

The Rico family, now in its fifth generation, is at a family reunion. (Courtesy of Vera Rico.)

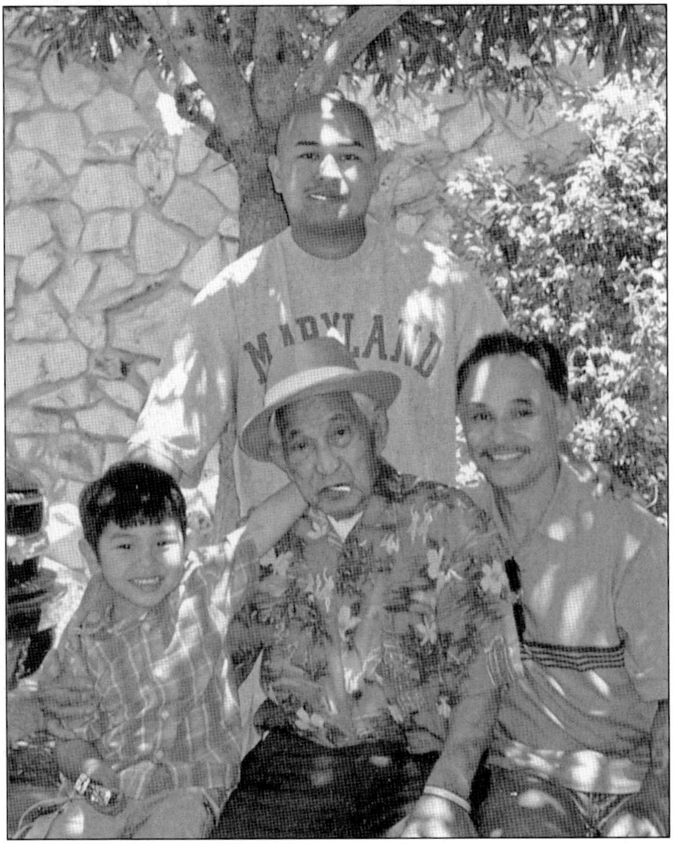

Michael Padua (center, with hat) arrived in Stockton via Hawaii in the 1930s. He is here with his son, George (right), grandson Cornell (above), and great-grandson Kyle (left). (Courtesy of Carlena Padua Rowell.)

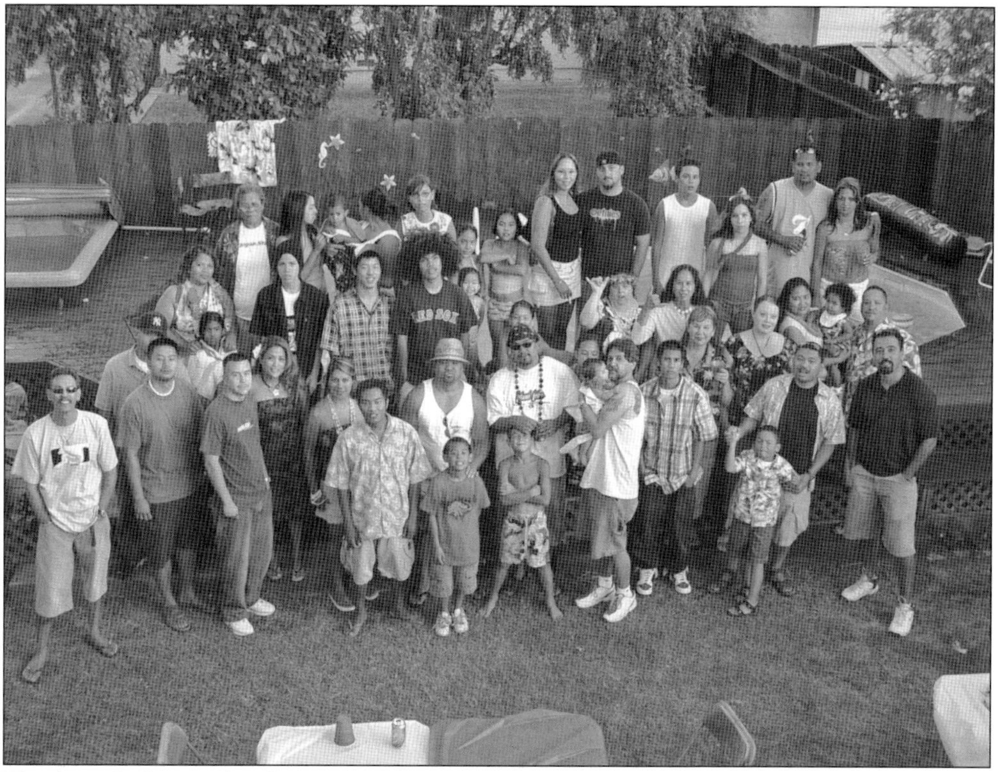

The large Rubianes family is at a reunion in Stockton in the early 2000s. (Courtesy of the Rubianes family.)

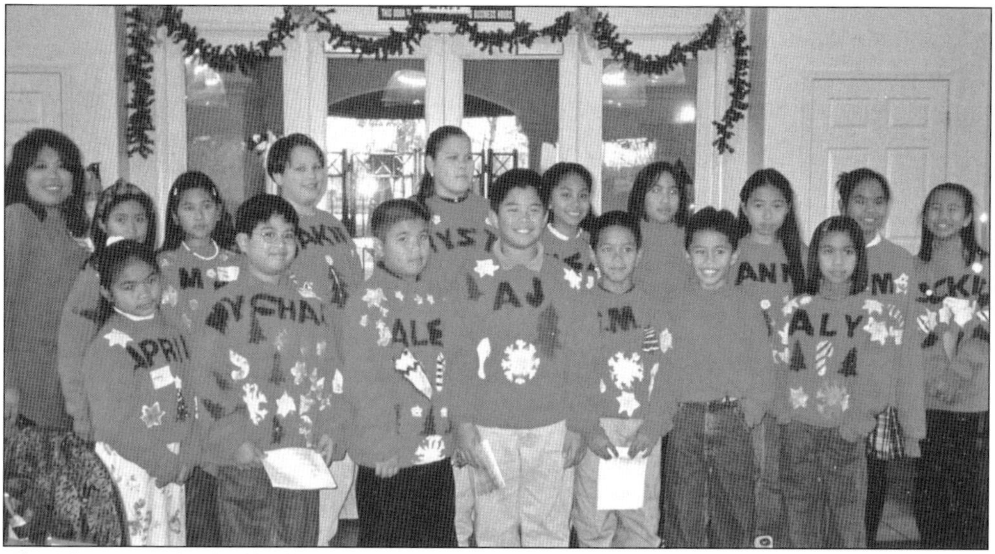

The Filipino Medical and Allied Professionals Society Youth Chorale and Dance Troupe perform at a recent holiday party. They are Eric Tauro, Mary Jael Sales, Andrew "AJ" Moya, Christine Moya, George Moya, Inez Galvez, April Somera, Leanne Orino, Marion Orino, Mark Orino, Alex Urbano, Carlo Garcia, Alysha Urbano , Krystle Kaye Jacobson, Sven Norman Jacobson III, Manieka Tamayo, Francisco Tamayo, and Winnie Ontiveros. (Courtesy of FILMAPS.)

Five

Coming Together
The Bonds of Community

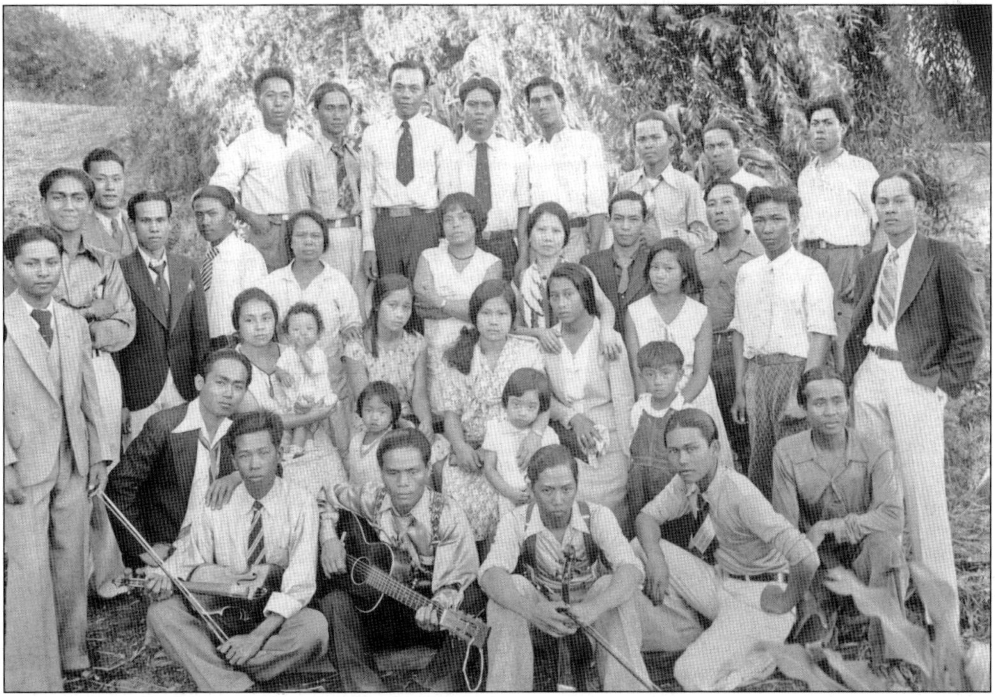

Here a group of friends, town mates, and relatives come together near the present site of Delta College for music and relaxation in the early 1930s. As soon as Filipinos arrived in Stockton, they looked for town mates and relatives, created social groups, and formed organizations for every purpose. Filipinos formed regional and hometown mutual aid associations, unions and protective associations, sports clubs, professionals support groups, and more. Four fraternal organizations—the Gran Oriente Filipino (GOF), Caballeros de Dimas Alang (CDA), the Legionarios del Trabajo (LDT), and the Filipino Federation of America—were among the most cohesive and powerful Filipino community organizations in Stockton. The Masonic GOF, the Masonic-style CDA, and LDT had historic and intellectual roots in the Philippine Revolution. For many Filipinos, the lodge became another family, offering a surrogate family, pride, and dignity to its members; lodge members respectfully and lovingly referred to one another as "Bro" and "Sis." Filipinos in Stockton, whatever their generation, immigration status, or background, celebrated many rituals together, creating strong bonds of community. (Photograph by Frank Mancao, courtesy of FANHS National.)

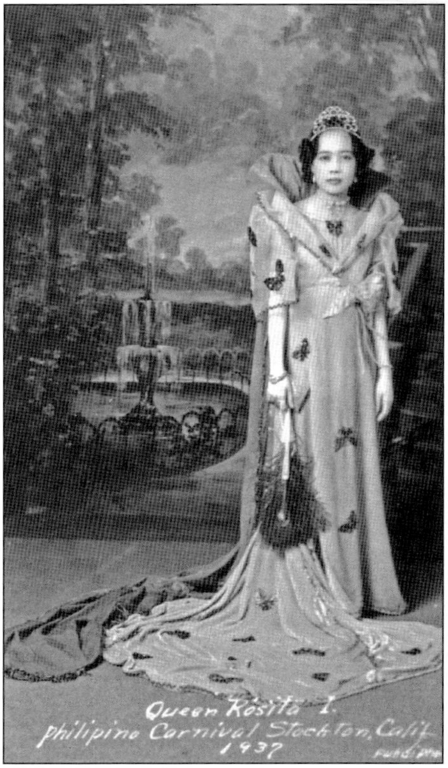

Queen contests were lucrative affairs for both the young ladies and the organizations, who would split ticket sales at the end of the contest. Thousands were raised in these annual affairs. Victory was not based, however, on beauty but rather on the power and influence of the candidate's family and community networks. Queen Rosita I was queen of the Philippine Carnival in Stockton in 1937. (Courtesy of FANHS National.)

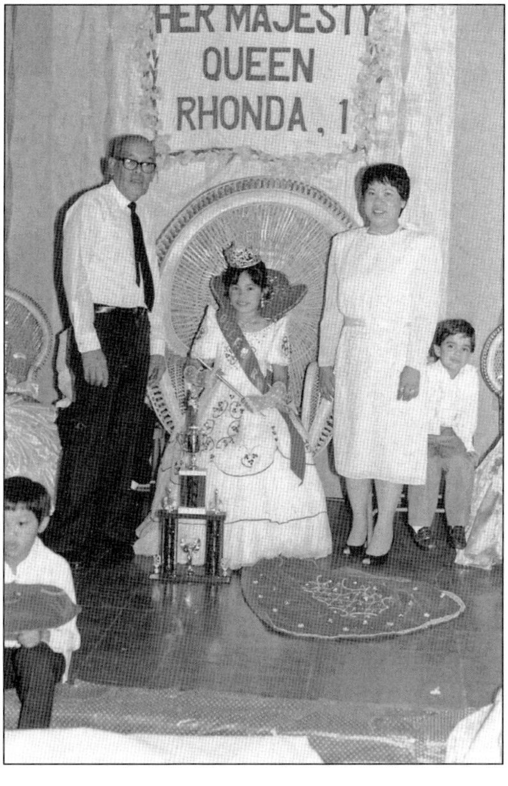

Rhonda Carranza, with her parents, is crowned queen of the annual Our Lady of Antipolo Fiesta in the 1980s at St. Mary's Hall. The Filipino Catholic Association has sponsored the annual queen contest since the 1950s. (Courtesy of the Carranza family.)

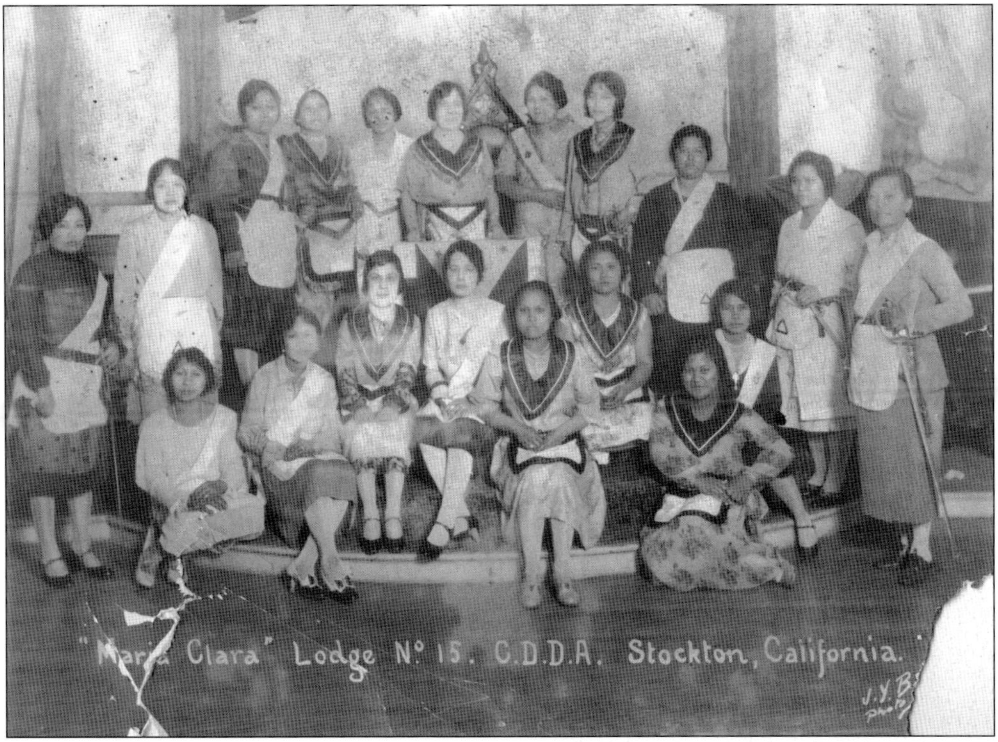

"Maria Clara" Lodge of the Caballeros de Dimas Alang in Stockton, shown in the mid-1920s, was named after a character in the novel *Noli Me Tangere* by Jose Rizal. (Photograph by John Y. Billones, courtesy of FANHS National.)

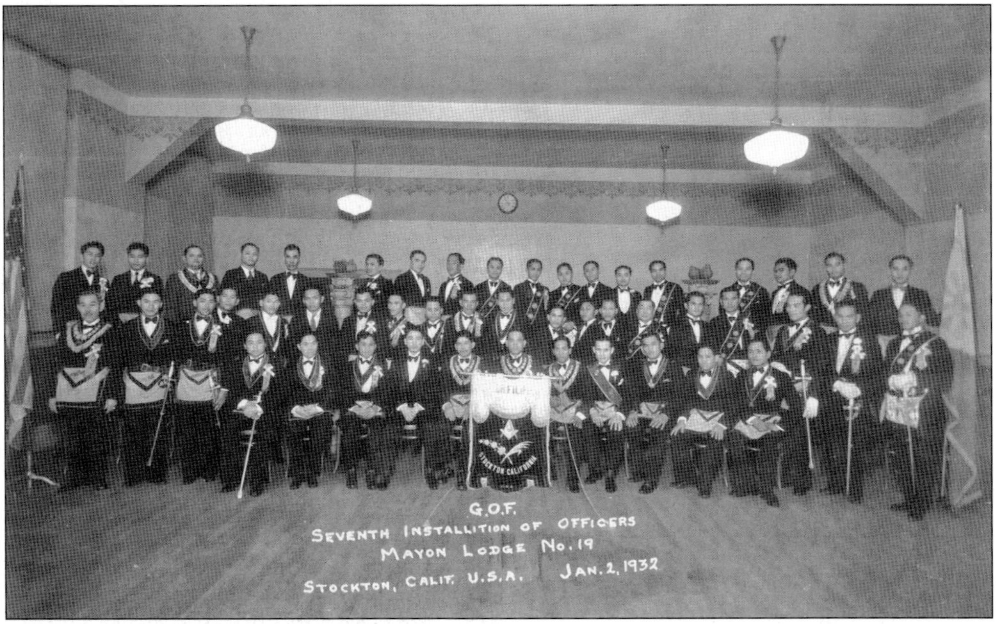

The Gran Oriente Filipino was a Masonic organization with members all over the West Coast. This is the Stockton-based Mayon Lodge in 1932. (Courtesy of Special Collections, University of the Pacific.)

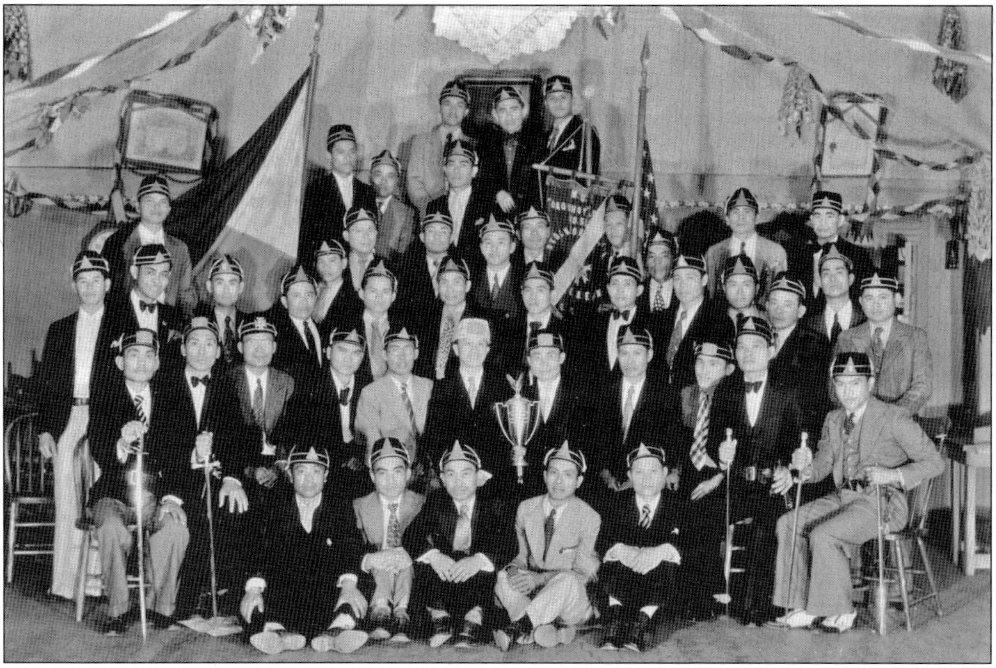

The Worshipful Daguhoy Lodge of the Legionarios del Trabalo was organized in Stockton in 1926 in the Mariposa Hotel, mainly by immigrants from Bohol. On Bohol, Francisco Daguhoy led the longest revolt against Spanish authorities. Here the lodge is pictured in the 1920s. (Photograph by Frank Mancao, courtesy of FANHS National.)

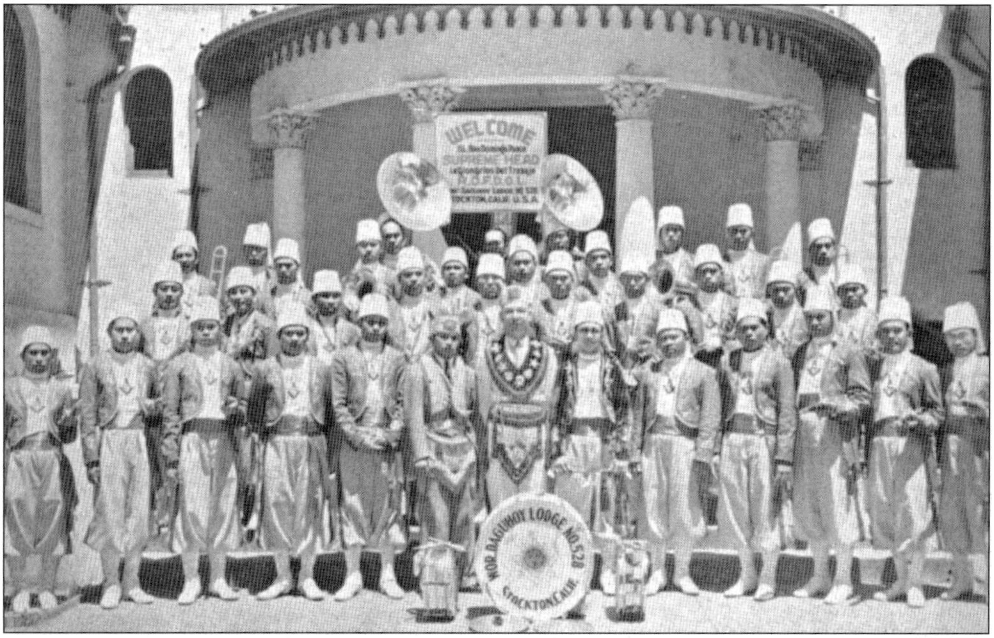

The Daguhoy Lodge Band of the Legionarios del Trabajo was a popular group that marched annually in the Fourth of July parade in Stockton and entertained at all lodge events. They are shown here in the late 1930s. In the center is LDT founder Domingo Ponce. (Courtesy of the Daguhoy Lodge, Legionarios del Trabajo, Inc.)

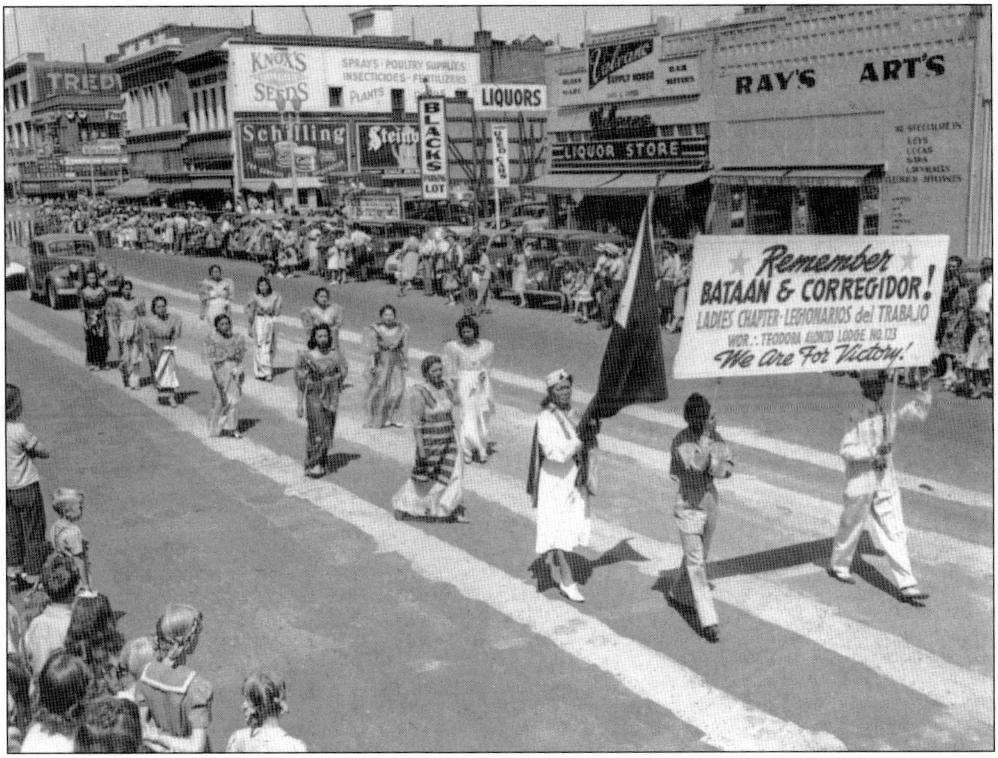

The Teodora Alonzo Lodge was organized in 1935; they quickly became leaders of the community. The lodge was named after Jose Rizal's mother. Here the lodge proudly marches during World War II in the 1942 Fourth of July parade in downtown Stockton. That year, the Filipino contingent marched proudly in Filipina dresses and in military uniform. (Courtesy of Tony Somera.)

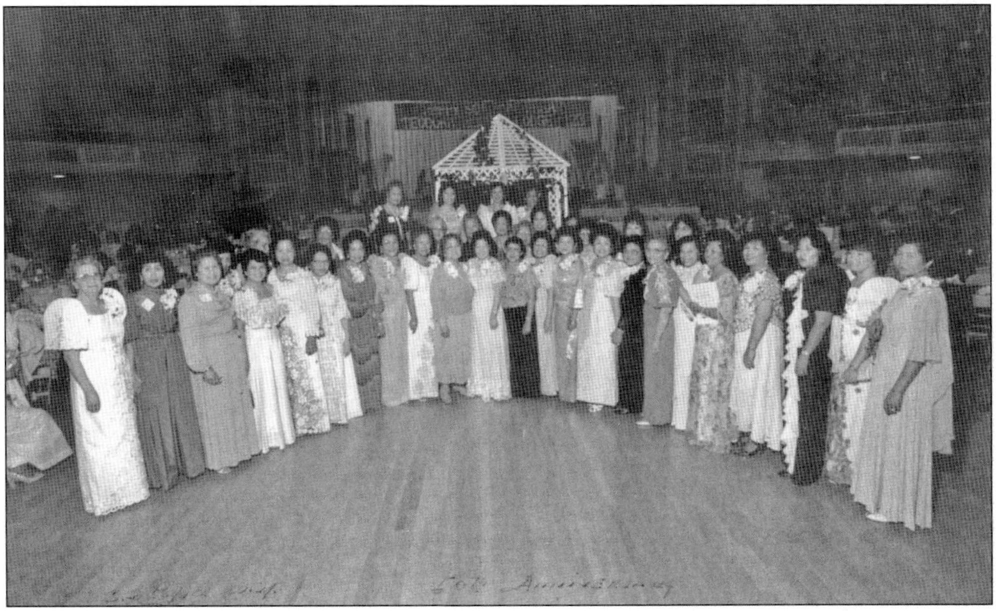

In 1985, the sisters of the Teodora Alonzo Lodge celebrated their 50th anniversary. They are still a lodge today. (Courtesy of Caroline Bulawit Gray.)

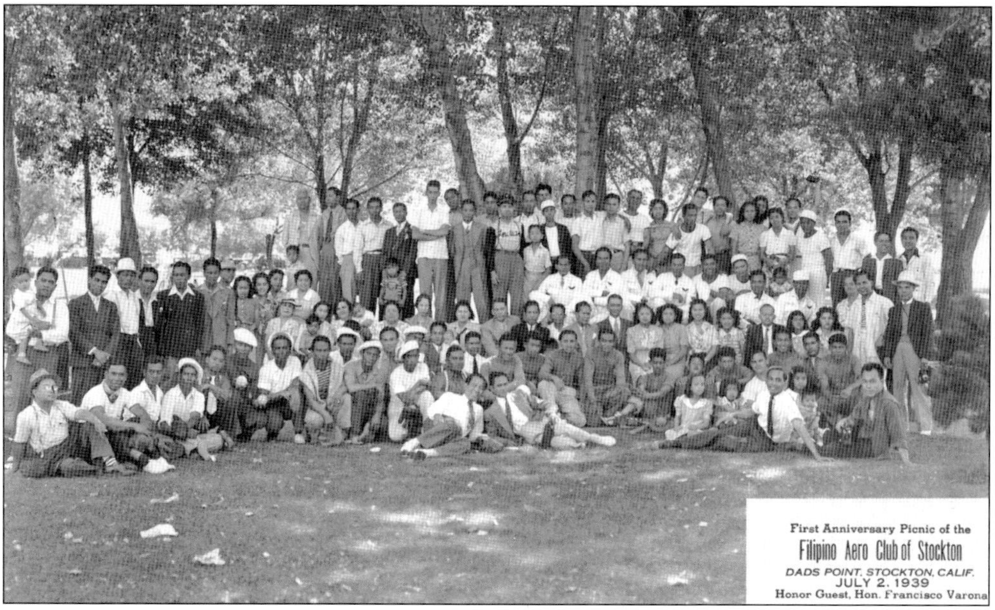

Aspiring pilots and community supporters in the Filipino Aero Club hold their first anniversary party at Dad's Point in Stockton in 1939. The honored guest was the hugely popular resident commissioner, Francisco Varona. (Courtesy of Rosaline Dickinson.)

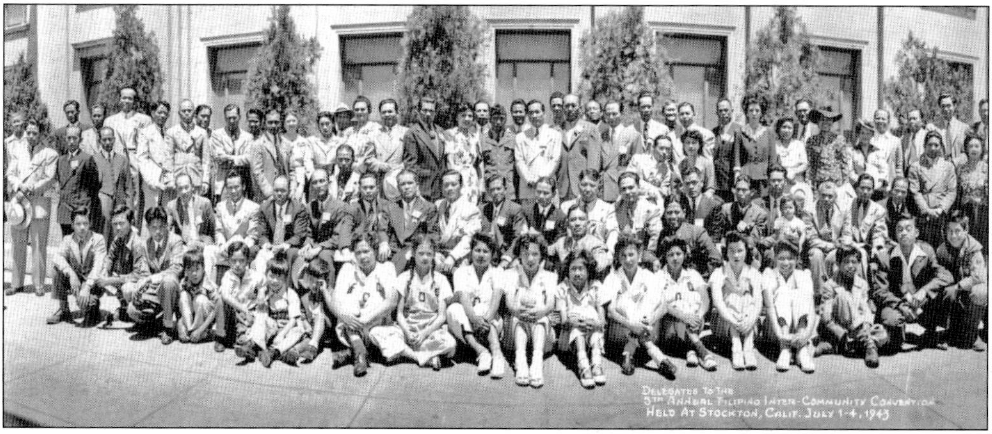

In the 1930s and 1940s, Filipino communities across the West Coast organized into community councils and held annual conventions. In 1943, Stockton was the site of the annual meeting. Stockton was the perfect choice for the wartime meeting. (Courtesy of FANHS Stockton.)

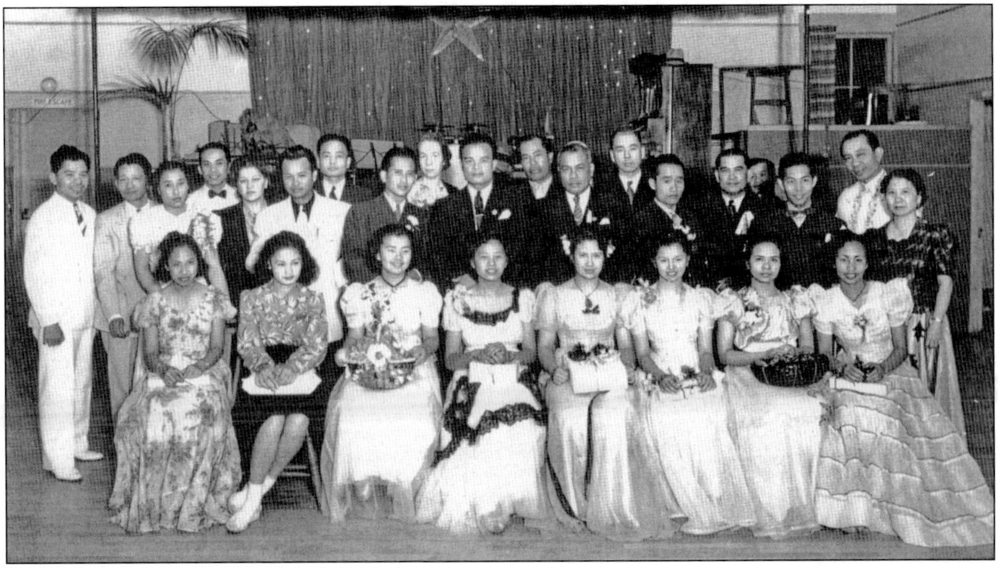

Next to queen contests, social box dances were the most lucrative fund-raisers for Filipino organizations. Men bid to dance with the *dalagas*, young women who were usually the daughters of Filipino community leaders. At the end of the dance, women split their winnings with the sponsoring organization. This social box occurred right before World War II. From left to right are (seated) Mary Caliso, Rosalie Flores, Angel Bantillo, Eleanor Galvez, Martha Ignacio, "Laling" Valderrama, Teofila Sarmiento, and Rebelina "Helen" Nava; (standing) Alfonso Gonzales, Sebastian Inosanto, Mary Inosanto, unidentified, Anne Dionisio, unidentified, Johnny Dionisio, Pete Tantiado, Verdella Bautista, Eddie Olamit, Olympio Manubat, unidentified, Dr. Macario Bautista, unidentified, Vicente Roldan, two unidentified, and Placido and Juliana Lazaro. (Courtesy of the Magdael family.)

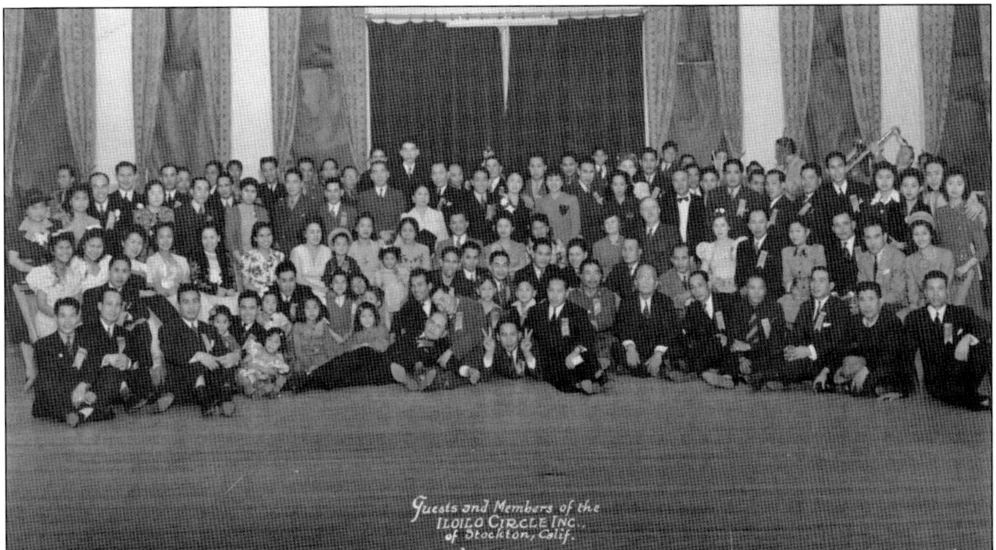

Immigrants with roots in the Iloilo area, a major city on the island of Panay, formed this popular organization, which took root in the *campo* in the late 1930s. This is one of their get-togethers in 1943. They maintain their headquarters today on Sonora Street in Little Manila. (Courtesy of Violet Dutra.)

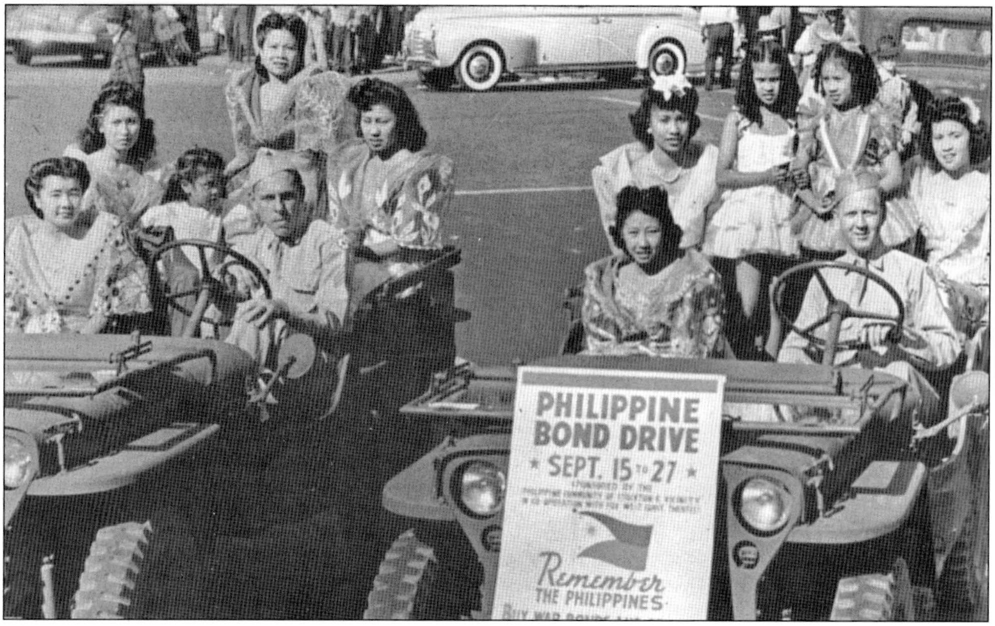

The Regidor Lodge of the Caballeros de Dimas Alang (CDA) held a hugely successful war bond drive in the summer of 1942. Women sang patriotic songs at the corner of Lafayette and El Dorado Streets to sell war bonds. The CDA bought two fighter planes for the war. From left to right are Angelina Bantillo (Magdael), Mary Mabia, Norma Suarez, Asuncion Nicolas, Lourdes Soledor (Pasco), Remedios Soledor, Helen Nava, Sally Revillar (Gacer), Martha Braga, and Rosemary Quitiquit. (Courtesy of Angelina B. Magdael.)

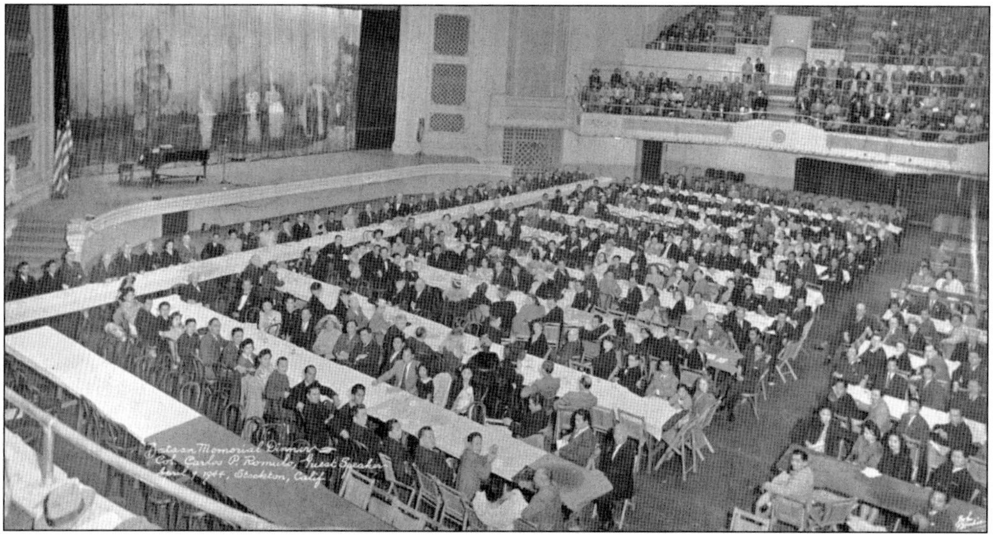

Thousands of Stocktonians attended a dinner for Bataan Day on April 9, 1944, at the Civic Auditorium, where Philippine Commonwealth cabinet member Col. Carlos P. Romulo challenged white Stocktonians to stop discriminating against Filipinos, to "take them in your hearts as the 17 million Filipinos took into their hearts the 7,000 American soldiers who fought in Bataan." He was the first Philippine official who challenged the racial status quo in California. Romulo later served as president of the UN General Assembly and chair of the UN Security Council. (Photograph by Bob's Studio, courtesy of Photographic Collections, Visual Communications.)

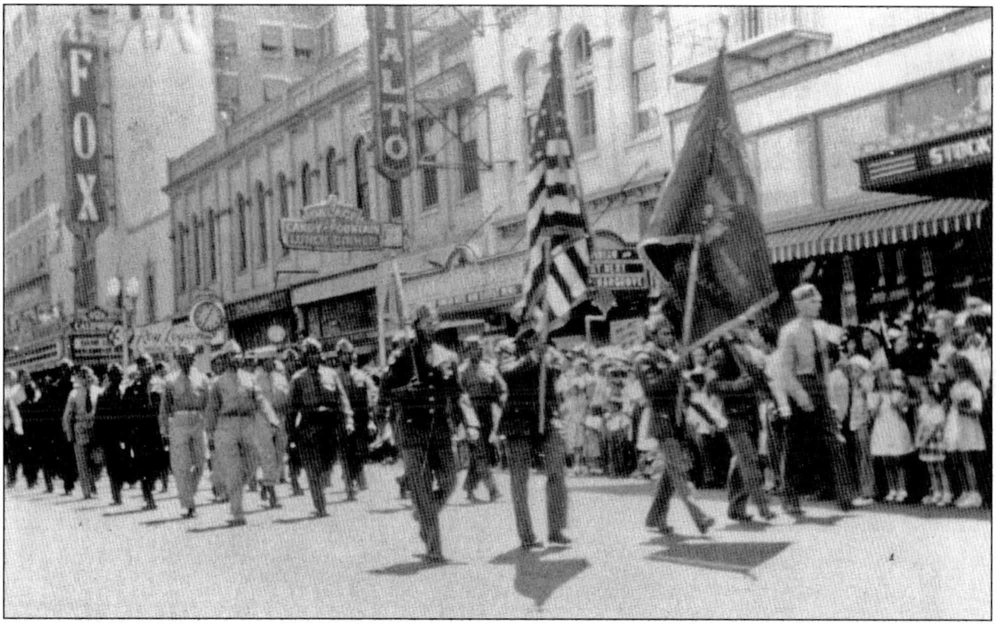

Filipino veterans marched proudly down Main Street in Stockton after World War II. Filipino American veterans could now take advantage of every right afforded to U.S. veterans: citizenship, the GI Bill, VA benefits, and more. Their counterparts in the Philippines would not be so lucky; U.S. Armed Forces in the Far East veterans were stripped of all benefits by the 1952 Rescission Act. (Courtesy of FANHS Stockton.)

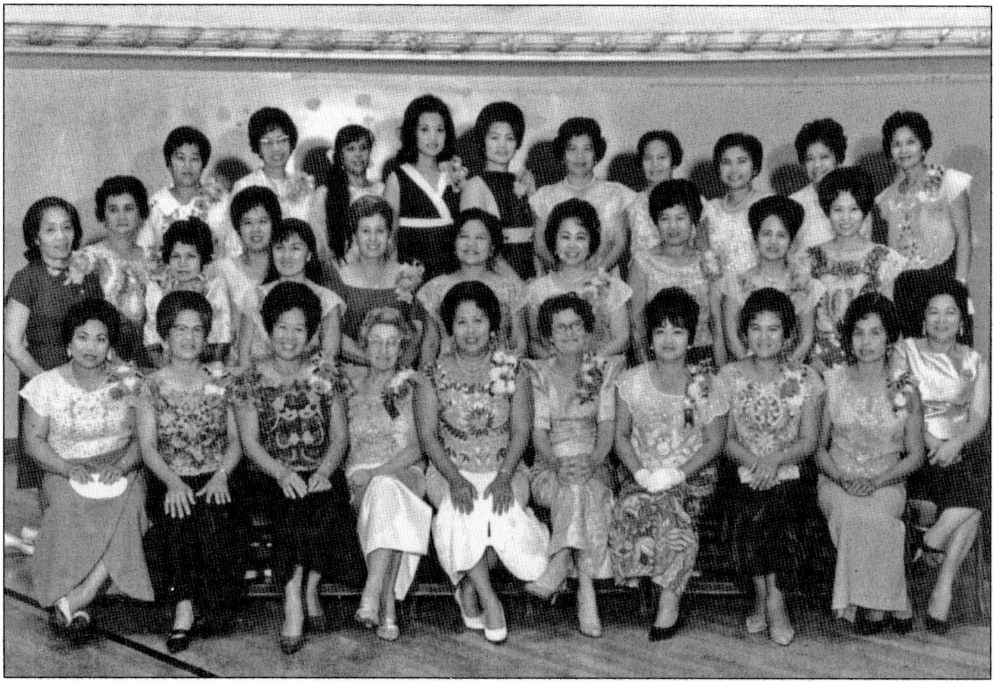

The wives of veterans of World War II and the Korean War created an active auxiliary that is still vibrant. The Manuel Roxas Post Auxiliary is shown here in 1968. (Courtesy of Concepcion M. Bohulano.)

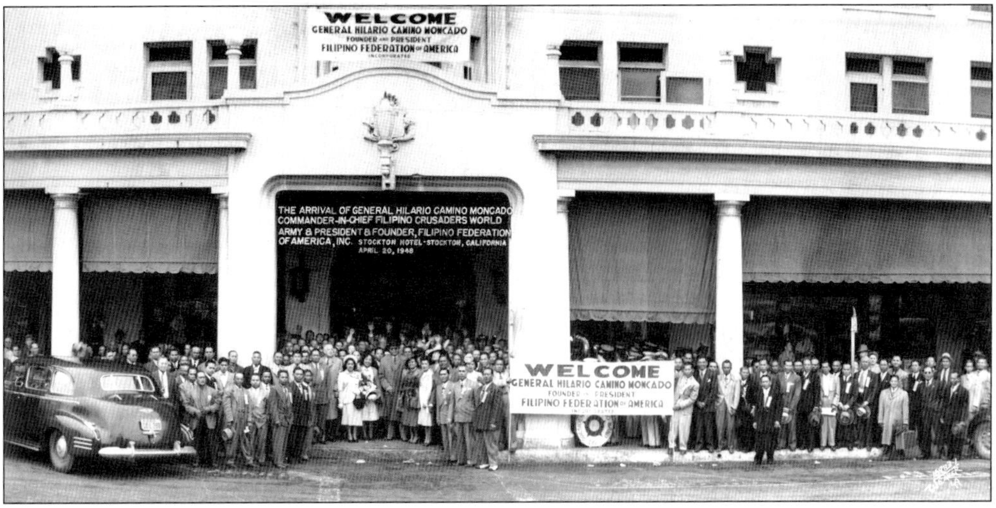

Members of the Filipino Federation of America welcome their leader, Los Angeles–based Hilario Moncado, at the Hotel Stockton in 1948. (Courtesy of Purita Talisayan.)

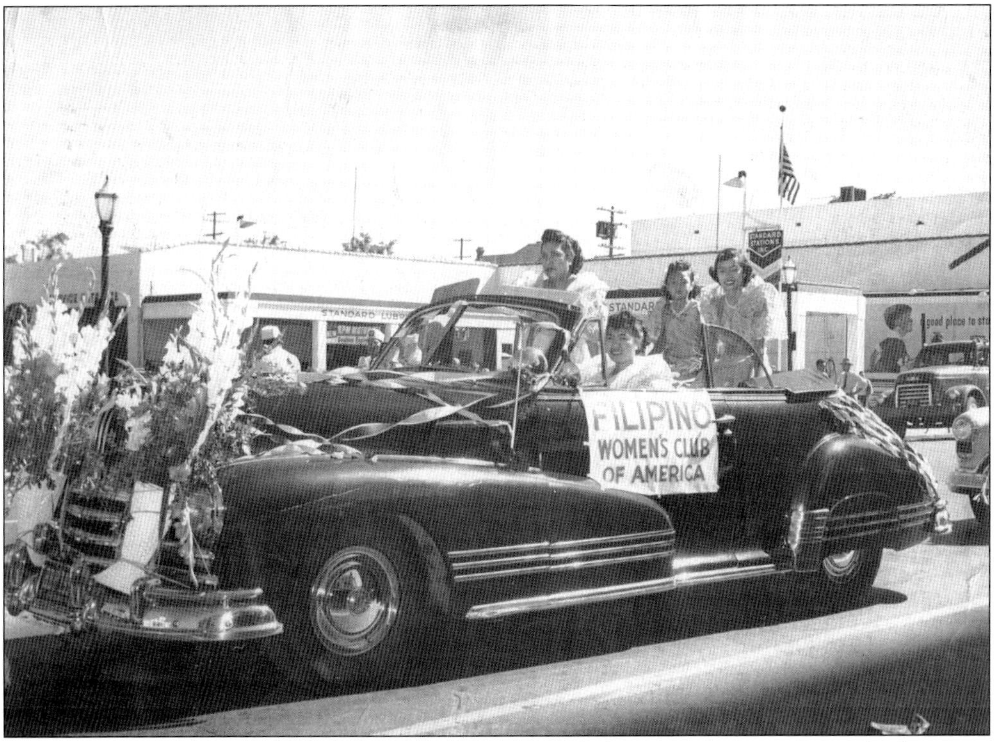

Fourth of July was a major celebration in Stockton, and almost every organization had its own float or marching contingent in the annual parade. Irene Plaza (Edralin) rides on the left in the back of the Filipino Women's Club float in the 1950s. (Courtesy of Irene Edralin.)

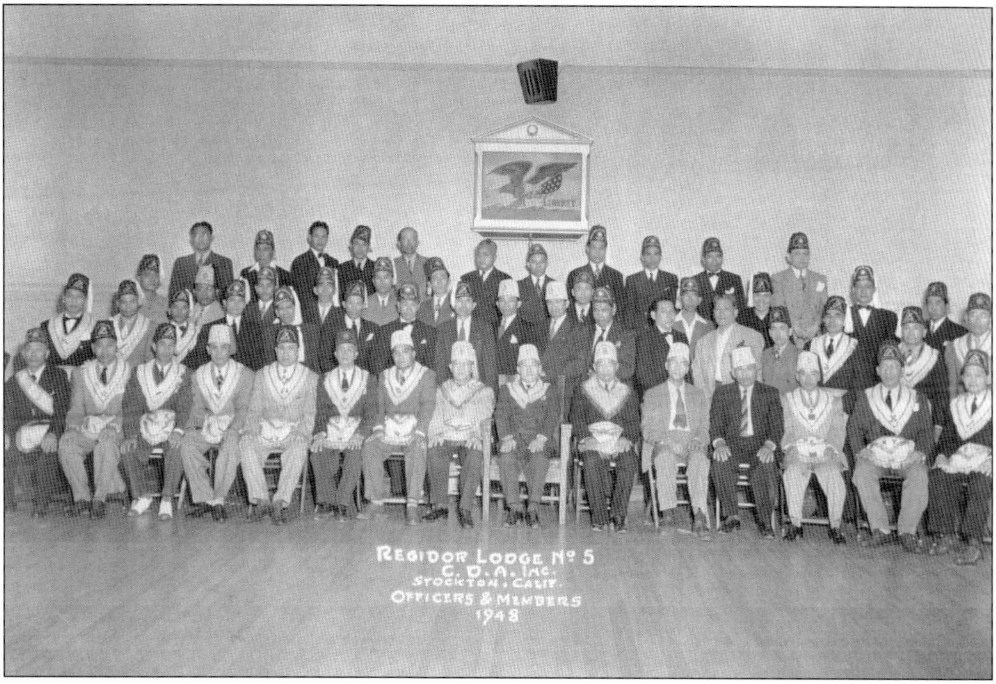

The Regidor Lodge Caballeros de Dimas Alang (CDA), poses for a photograph in 1948. They raised funds to build a headquarters and home through the war and the 1950s, finally achieving their dream. The home is at 204 South Hunter Street in Little Manila. (Courtesy of FANHS Stockton.)

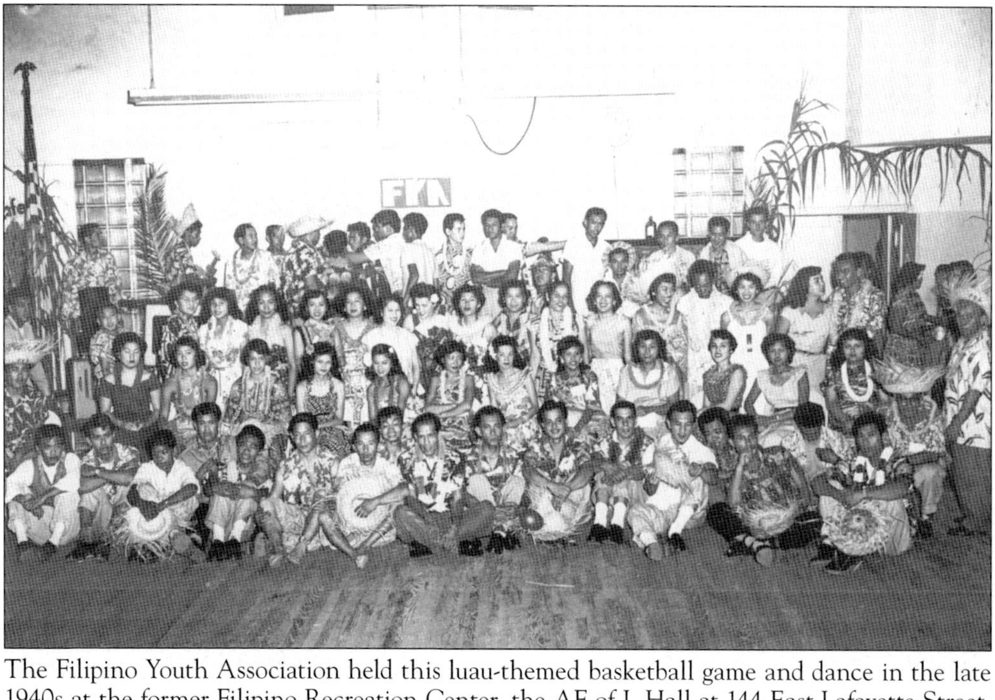

The Filipino Youth Association held this luau-themed basketball game and dance in the late 1940s at the former Filipino Recreation Center, the AF of L Hall at 144 East Lafayette Street. Second- and third-generation Filipinos from all over the state made lifelong friends and met spouses through these sports networks. (Courtesy of Jay Gesulga.)

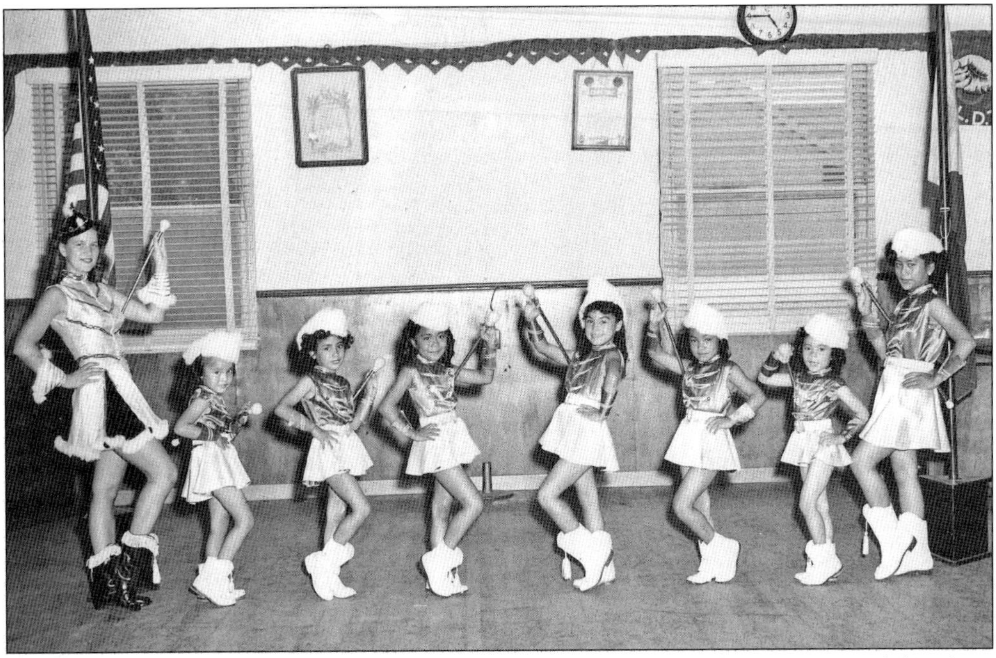

The children of community members participated in many events. The Legionarios del Trabajo Drum and Bugle Corps majorettes in the 1950s were, from left to right, unidentified, Maria Olamit, Susan Riberal, Berttha Navarro, Cecilia ?, Carol Rubia, Vicky Lazaro, and Gloria Carido. (Courtesy of the Olamit family.)

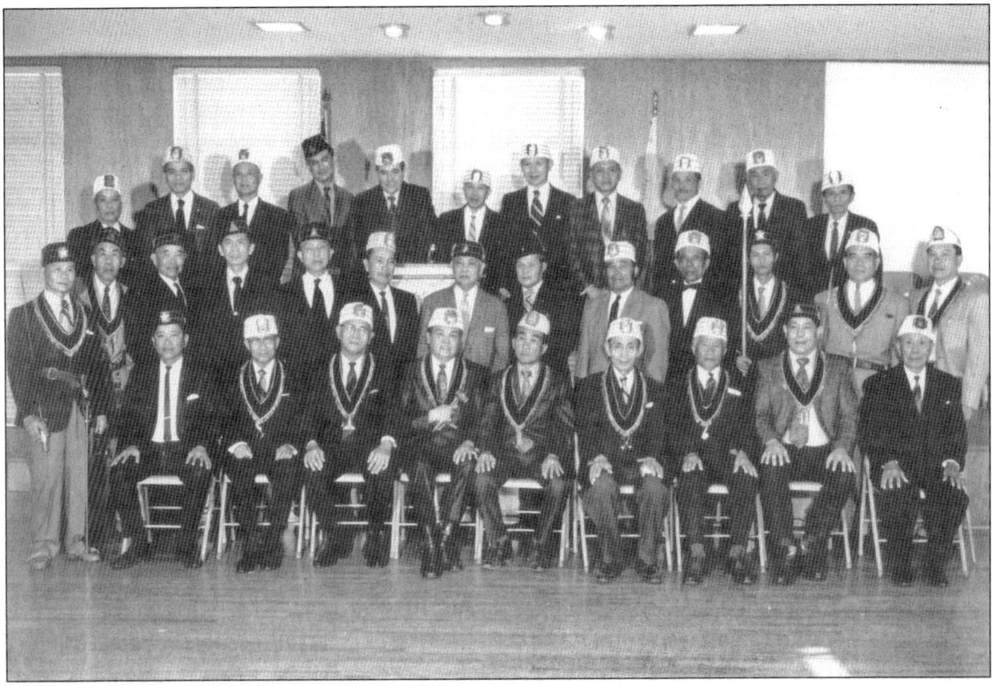

Several more lodges were created in the 1930s and 1940s, and the Legionarios del Trabajo bought a headquarters building on San Joaquin Street. This is the Mabini Lodge of the Legionarios del Trabajo in the 1960s. (Courtesy of FANHS Stockton.)

Filipinos had two reasons to celebrate Fourth of July: the independence of the United States and the independence of the Philippines from the United States. Here Christine Bohulano (holding the flag) prepares to sing on July 4, 1961, at the Filipino-American Friendship Day program at the Civic Auditorium with her mother, Concepcion, and her cousin, Marcy Roldan (kneeling). (Courtesy of Concepcion M. Bohulano.)

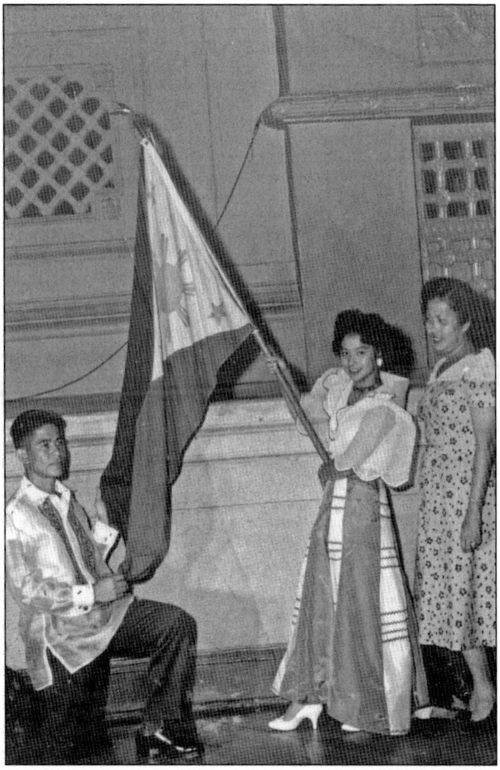

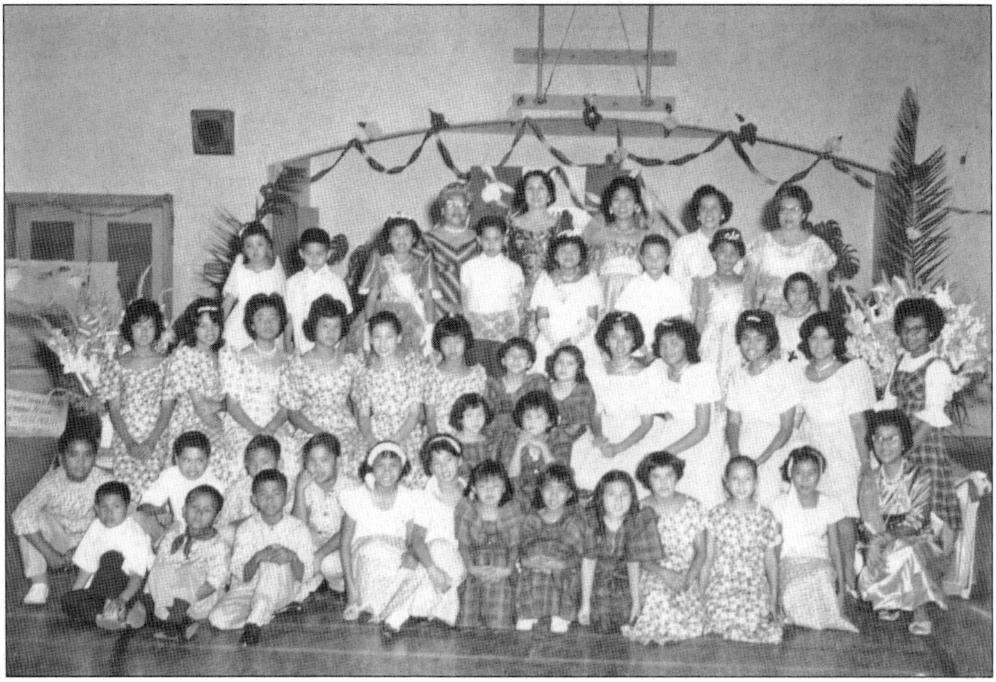

The Filipino Catholic Association's annual festival for Our Lady of Antipolo features folk dances and coronation of the festival queen. Here folk dancers and the royal court pose on July 4, 1961, at St. Mary's Hall. (Courtesy of Sharon Monton Robinson.)

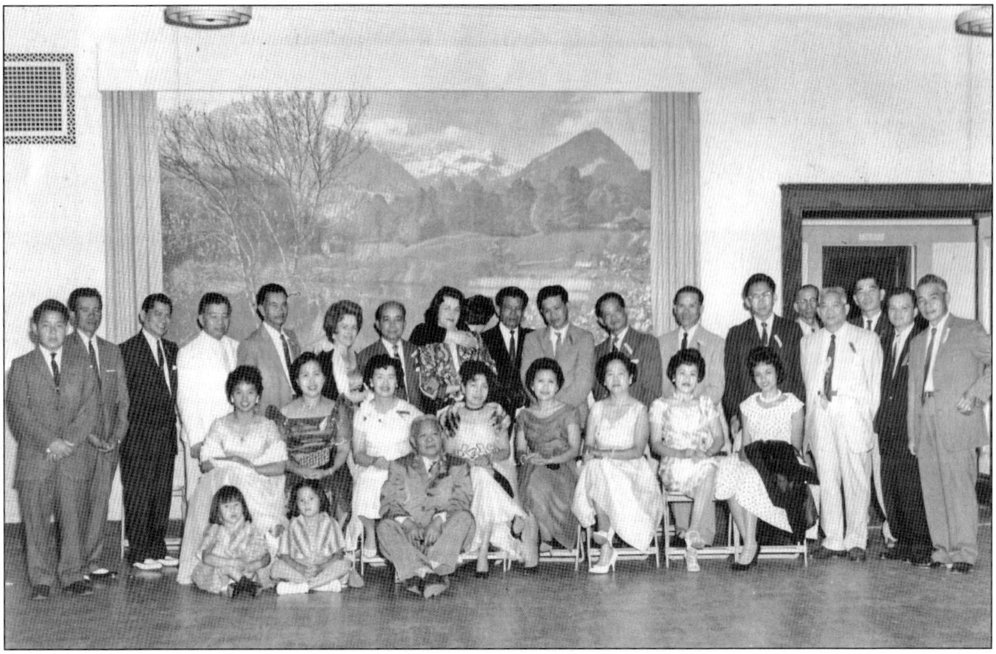

By the time this dance was held in the South Hall of the Civic Auditorium in the early 1960s, the Numancia Aid Association was more than 30 years old. The organization was founded by immigrants from Numancia, Aklan province, on the island of Panay, and celebrated its 75th anniversary in 2007. (Courtesy of the Numancia Aid Association.)

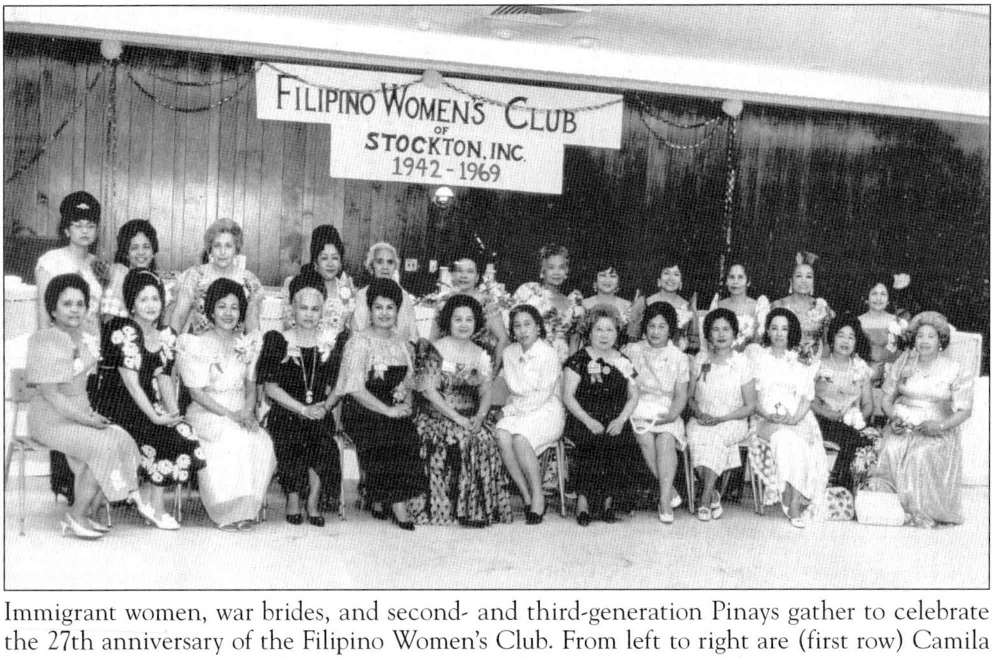

Immigrant women, war brides, and second- and third-generation Pinays gather to celebrate the 27th anniversary of the Filipino Women's Club. From left to right are (first row) Camila Carido, unidentified, Conching Lagura, Paula Daclan, Soling ?, Segunda Reyes, Mary Inosanto, Juliana Lazaro, Mary Ely, Helen Panis, Rose Orello, and two unidentified; (second row) Carmen Carido, second from right, Carmen Tomek, and Eufemia Macahilas. (Courtesy of Caroline Bulawit Gray.)

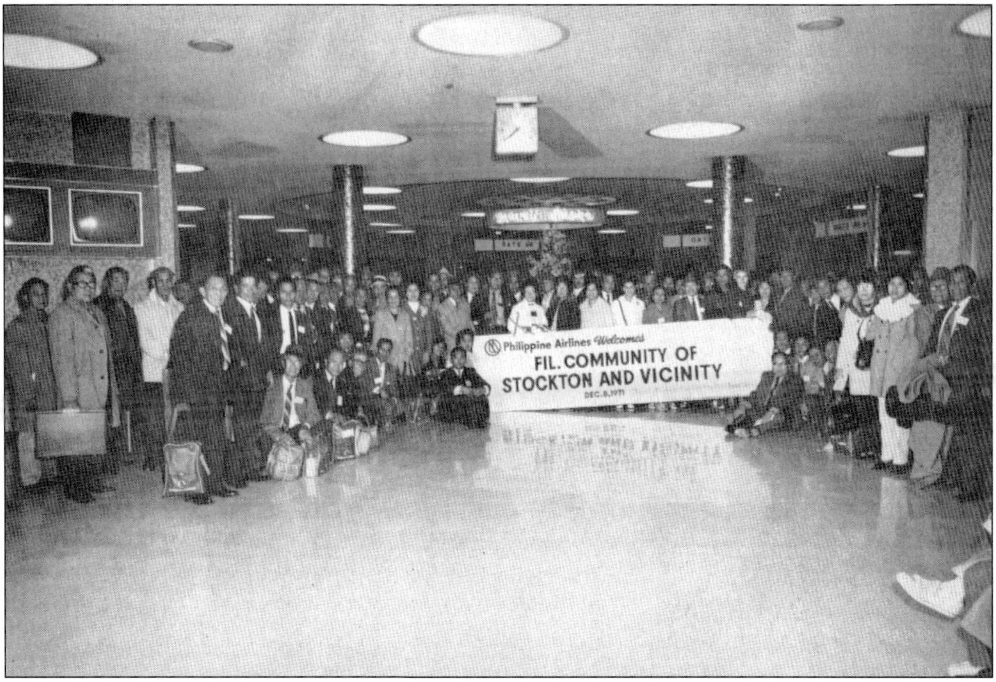

The Filipino Community of Stockton sent a contingent to the Philippines on Philippine Airlines on December 8, 1971. (Courtesy of FANHS Stockton.)

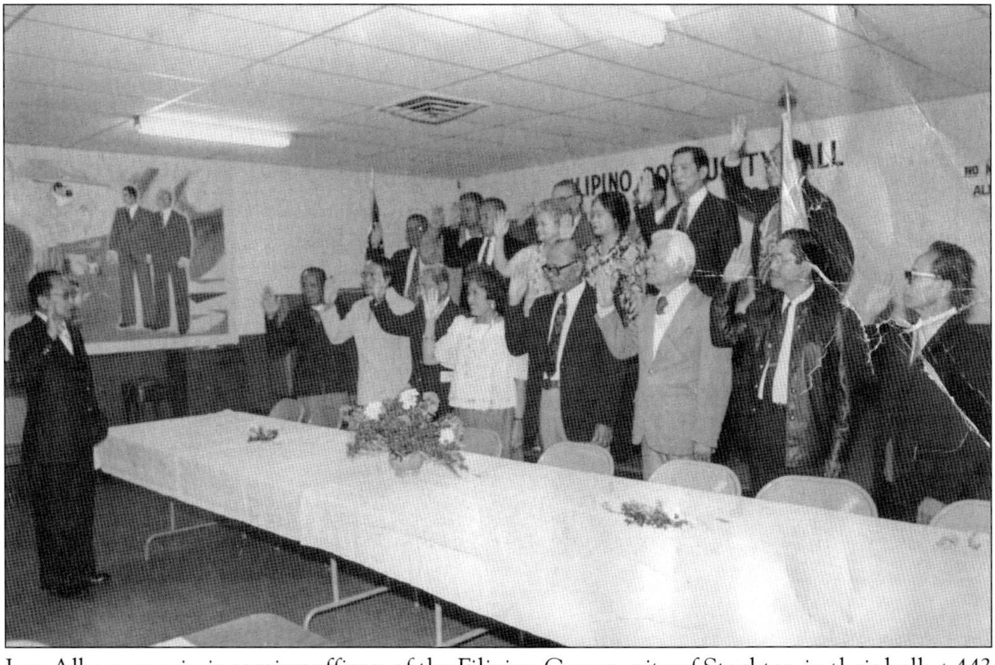

Jose Alba swears in incoming officers of the Filipino Community of Stockton in their hall at 443 East Sonora Street in the late 1970s. From left to right are (first row) three unidentified, Carmen Tomek, Pres. Jaun "Johnny" Latosa, Rev. Apolinar Sangalang, Ernesto T. Mabalon, and Angel Cabales; (second row) Urbano Barcenas, two unidentified, Segunda Reyes, and five unidentified. (Courtesy of the Ernesto T. Mabalon.)

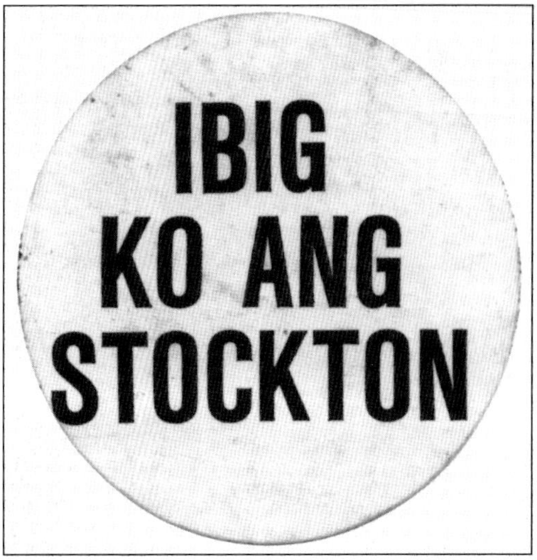

American Filipino youth distributed these stickers, which have "I love Stockton" loosely translated into Tagalog, the Philippine national language, during the Second Annual Far West Convention, held at University of the Pacific in 1972. The convention brought several hundred Filipino American youth to Stockton. (Courtesy of Adeline B. Suguitan.)

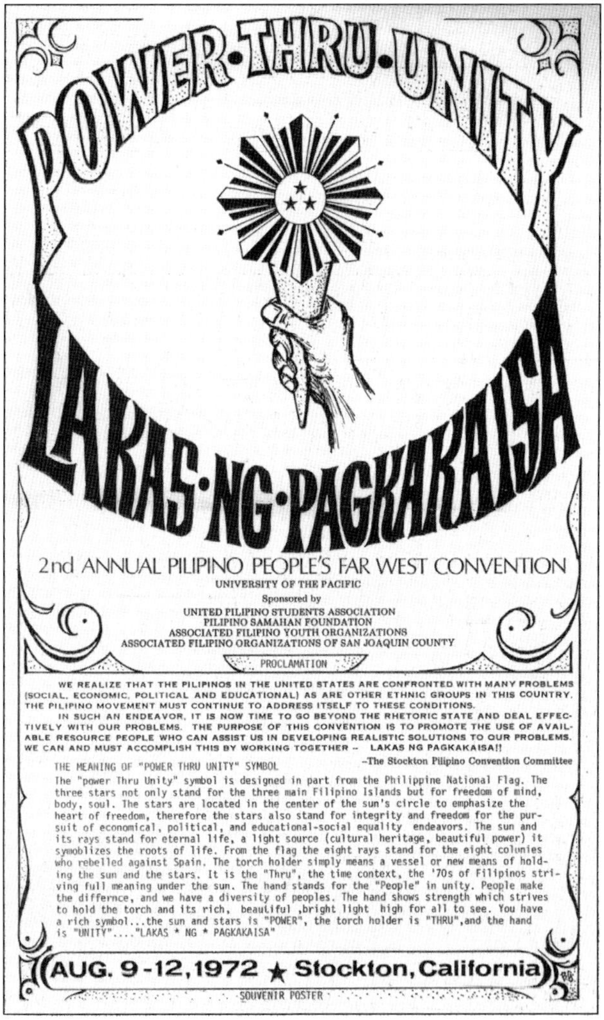

"Lakas ng Pagkakaisa," or "Strength in Unity," was the theme for the Second Annual Pilipino People's Far West Convention, held in Stockton in August 1972. The convention featured workshops on identity, arts, culture, and political empowerment. (Courtesy of FANHS National.)

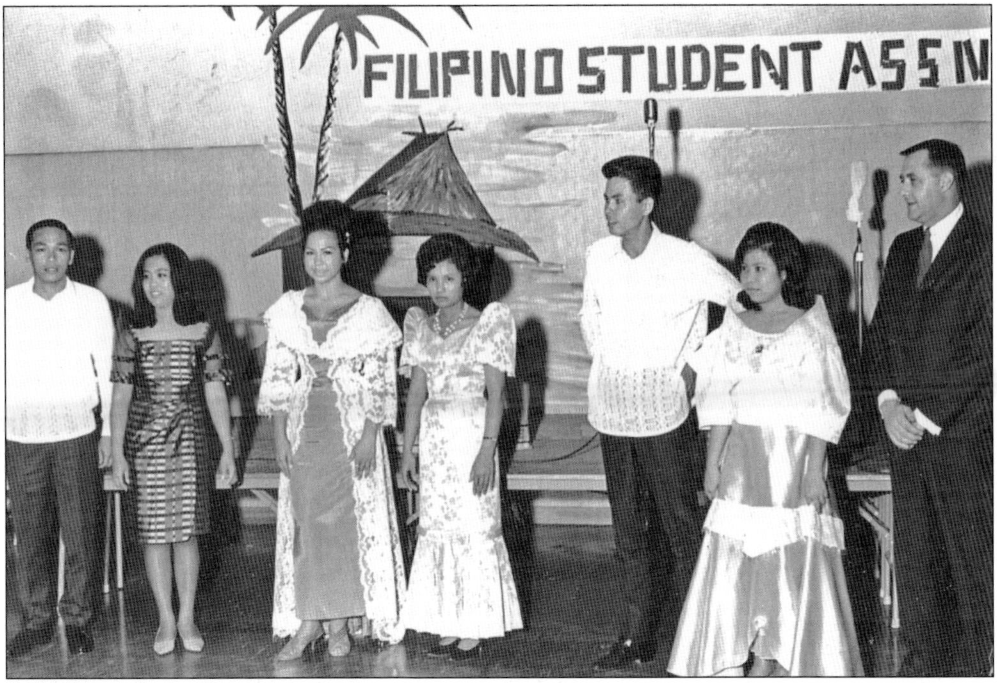

Filipino organizations proliferated wherever a critical mass (more than three) of Filipinos congregated. This is one of the first events of the Filipino Student Association at Delta College in the 1960s. (Courtesy of Florence Quilantang.)

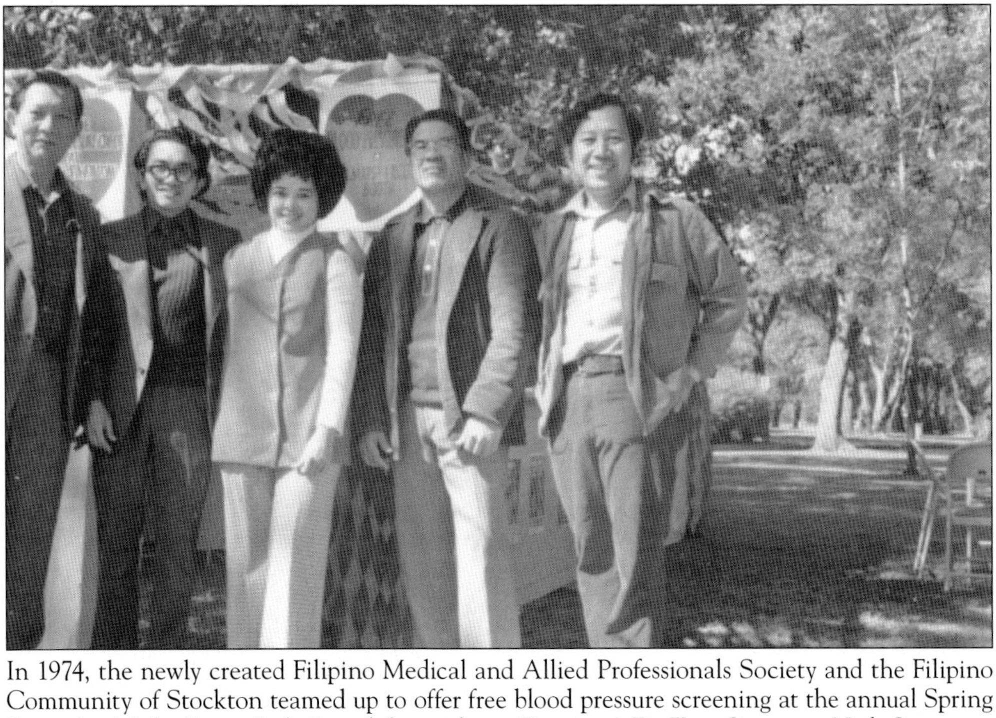

In 1974, the newly created Filipino Medical and Allied Professionals Society and the Filipino Community of Stockton teamed up to offer free blood pressure screening at the annual Spring Festival at Micke Grove Park. From left to right are Doming ?, Dr. Tony Saqueton, Nady Saqueton, Art Almendral, and Jose Bernardo. (Courtesy of Carolina Saqueton Luces.)

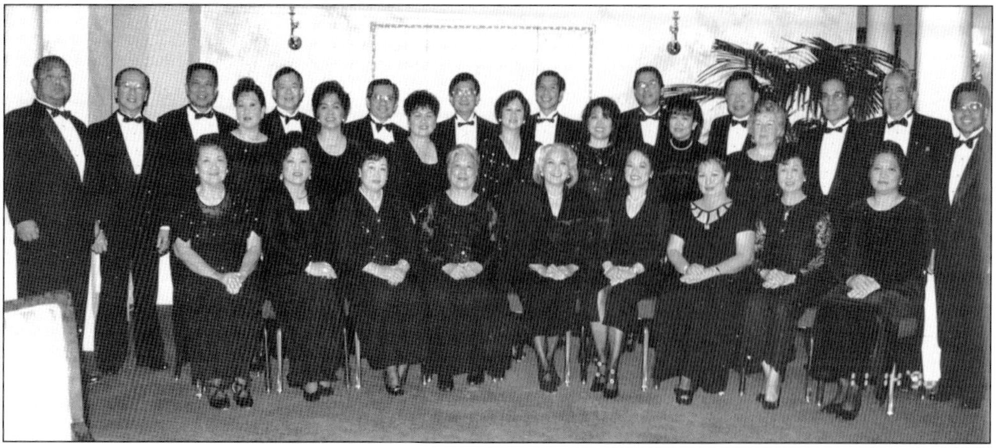

The Filipino Medical and Allied Professionals Society's chorale members, shown here at a recent performance in Stockton, include Leticia Amida, R.N.; Virgilio Ambida, D.M.D.; Nancy Andres; Enrique Bacani; Albina Benabaye, M.D.; Ellen Escobar; Virgilio Escobar; Marcelo Espiritu, M.D.; Norma Espiritu, M.D.; Corazon Galvez, D.M.D.; Jose Galvez, D.M.D.; Ellen Gregorio; Winnie Jacobson; Luis Nosce, M.D.; Margarita Nosce, M.D.; Eunice Oh, R.N.; Mario Oribello; Perla Oribello, R.N.; Thelma Ramseyer; Helen Reyes, M.D.; Hope Rigunan, O.D.; Cecilia Simeon; Rolando Simeon; Delores Soderfeldt; Rachel Strack, R.N.; Eduardo Sumaquial, M.D.; Marietta Sumaquial, M.D.; and Grace Tolentino, R.N. (Courtesy of Grace Tolentino and FILMAPS.)

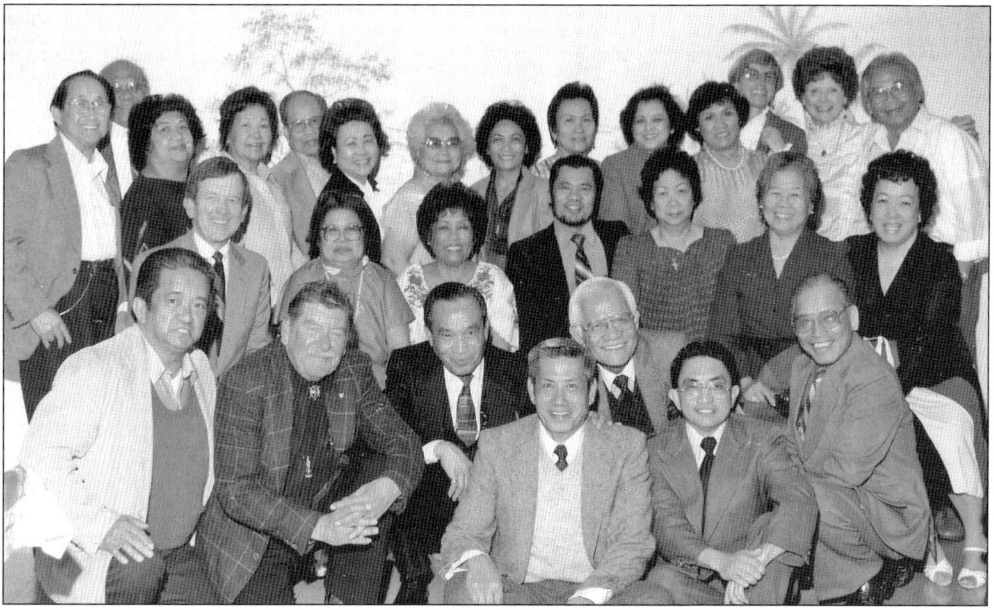

The Filipino Chamber of Commerce installed officers in February 1985 at the Barrio Fiesta Restaurant at Filipino Plaza. From left to right are (first row) Ben Ramos, Adolph Tomek, Frank Perez, Vic Hernandez, Apolinar Sangalang, Tony Saqueton, and Urbano Barcenas; (second row) Dave Smith, Caridad Dulay, Carmen Tomek, Narcy Giva, Letty Amigable, Cosette Barcenas, and Bernie M. Giva; (third row) Joseph Antonio, Bill Calip, Mrs. Antonio, Bernice Vera Cruz, Martin Castillo, Fely Castillo, Segunda Reyes, Stella Hand, Mrs. Calipe, Nady Saqueton, Linda Hernandez, Doris Beckwith, unidentified, and Al Felizardo. (Courtesy of Bernie M. Giva.)

Six

Creating Cultures
Filipino American Ethnicity and Cultural Identities

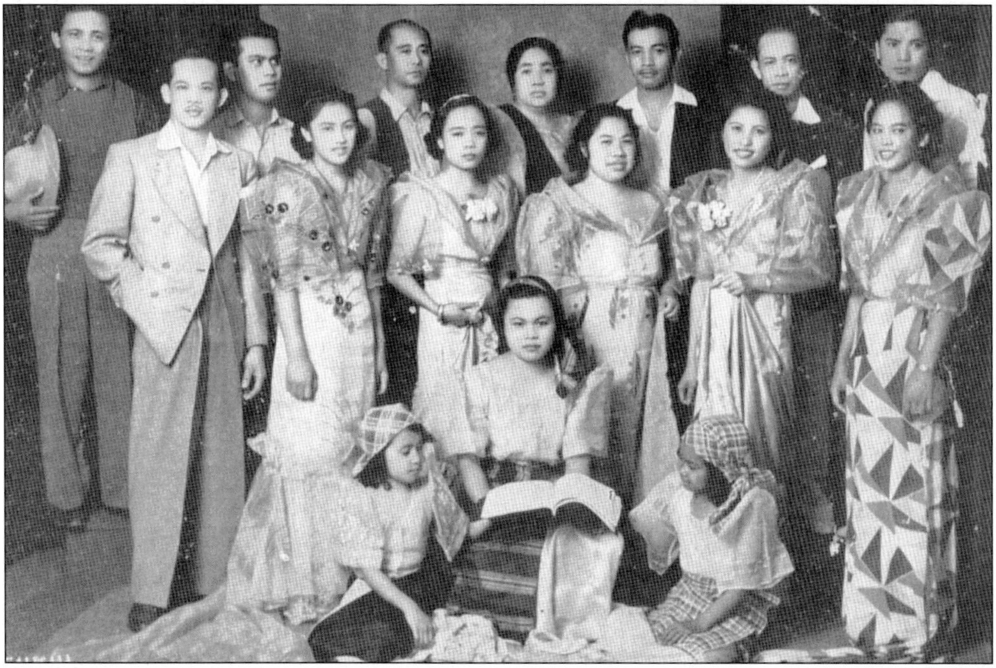

Lucia Cordova (third row, fourth from left), a native of Numancia, Aklan, taught a Tagalog class in Little Manila. In 1937, she wrote and directed an original acclaimed Tagalog play, or *zarzuela*: *Walang Kamatayang Pagibig* (*Love Eternal*). Few Filipinos in Stockton at that time spoke Tagalog, now the national language of the Philippines. The Philippines is an archipelago of more than 7,000 islands, and its people speak more than 100 languages and dialects. It was only after the Philippine Revolution that "Filipino" was used to refer to residents of the archipelago. Filipinos who immigrated to Stockton brought with them their regional languages and dialects, traditions, culture, and religious customs. Over the decades, however, Ilocano, Visayan, and Tagalog immigrants struggled together to survive in the United States, and became Filipino, and then Filipino American. Filipinos in Stockton created a unique cultural identity that forged the values and customs from the provinces of the Philippines with the political and cultural identities they were forming in the United States. Through photographs of historic Filipino American churches, queen contests, sports teams, escrima masters, jazz bands, folk dances, and hip hop performances, this chapter features rich and unique Stockton Filipino American cultural identities and their dynamic evolutions through the decades. (Courtesy of FANHS Stockton.)

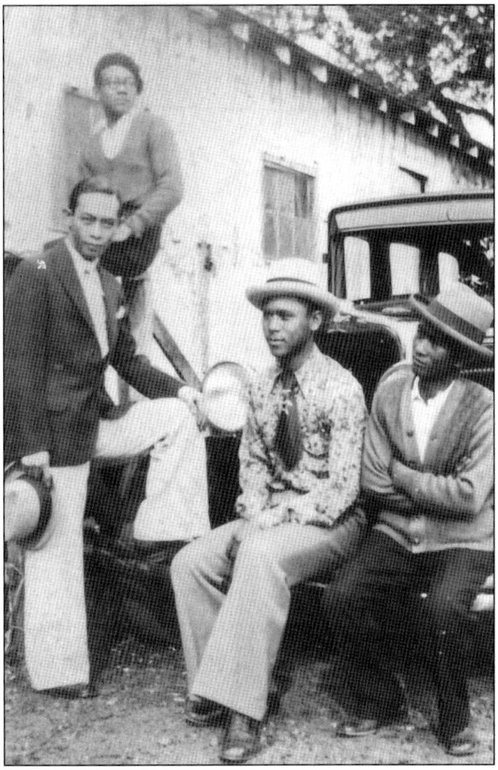

Some debate that Hollywood in the 1930s and 1940s was just as influenced by Pinoy style as vice-versa. Pinoys took great pride in wearing the latest trends. Here friends gather for a photograph in their casual, yet fashionable, dress in 1930. (Courtesy of FANHS Stockton.)

For almost 100 years, Filipinos in the Delta/Central Valley have gathered in secret spots to "camp" for *sabong*, or cockfighting. Police in Stockton busted a huge cockfight during World War II near Stockton. This chicken fight took place in Livingston, near Stockton in 1941. (Courtesy of Caroline Bulawit Gray.)

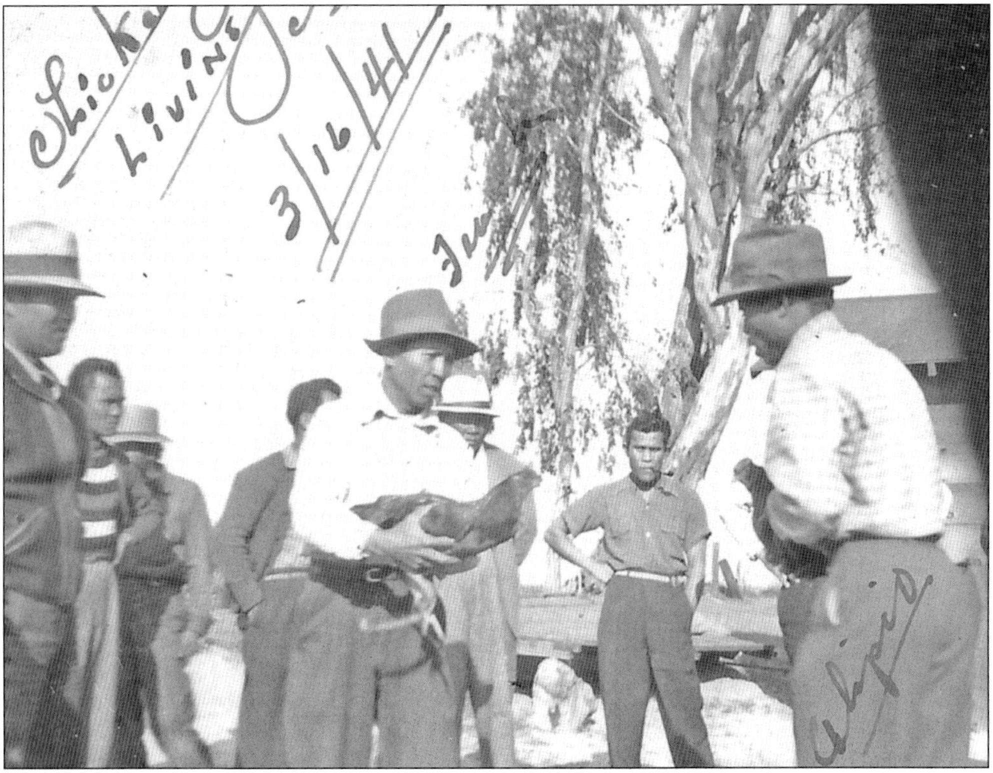

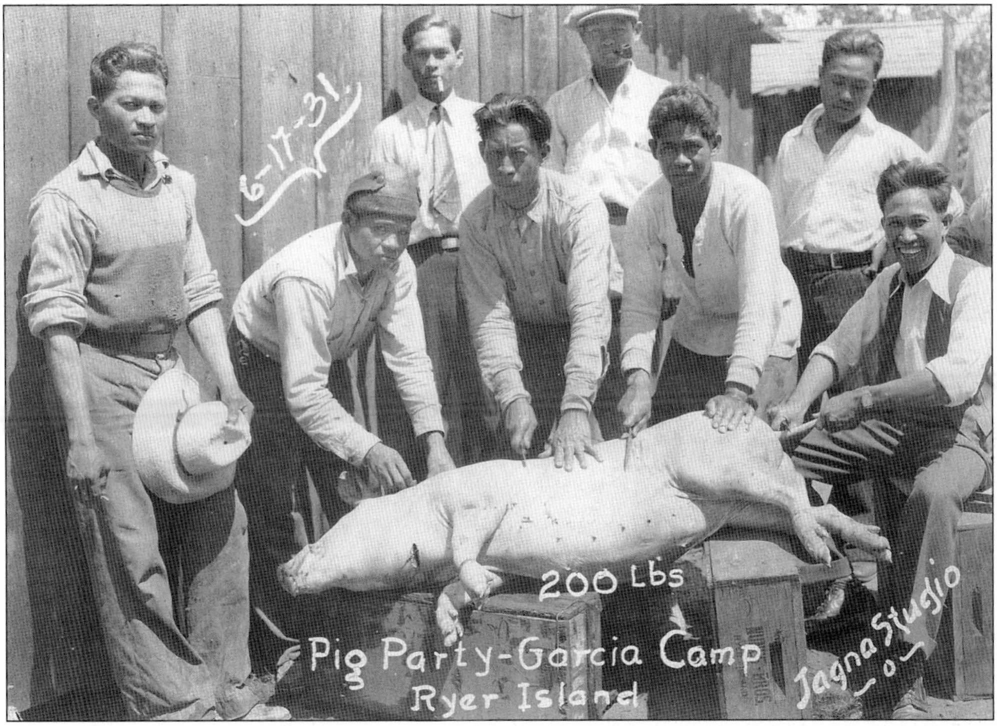

The highlight of every end-of-season *campo* party was a lechon, a whole roast pig. Here Pinoys roast a 200-pounder on Ryer Island. (Courtesy of Tony Somera.)

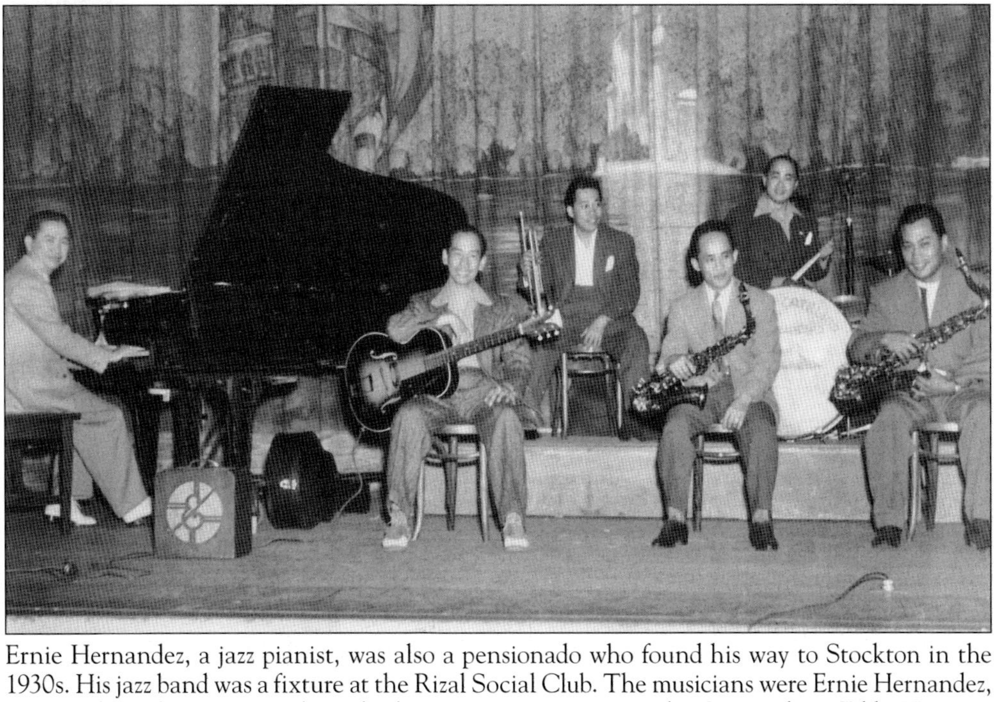
Ernie Hernandez, a jazz pianist, was also a pensionado who found his way to Stockton in the 1930s. His jazz band was a fixture at the Rizal Social Club. The musicians were Ernie Hernandez, piano; Eddie, alto sax; Cornelio "Charlie" Bautista, tenor sax; Pedro Corpuz, bass; Eddie Navarro, trumpet; Patero Bolong, trumpet; and "Jimmy" on drums. (Courtesy of Anelina B. Magdael.)

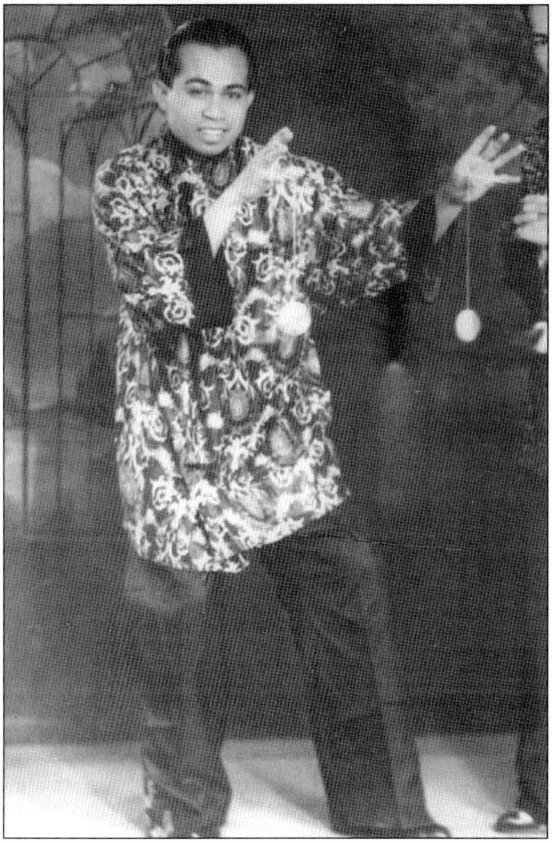

After Duncan bought the rights to the yo-yo from Filipino immigrant Pedro Flores in 1929, the company assembled a group of Pinoy yo-yo experts to travel and demonstrate the ancient toy. In this group was yo-yo world champion Raymond R. Lapitan, who also worked as a farm labor contractor in Stockton, where he raised his family. (Courtesy of Kathi Bravo.)

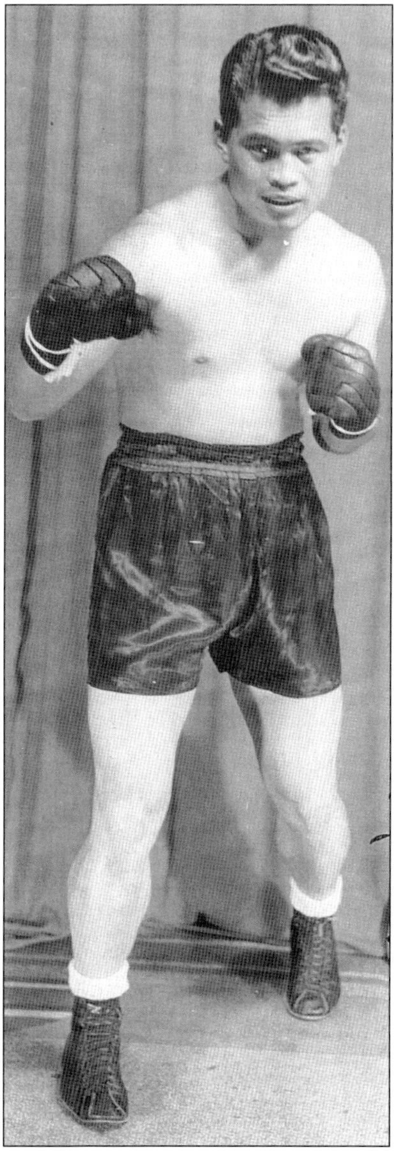

Boxing was an enormously popular sport among Filipinos in Stockton, who would flock to the Civic Auditorium for matches. Joseph "Joey" Caballero fought 500 and lost only 50 matches in his prime in the 1940s and 1950s. He was a native of Carcar, Cebu. (Courtesy of the Caballero-Pimental family.)

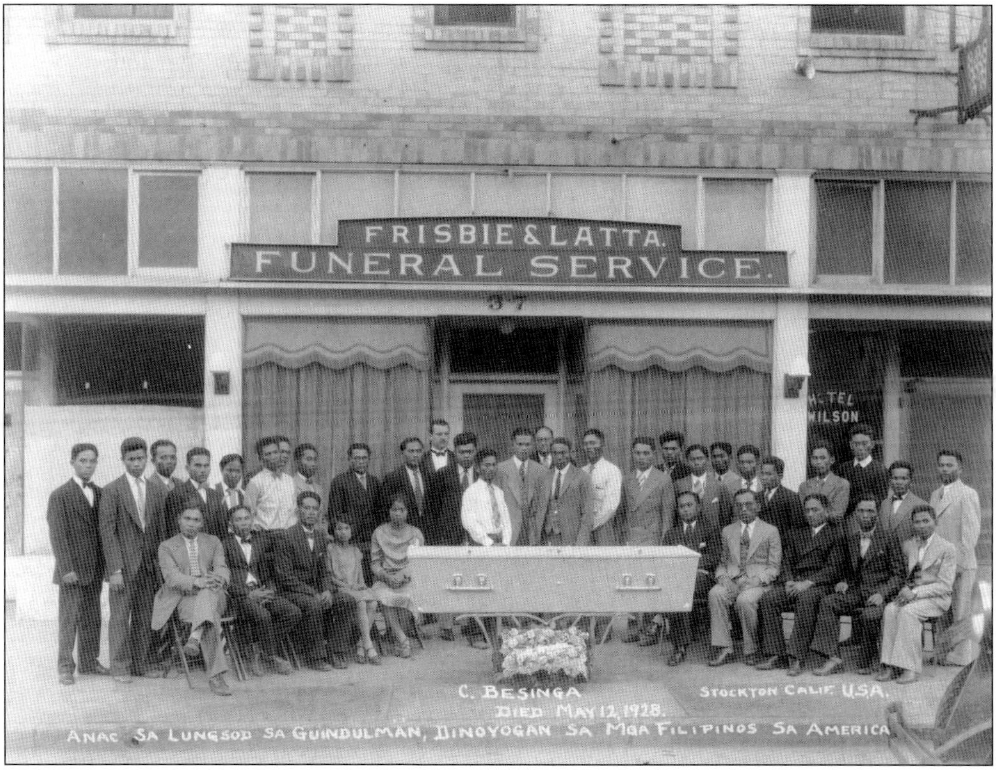

When C. Besinga died on May 12, 1928, his town mates from Guindulman, Bohol, provided the funeral and services for their brother. Whether Protestant, Catholic, or Muslim, Filipinos in Stockton all practice elaborate and meaningful funeral rites. Lodges also buried their members with complex rituals. (Courtesy of Special Collections, University of the Pacific.)

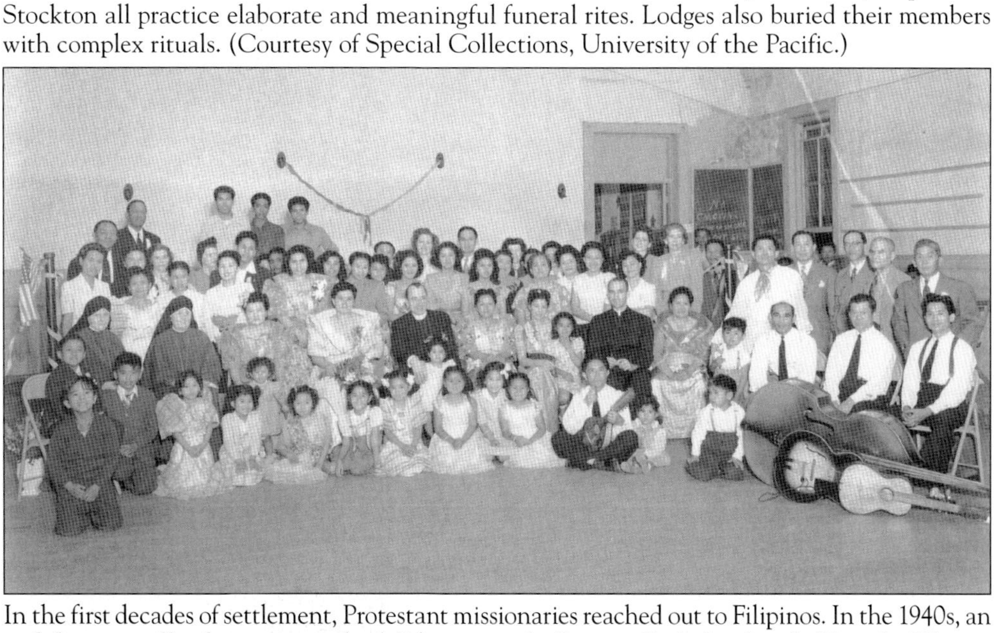

In the first decades of settlement, Protestant missionaries reached out to Filipinos. In the 1940s, an archdiocesan effort began to win back Filipinos to the Roman Catholic church. Here the Filipino Catholic Society of Stockton (now the Filipino Catholic Association) holds a get-together in the 1940s at St. Mary's Hall. (Courtesy of FANHS Stockton.)

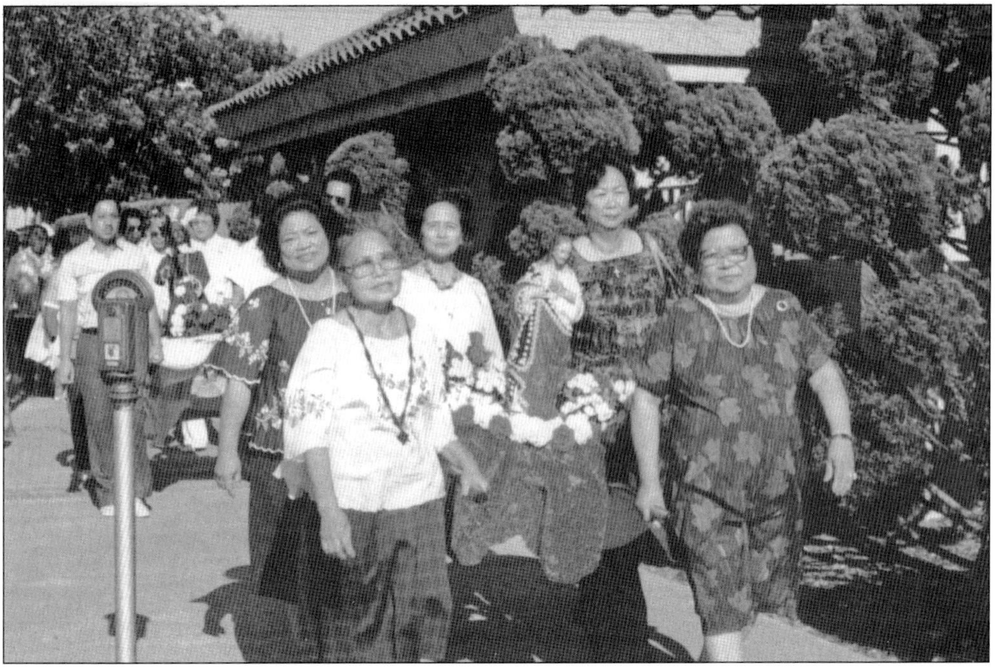

During the Barrio Fiesta, members of the Filipino Catholic Association hold a mass and religious procession around the block. This photograph was taken in the 1980s. From left to right are Emerita Estandian, Rafaela Sumabon, Prima Adiong, Letty Amigable, and Charito Dulay. (Courtesy of Concepcion M. Bohulano.)

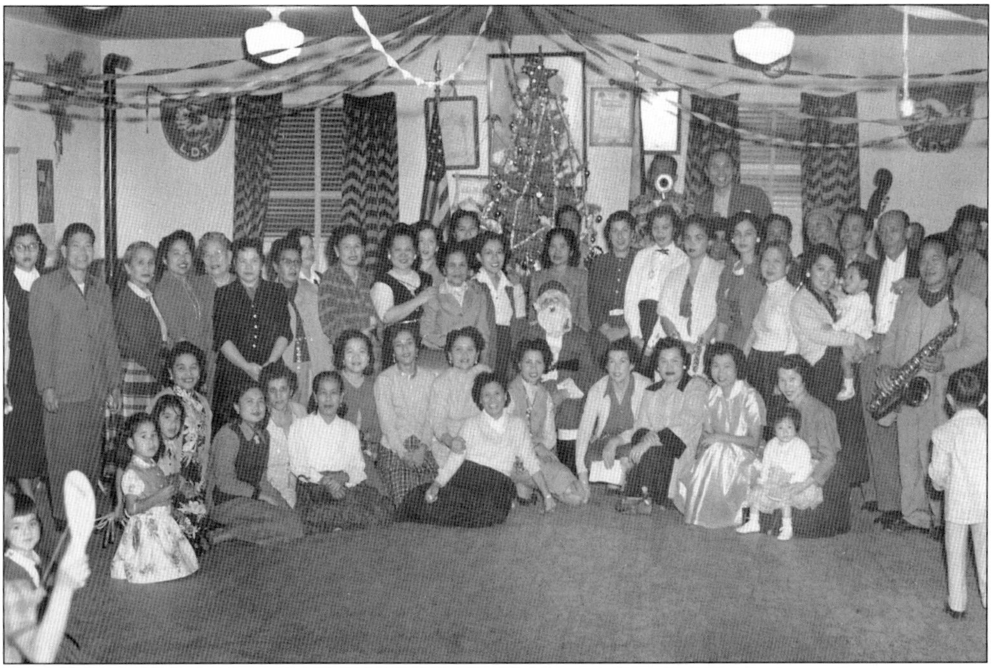

Annual Christmas parties at the Daguhoy Lodge hosted by different organizations brought together generations for gifts and celebration. The little boy at the far right with his back to the camera is Vince Reyes. This celebration took place in the 1950s. (Courtesy of the Vince Reyes.)

Grandmaster Angel Cabales was born in 1917 in Antique, Panay, and lived in Stockton until his death at age 83. His mentor, Felicisimo Dizon, taught him *de cuerdos escrima*, the ancient indigenous martial art that utilizes sticks, bladed weapons, and empty hand fighting techniques. Widely known as the father of escrima in America, Cabales founded the Filipino School of Self Defense on Harding Way in 1968 and trained martial arts notables Rene Latosa, Dan Inosanto, Leo Fong, and his son, Vincent Cabales. (Courtesy of FANHS Stockton.)

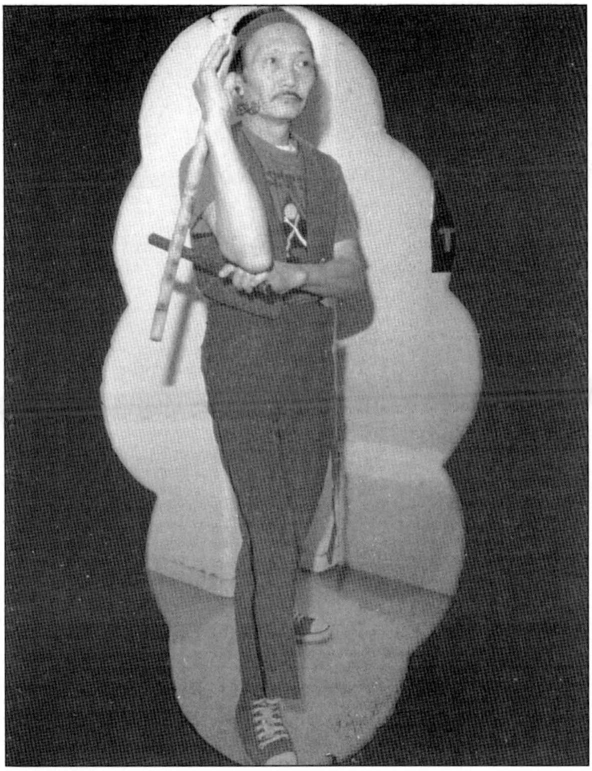

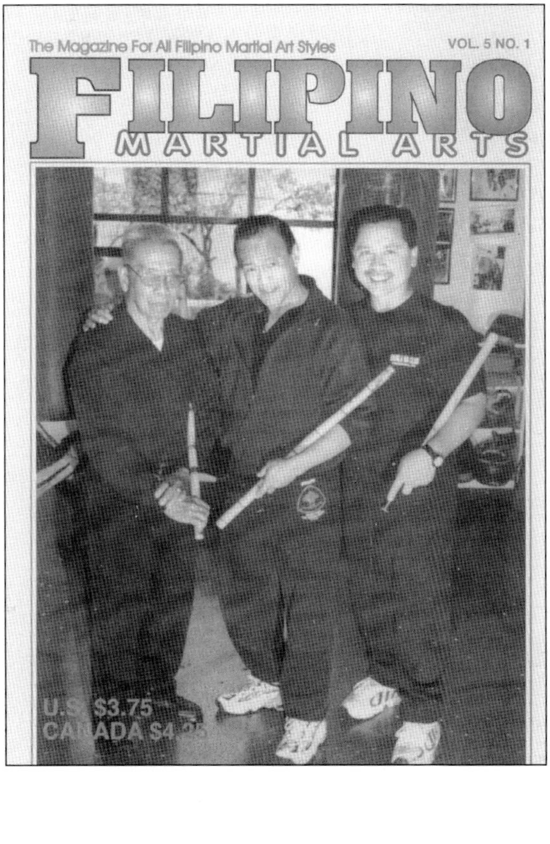

Grandmaster Leo Giron (left) and his students Dan Inosanto (center) and Tony Somera (right) are among those from Stockton who have taken escrima to the next level and worldwide. Leo Giron's Largo Mano system has been globally influential. (Courtesy of Tony Somera.)

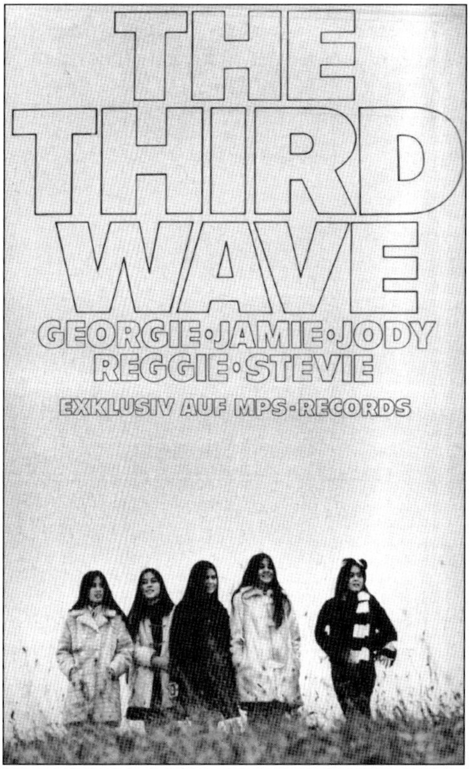

Georgie, Jamie, Jody, Reggie, and Stevie Tenio's 1960s vocal group called the Third Wave performed with Carmen McRae at the Monterey Jazz Festival. Here the five girls pose on the cover of their German record release. (Courtesy of FANHS National.)

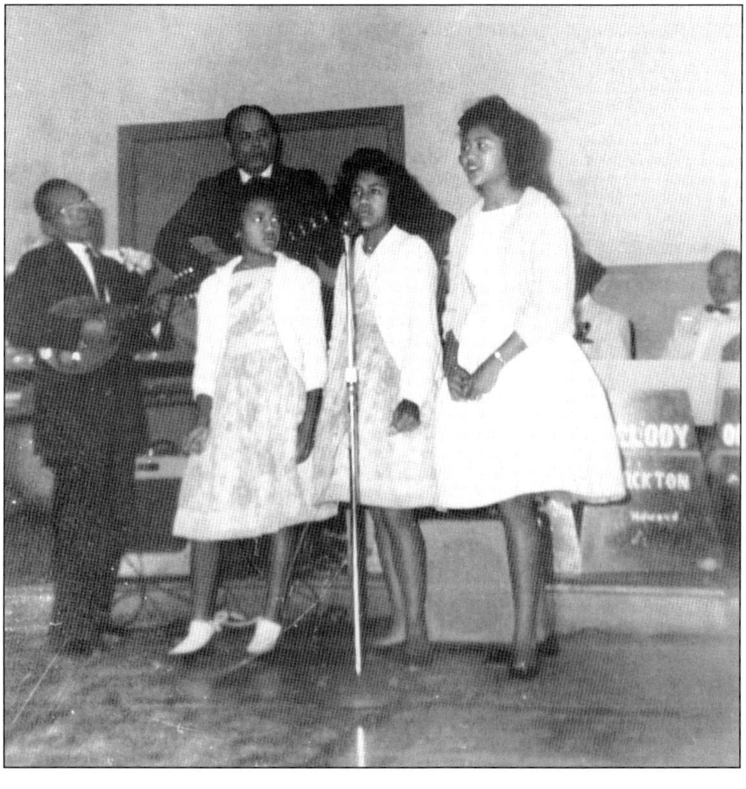

At St. Mary's Hall *c.* 1962, "Eking" Bascones on mandolin accompanies the three singing Thomas sisters, from left to right, Lorita, Erlinda, and Evangeline Thomas. (Courtesy of Evangeline Thomas.)

Led by former Bayanihan Dance Company dancer Voltaire Gungab, and locals Rosie Tolentino, and Arthur Zulueta, the Luzviminda Dance Troupe performed for the community throughout the early 1970s. Pictured here is Betty Aynaga and Ken Estrella, performing the Mountain province dance *salip*. (Courtesy of Betty Aynaga.)

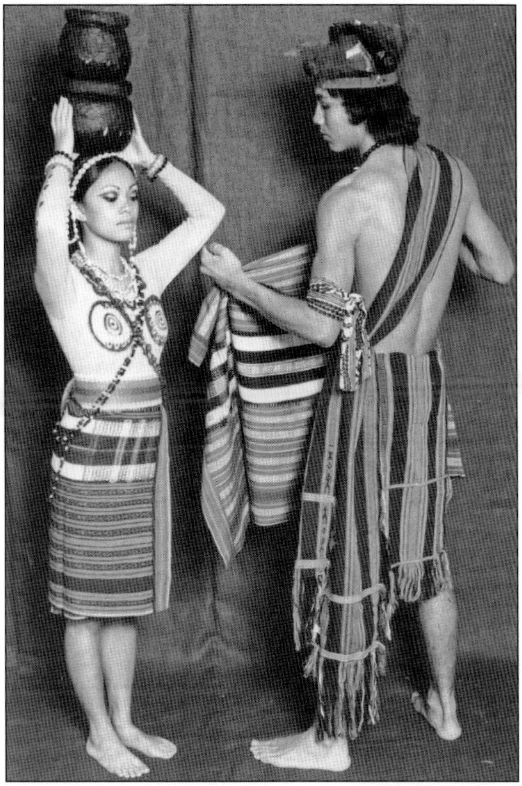

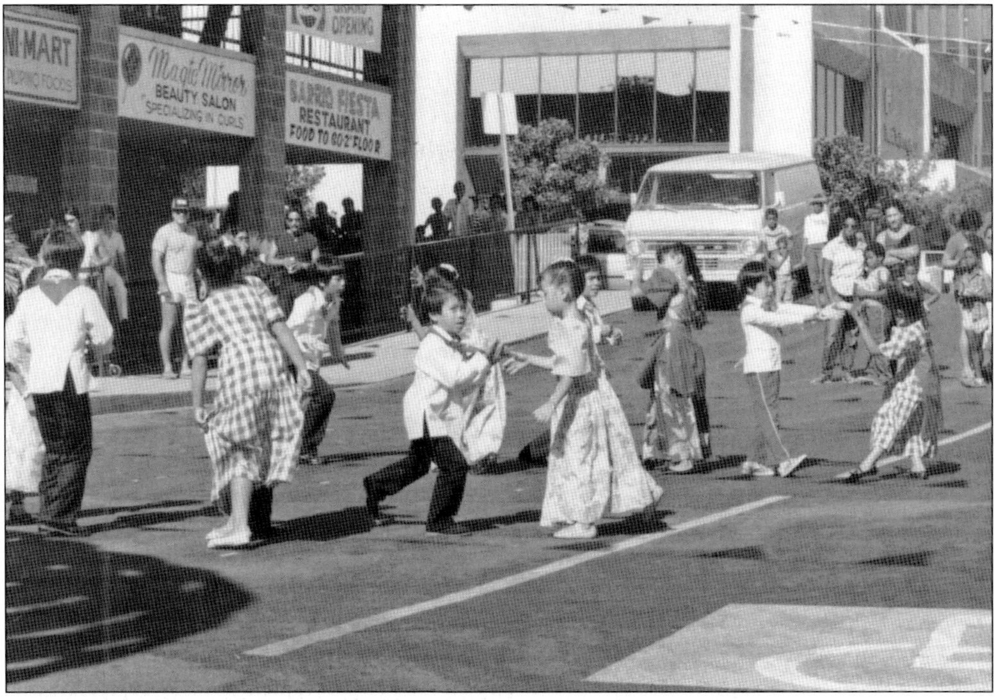

The Maharlika Dance Troupe, led by Virgina Navarro, performs at the Barrio Fiesta in the 1980s. (Courtesy of Virginia Navarro.)

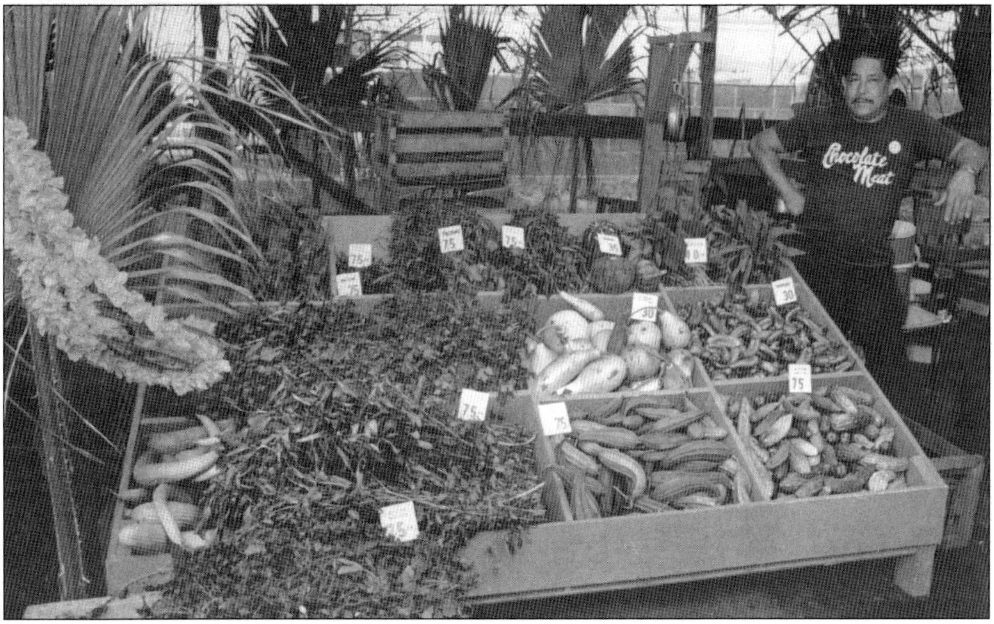

Lathrop farmer Cecil Bonzo was a founder of the Farmer's Market under the Crosstown Freeway. Here he is pictured with his vegetable booth at the Barrio Fiesta in the 1980s. (Courtesy of Stockton FANHS.)

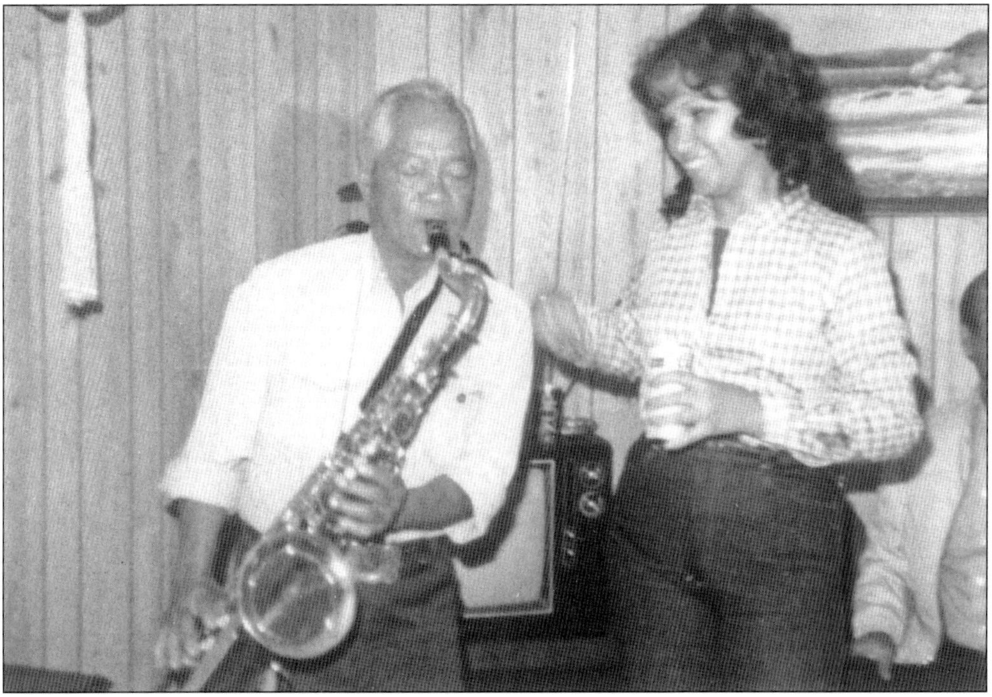

Paterno Bolong was a trumpeter and sax player who played with several Filipino bands, including the Ernie Hernandez Jazz Band. Here he plays for his daughter Helene Nunes in the 1980s. (Courtesy of Helene Bolong Nunes.)

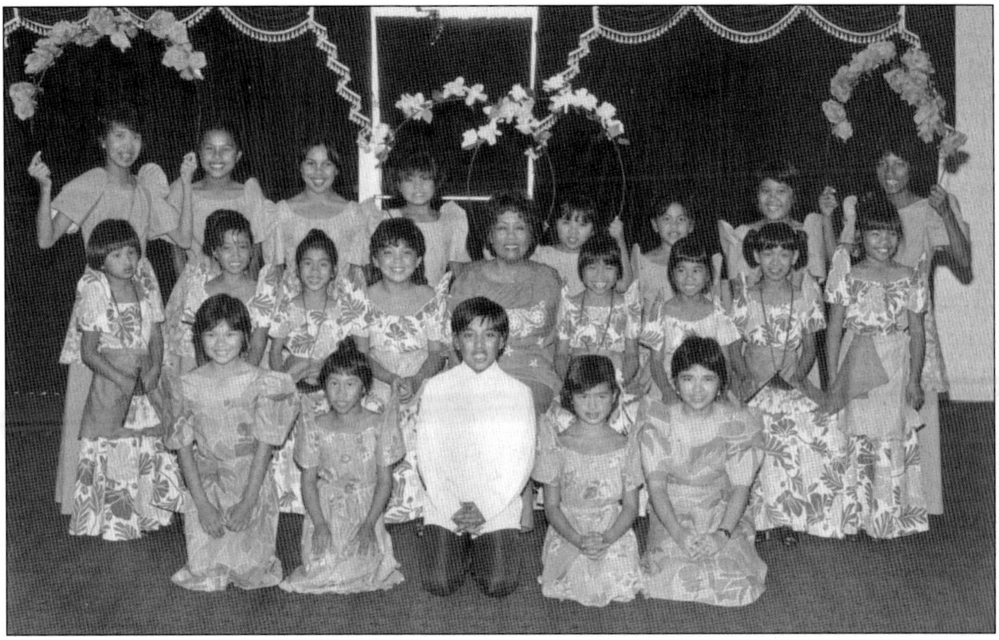

From the 1950s to her retirement in the 1990s, Carmen Tomek (center) taught Filipino folk dances to three generations of Filipinos in Stockton. This is her Sampaguita Dance Troupe in 1984. (Courtesy of Carolina Saqueton Luces.)

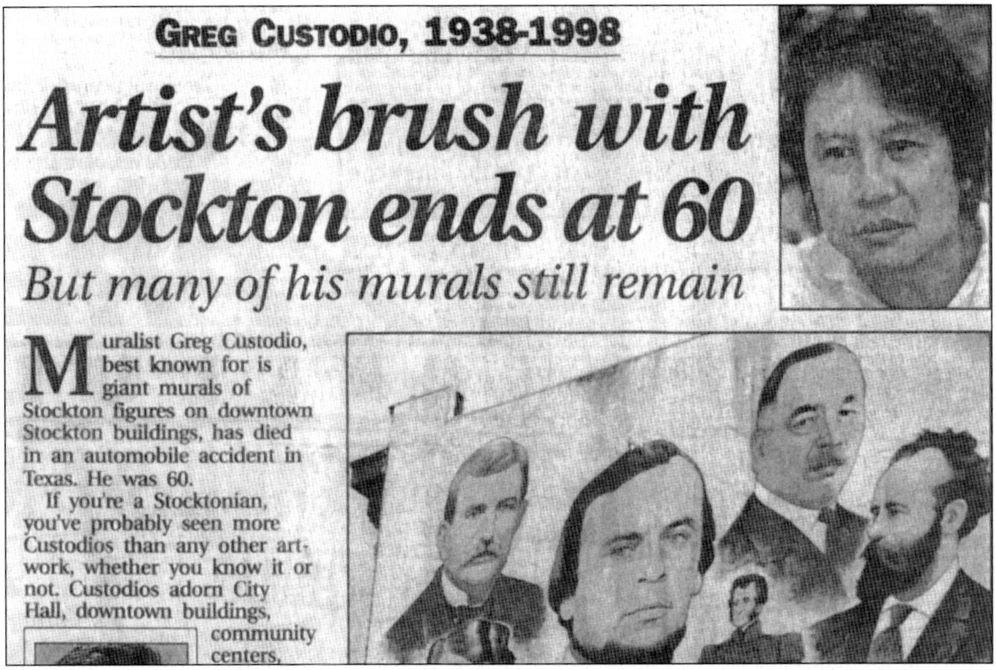

GREG CUSTODIO, 1938-1998

Artist's brush with Stockton ends at 60

But many of his murals still remain

Muralist Greg Custodio, best known for is giant murals of Stockton figures on downtown Stockton buildings, has died in an automobile accident in Texas. He was 60.

If you're a Stocktonian, you've probably seen more Custodios than any other artwork, whether you know it or not. Custodios adorn City Hall, downtown buildings, community centers,

Until his death in 1998, Greg Custodio was one of the most noted Filipino visual artists in the United States and the city of Stockton's first and only salaried muralist. Born in 1938 in Manila, Custodio organized the Filipino Artists Guild in the Philippines. He left the Philippines and came to Stockton in 1968. He became the city's artist-in-residence from 1974 to 1994, painting several murals for private and public buildings. (Courtesy of FANHS Stockton.)

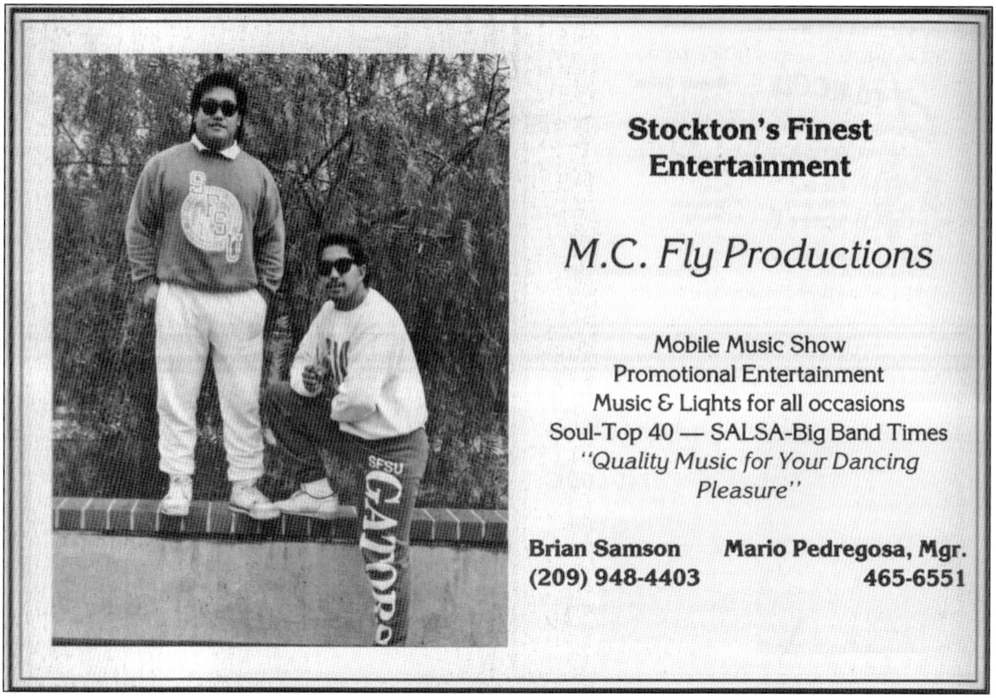

Filipino Americans have been highly influential in the development of West Coast hip hop culture. Dance crews and mobile DJ crews, like the pioneering MC Fly Productions of Stockton, have made an indelible mark on hip hop culture. Mario Pedregosa and, on left, Brian Samson provided DJ music for parties and celebrations. The West Coast DJ culture grew out of such crews. (Courtesy of the Mabalon family collection.)

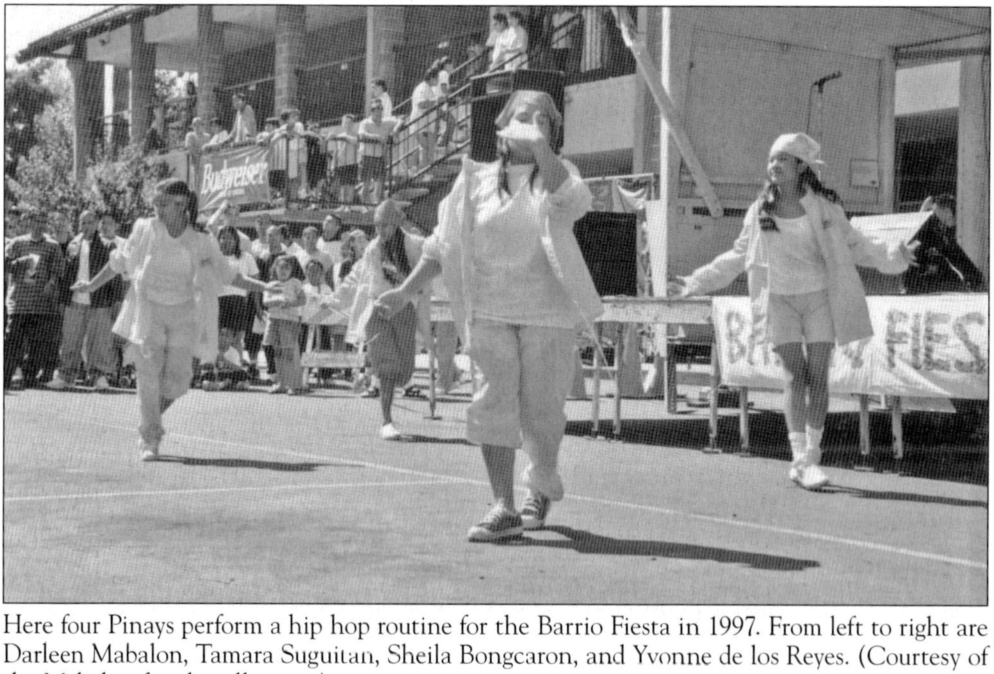

Here four Pinays perform a hip hop routine for the Barrio Fiesta in 1997. From left to right are Darleen Mabalon, Tamara Suguitan, Sheila Bongcaron, and Yvonne de los Reyes. (Courtesy of the Mabalon family collection.)

Weddings became even larger as the community grew. Philippine traditions such as the money dance, in which guests danced with and pinned good-luck money on the bride and groom, became cherished Filipino American traditions. Here Addie Bohulano Suguitan and Mel T. Suguitan dance at their wedding, which drew more than 1,000 guests at the Civic Auditorium in 1977. (Courtesy of Adeline Suguitan.)

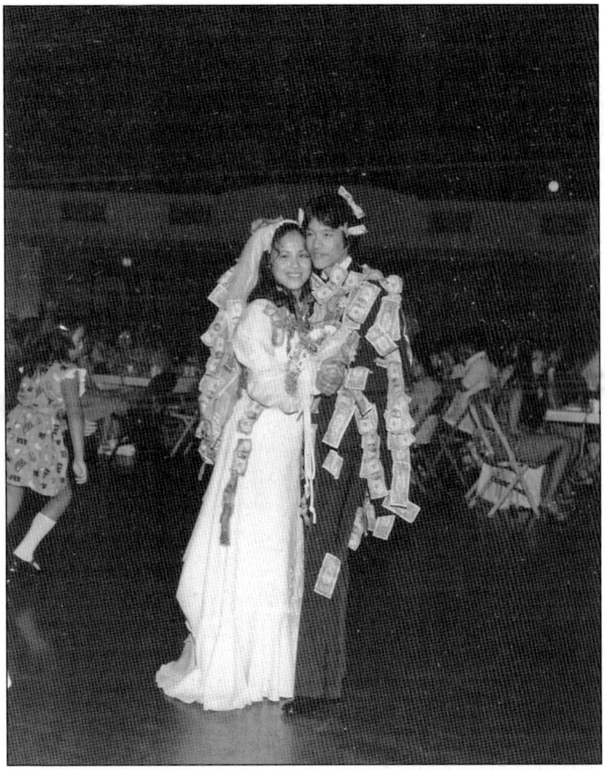

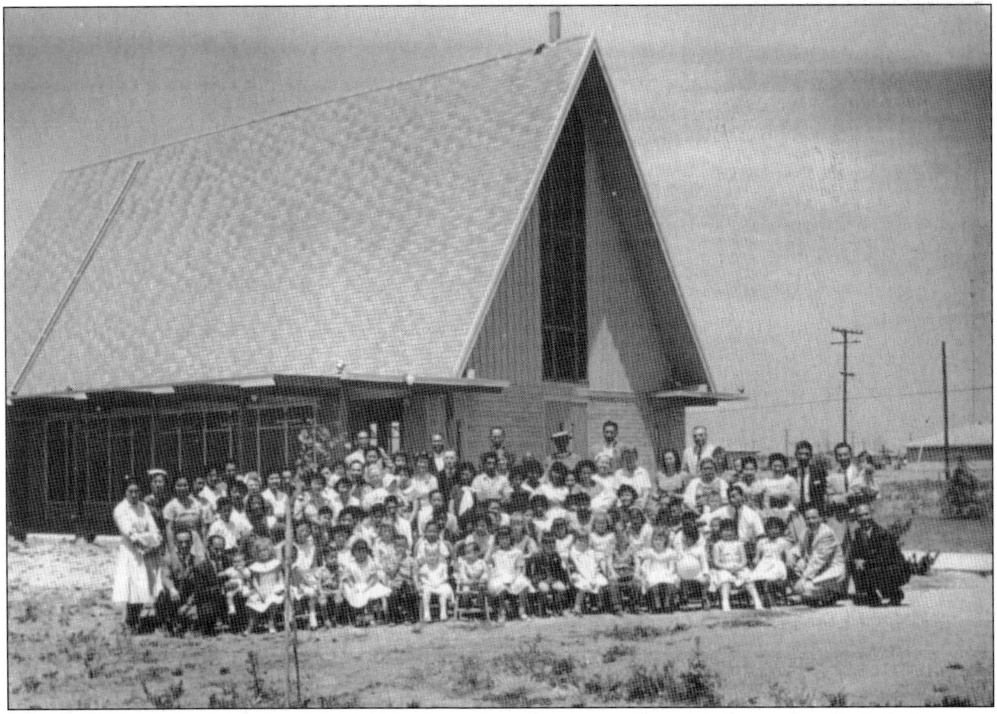

After years in downtown Stockton, the Trinity Presbyterian Church relocated to Eighth Street in south Stockton in the 1960s. This is their dedication ceremony. (Courtesy of FANHS Stockton.)

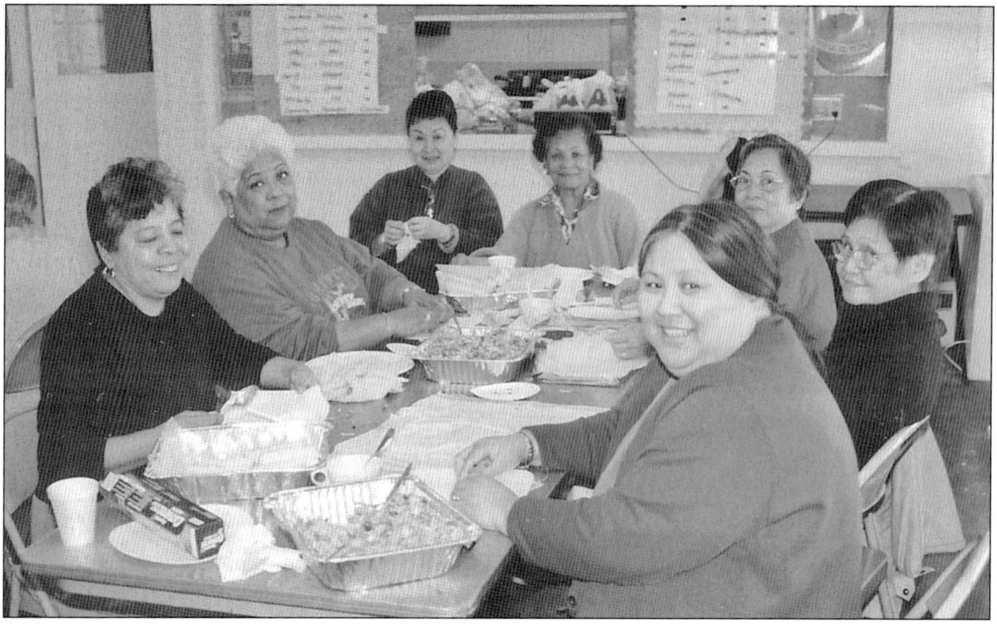

In Stockton, regional cooking methods and the bounty of local ingredients have created a new Filipino American cuisine unique to the delta area. Here Trinity Presbyterian Church members make and wrap lumpia to raise money for the church in the late 1990s. They continue a generations-old tradition in the church. (Courtesy of Adeline Suguitan.)

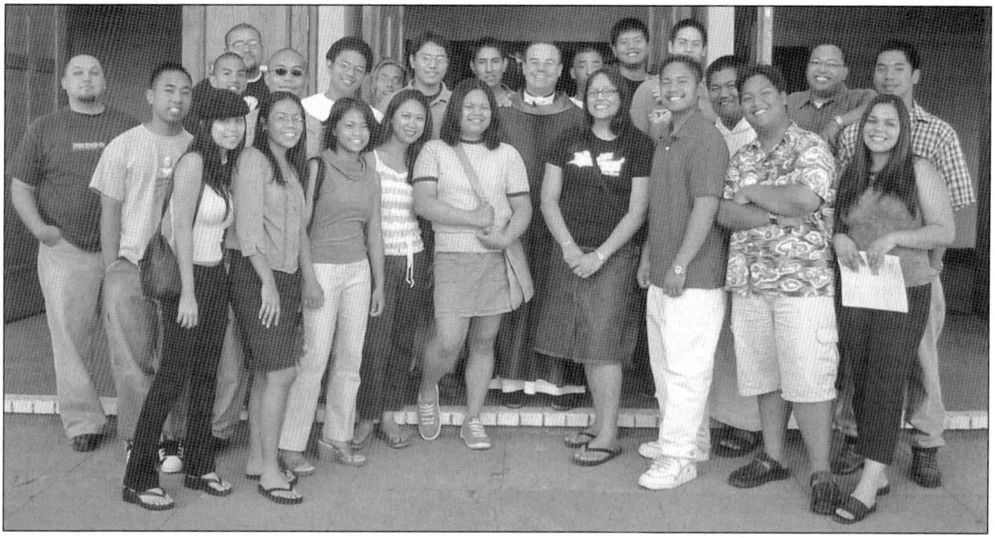

St. George's Catholic Church and School have served the Stockton Filipino community since the 1950s. Here the St. George's Youth Group poses in front of the church in 2002. Led by Dillon Delvo, the activist-oriented youth group has campaigned for many issues, including affordable housing and preservation of Little Manila and against the death penalty. From left to right are (first row) Anna Sison, Debbie Johnston, Rebecca Abellana, Marie Erguiza, Sarah May Olarte, Celena Foronda, Patrick Foronda, Ace Alcantara, and Faith ?; (second row includes) Robert Johnston, John Hernando, R. J. Ricacho, Simon Gomez, Marlo Villadores, Chad Cordero, Derrick Canton, Gustavo Medina, Fr. Ramon Bejarano, Jorge Ramirez, Chris Legaspi, John Thomason, Manuel Farinas, Dillon Delvo, and Gilbert Menor. (Courtesy of Dillon Delvo.)

Legendary jazz pianist and vocalist Rudy Tenio has performed nationwide and released his first CD in 1999, *I Listen to My Heart*. The son of immigrants from Bohol, Tenio continues the legacy of Stockton Filipino American jazz. (Courtesy of Rudy Tenio.)

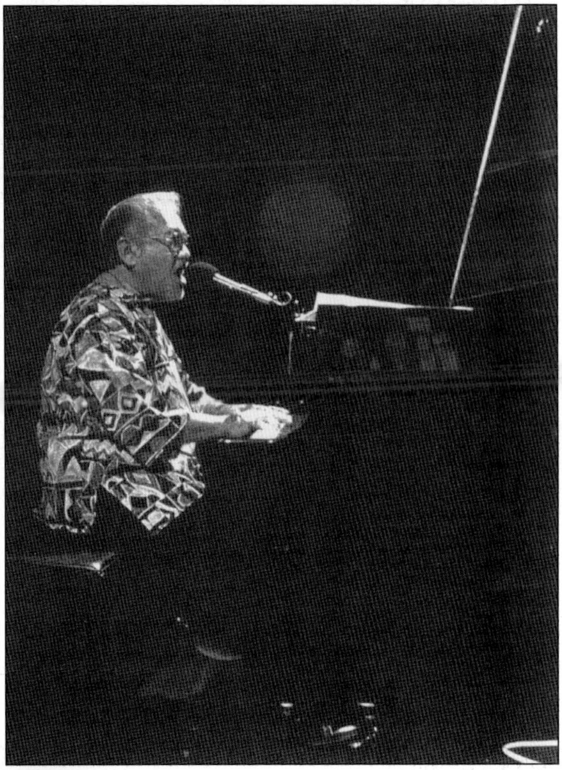

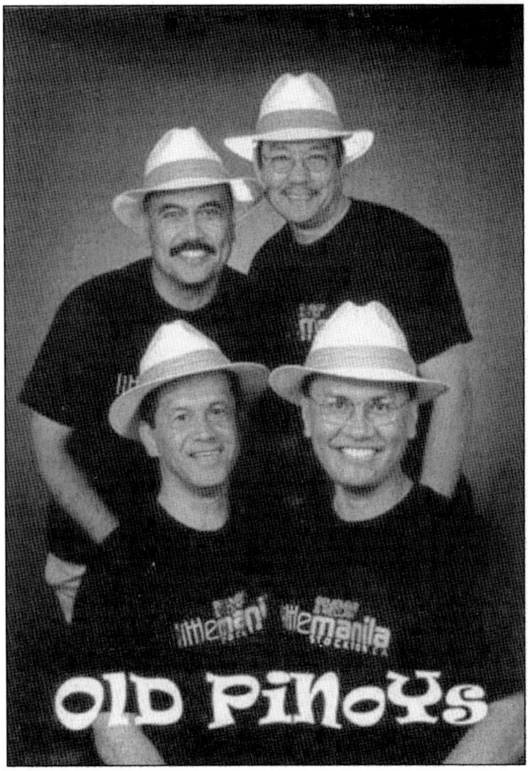

Sons of pioneer Pinoys formed a popular singing group in the 1990s, the Old Pinoys. The group has performed all over the state. From left to right are (seated) Fred Yurong and Geoff Aspiras; (standing) Oscar Aban and Mel Suguitan. The group's inspiration and name come from their memories of the old-timers singing on the sidewalks of Little Manila. (Courtesy of Adeline B. Suguitan.)

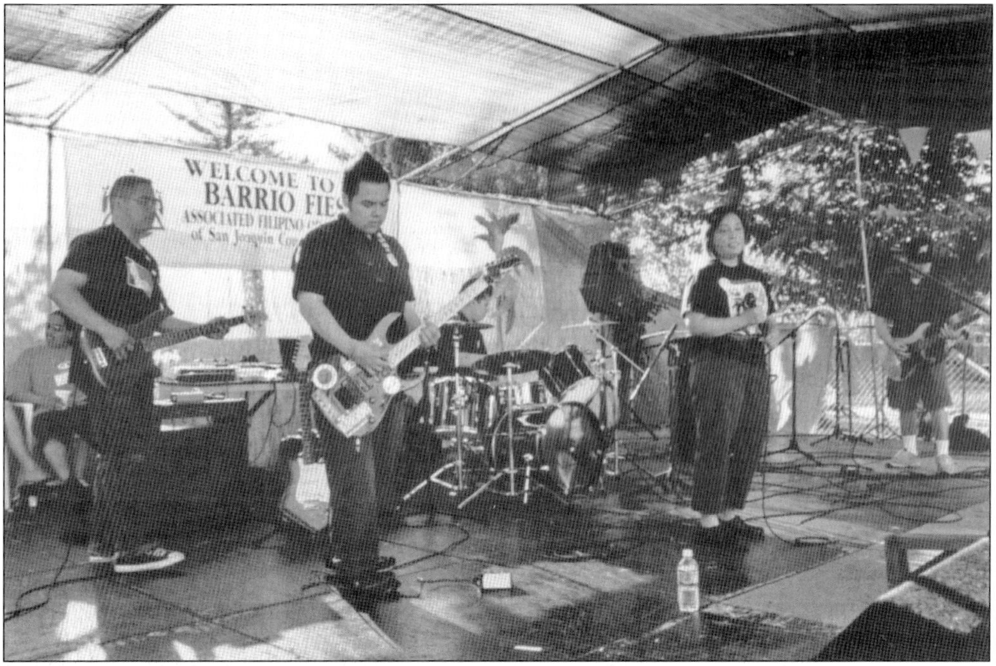

The Skyflakes, an indie underground pop group, perform at the Barrio Fiesta in 2003. The three Saria siblings hail from Stockton. From left to right are Jesus "Jesse" Gonzales, Jericho Saria, Oliver Saria, Tricia Saria Ramos, and Ron Ramos. (Courtesy of the Mabalon family collection.)

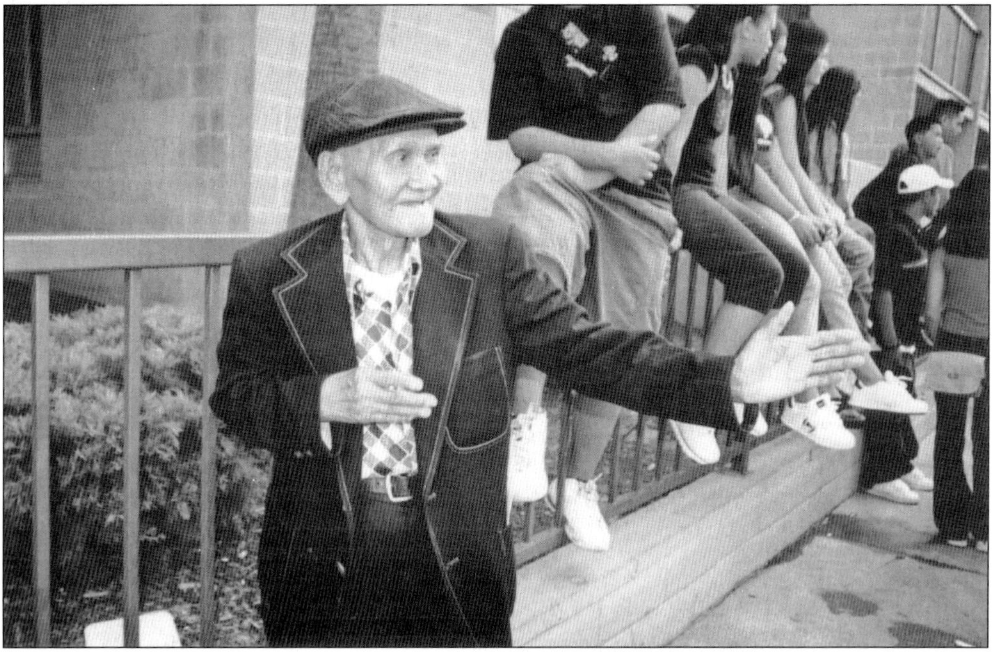

Longtime residents, new immigrants, and youth come together at the annual Barrio Fiesta. Jesus "Jesse" Corralles, who arrived in Stockton in the 1930s, was a fixture at the Barrio Fiesta until his death. In 2003, he keeps up with the hip hop dancers and shows the younger generation how it's done. (Courtesy of the Mabalon family collection.)

Seven

Preserving Our History for the Future Generations

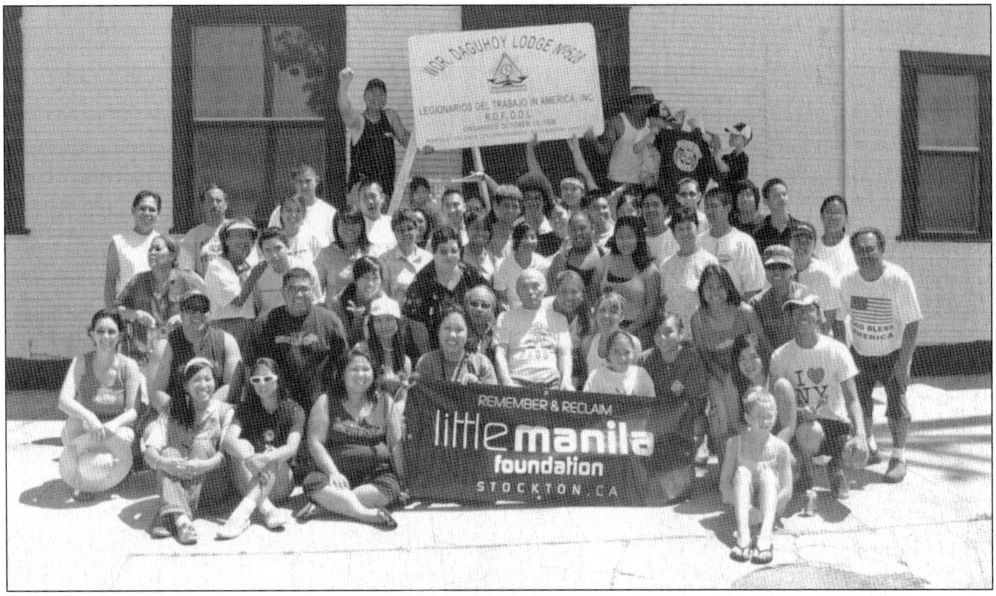

When, in 1999, the city demolished another block of Little Manila for a gas station and fast-food development, the Stockton Chapter of FANHS pushed to save the remaining buildings of the neighborhood. The Little Manila Historic Site, designated in 2000, is the country's first Filipino American city-designated historic district. In 2000, the Little Manila Foundation was created; they placed banners and historic markers in the area. The Filipino American National Historical Society is planning their Filipino American National Museum for the area. Every year, Bahala Na Escrima, the Little Manila Foundation, and community volunteers revitalize a Little Manila historic building. In 2006, they repainted and cleaned the historic Daguhoy Lodge (shown here) for the annual Fight the Blight event in August. Original lodge member Modesto Lagura, center, attended the cleanup. In addition to the lodge, only three original Little Manila buildings remain, and the Little Manila Foundation continues to fight demolition and displacement in the neighborhood. The Filipino American community of Stockton, the historic heart of Filipino America, is committed to preserving its history for the generations to come. (Courtesy of the Little Manila Foundation.)

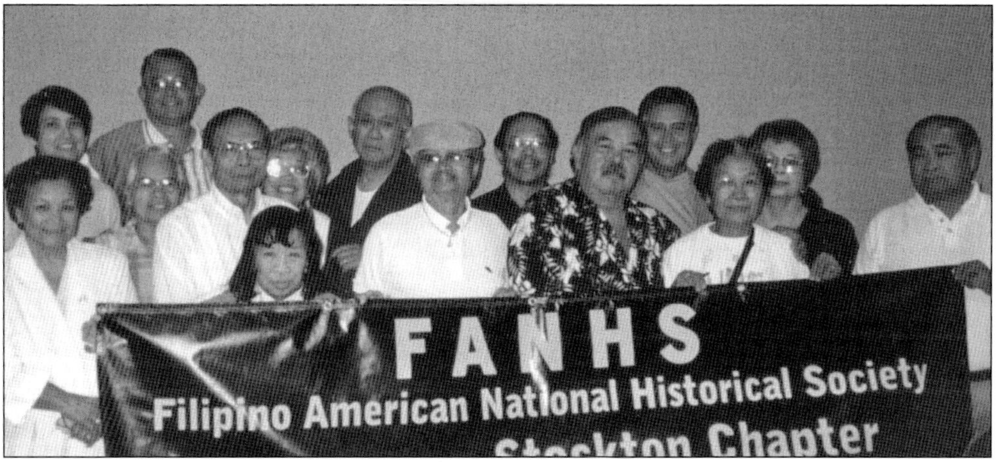

The Stockton Chapter of FANHS was formed in 1992. The chapter is dedicated to the preservation and dissemination of local Filipino American history. Here chapter members pose for a photograph in 1999. From left to right are Leatrice Perez, Marilyn Guida, Violet Dutra, Mel Lagasca, Moreno Balantac, Virgie Melear, Deanna Balantac, Jerry Paular, Sleepy Caballero, James Villadores, Bob Cabigas, Richard Tenaza, Maria B. Vea, Anita Bautista, and Frank Tibon. (Courtesy of Maria B. Vea.)

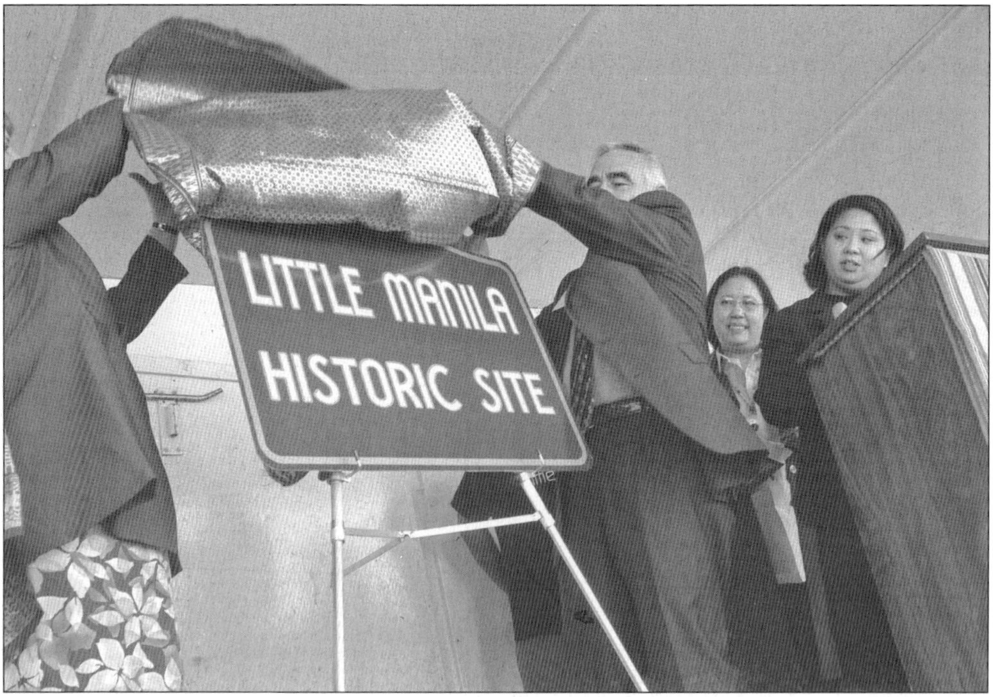

Cultural Heritage Board chair Leslie Crow (left) and Mayor Gary Podesto (center) unveil the Little Manila Historic Site signs to be placed around the four blocks surrounding Washington, Hunter, Sonora, and Center Streets in downtown Stockton, as Little Manila Foundation board members Elena Mangahas and Dawn Mabalon look on during the dedication ceremony on October 22, 2003. (Photograph by Calixtro Romias, courtesy of the *Record*.)

In 2003, the Little Manila Foundation placed historic banners around the Little Manila Historic Site. Eleven banners feature different aspects of the Filipino American experience in downtown Stockton in the early 20th century. In 2004, the local newspaper the *Record* printed a guide to the banners.

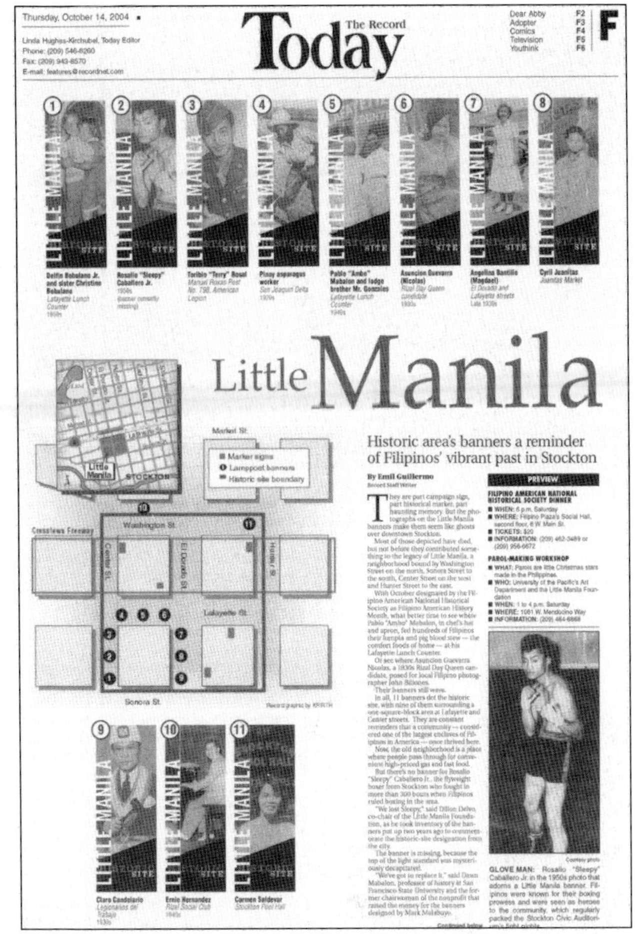

Thursday, October 14, 2004

Linda Hughes-Kirchubel, Today Editor
Phone: (209) 546-8260
Fax: (209) 943-8570
E-mail: features@recordnet.com

The Record **Today**

Dear Abby F2
Adopter F3
Comics F4
Television F5
Youthink F6

F

1. **Delfin Bobulano Jr. and sister Christine Bobulano** — *Lafayette Lunch Counter* 1950s
2. **Rosalio "Sleepy" Caballero Jr.** — 1950s (banner currently missing)
3. **Toribio "Terry" Rosal** — *Manuel Roxas Post No. 798, American Legion*
4. **Pinoy asparagus worker** — *San Joaquin Delta* 1920s
5. **Pablo "Ambo" Mabalon and lodge brother Mr. Gonzales** — *Lafayette Lunch Counter* 1940s
6. **Asuncion Guevarra (Nicolas)** — *Rizal Day Queen candidate* 1930s
7. **Angelina Bantillo (Magdael)** — *El Dorado and Lafayette streets* Late 1930s
8. **Cyril Juanitas** — *Juanitas Market*
9. **Claro Candelario** — *Legionarios del Trabajo* 1930s
10. **Ernie Hernandez** — *Rizal Social Club* 1940s
11. **Carmen Saldevar** — *Stockton Pool Hall*

Little Manila

Market St.
Marker signs
Lamppost banners
Historic site boundary
Crosstown Freeway
Washington St.
Center St.
El Dorado St.
Hunter St.
Lafayette St.
Sonora St.
Little Manila
STOCKTON
Record graphic by KRRITH

Historic area's banners a reminder of Filipinos' vibrant past in Stockton

By Emil Guillermo
Record Staff Writer

They are part campaign sign, part historical marker, part haunting memory. But the photographs on the Little Manila banners make them seem like ghosts over downtown Stockton.

Most of those depicted have died, but not before they contributed something to the legacy of Little Manila, a neighborhood bound by Washington Street on the north, Sonora Street to the south, Center Street on the west and Hunter Street to the east.

With October designated by the Filipino American National Historical Society as Filipino American History Month, what better time to see where Pablo "Ambo" Mabalon, in chef's hat and apron, fed hundreds of Filipinos their lumpia and pig blood stew — the comfort foods of home — at his Lafayette Lunch Counter.

Or see where Asuncion Guevarra Nicolas, a 1930s Rizal Day Queen candidate, posed for local Filipino photographer John Billones.

Their banners still wave.

In all, 11 banners dot the historic site, with nine of them surrounding a one-square-block area at Lafayette and Center streets. They are constant reminders that a community — considered one of the largest enclaves of Filipinos in America — once thrived here.

Now, the old neighborhood is a place where people pass through for convenient high-priced gas and fast food.

But there's no banner for Rosalio "Sleepy" Caballero Jr., the flyweight boxer from Stockton who fought in more than 300 bouts when Filipinos ruled boxing in the area.

"We lost Sleepy," said Dillon Delvo, co-chair of the Little Manila Foundation, as he took inventory of the banners put up two years ago to commemorate the historic-site designation from the city.

The banner is missing, because the top of the light standard was mysteriously decapitated.

"We've got to replace it," said Dawn Mabalon, professor of history at San Francisco State University and the former chairwoman of the nonprofit that raised the money for the banners designed by Mark Malabuyo.

Continued below

PREVIEW

FILIPINO AMERICAN NATIONAL HISTORICAL SOCIETY DINNER
- **WHEN:** 6 p.m. Saturday
- **WHERE:** Filipino Plaza's Social Hall, second floor, 8 W. Main St.
- **TICKETS:** $20
- **INFORMATION:** (209) 462-3489 or (209) 956-6672

PAROL-MAKING WORKSHOP
- **WHAT:** Parols are little Christmas stars made in the Philippines.
- **WHO:** University of the Pacific's Art Department and the Little Manila Foundation
- **WHEN:** 1 to 4 p.m. Saturday
- **WHERE:** 1081 W. Mendocino Way
- **INFORMATION:** (209) 464-6868

Courtesy photo

GLOVE MAN: Rosalio "Sleepy" Caballero Jr. in the 1950s photo that adorns a Little Manila banner. Filipinos were known for their boxing prowess and were seen as heroes to the community, which regularly packed the Stockton Civic Auditorium's fight nights.

In May, 2003, community members gather in front of the former Rizal Social Club as Anthony Veerkamp of the National Trust for Historic Preservation announces that Little Manila is one of the 11 Most Endangered Historic Places in the United States. The designation has helped to save the buildings from demolition, at least for the time being. From left to right are Marilyn Guida, Levin Sy, Veerkamp, Dawn Mabalon, Nelson Nagai, Leatrice Bantillo Perez, and Concepcion M. Bohulano. (Photograph by Elena Mangahas, courtesy of the Little Manila Foundation.)

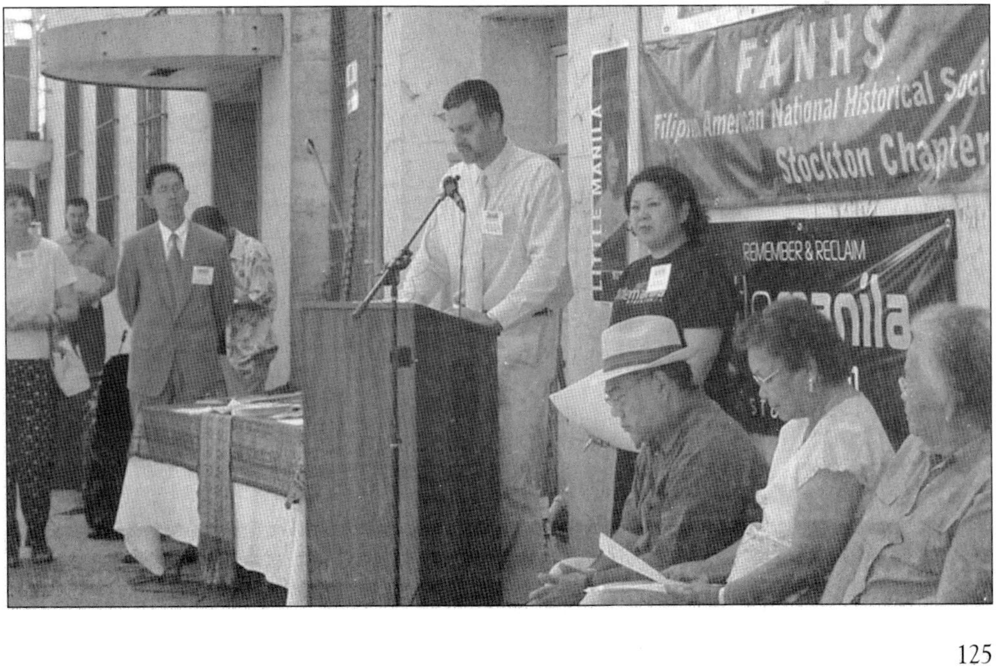

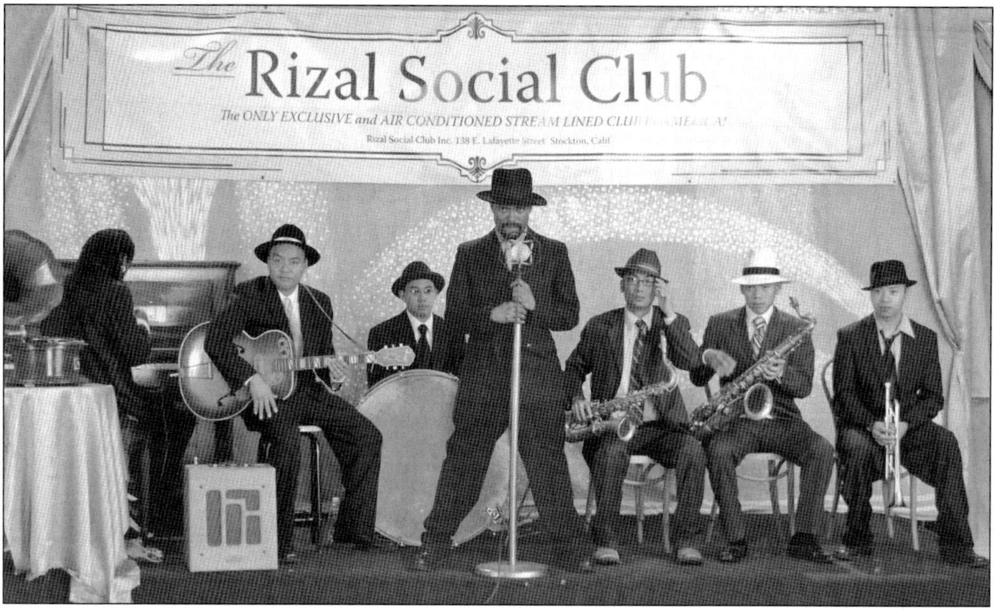

In 2006, Black Eyed Peas member Apl de Ap and director Patricio Ginelsa paid tribute to Stockton's Little Manila and re-created the Rizal Social Club for the video for "Bebot." Historic photographs of the time period inspired the video, which called attention to the campaign to preserve Little Manila. Though interiors were shot in Historic Filipinotown in L.A., exteriors were filmed in Little Manila. The California Preservation Foundation awarded the Peas, Ginelsa, and the Little Manila Foundation its Presidents Award for the video. (Courtesy of Sthanlee B. Mirador.)

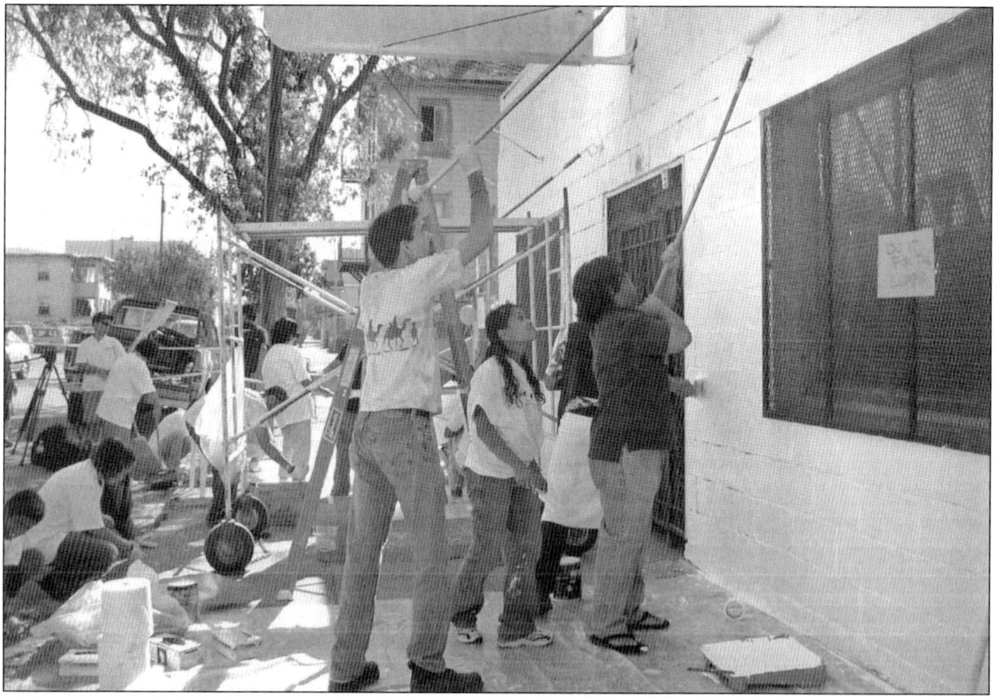

Volunteers with Bahala Na Escrima and the Little Manila Foundation paint and refurbish the exterior of the Iloilo Circle for the first annual Fight the Blight event in August 2005.

(X) Oscar + (X) Winnie

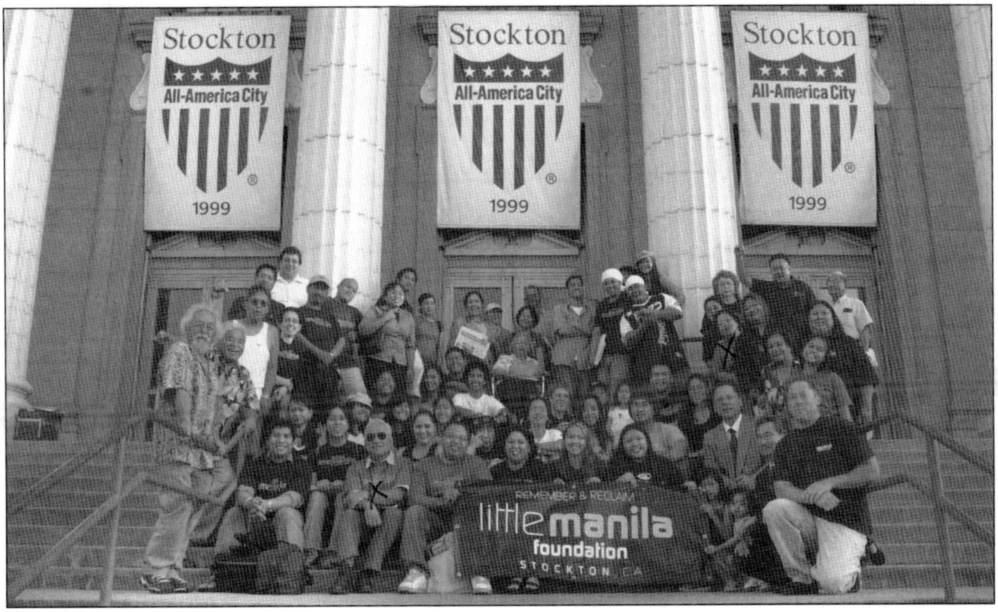

Little Manila, FANHS, and community supporters gather on the city hall steps in October 2003 to present an alternative redevelopment plan for Little Manila. When a strip mall developer threatened the area, the community responded with a plan that included a cultural center, the Filipino American National Museum, and affordable housing. The strip mall plan has failed, and the community continues toward their vision. (Courtesy of the Little Manila Foundation.)

ABOUT THE AUTHORS

Dawn Bohulano Mabalon, Ph.D., is a third-generation Pinay born and raised in Stockton, California. She is assistant professor of history at the Department of History at San Francisco State University. She received her M.A. in Asian American Studies at UCLA and her Ph.D. in History from Stanford University. She cofounded the Little Manila Foundation and is a National Trustee of the Filipino American National Historical Society. She lives in San Francisco with her partner, Jesus P. Gonzales.

Rico J. Reyes is a multimedia artist and curator born in Quezon City, Philippines, and raised in Manteca, California. He received his B.A. in Studio Art from UC Berkeley and his M.F.A. in New Genres from UCLA. A founding board member of the Little Manila Foundation, he is a Ph.D. candidate in Cultural Studies at Goldsmiths College, University of London.

Founded in 2000, the Little Manila Foundation advocates for the historic preservation and revitalization of the Little Manila Historic Site in Stockton, California, the historic heart of Filipino America. More information can be found at www.littlemanila.net or by writing to email@littlemanila.net.

The mission of the Filipino American National Historical Society is "to promote understanding, education, enlightenment, appreciation, and enrichment through the identification, gathering, preservation and dissemination of the history and culture of Filipino Americans in the United States." The Stockton Chapter was founded in 1992. Information is available by contacting stocktonfanhs@aol.com or visiting www.geocities.com/tokyo/pagoda/4534/.

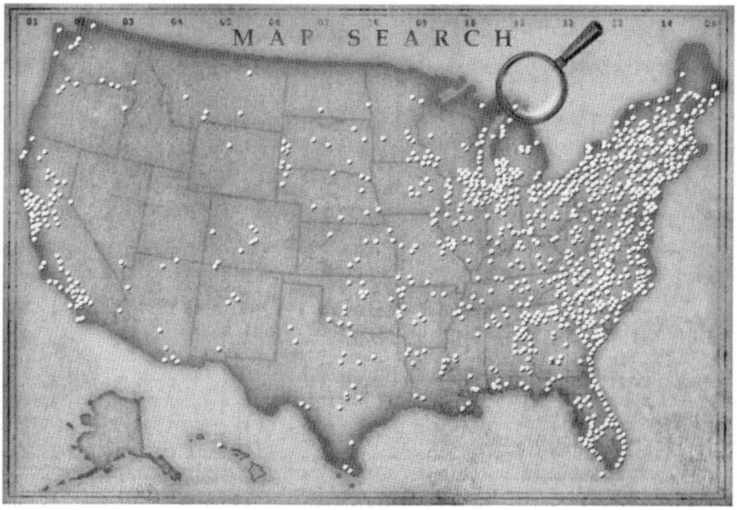
MAP SEARCH